FOR ARGUMENT'S SAKE

FOR ARGUMENT'S SAKE

A Guide to Writing Effective Arguments

SECOND EDITION

KATHERINE J. MAYBERRY
Rochester Institute of Technology

ROBERT E. GOLDEN
Keene State College

HarperCollins*CollegePublishers*

Executive Editor: Anne Elizabeth Smith
Project Editor: Edith Baltazar
Design Supervisor: Mary Archondes
Text and Cover Designer: Sarah Johnson
Electronic Production Manager: Valerie A. Sawyer
Desktop Administrator: Hilda Koparanian
Manufacturing Manager: Helene G. Landers
Electronic Page Makeup: BookWorks
Printer and Binder: RR Donnelley & Sons Company
Cover Printer: The Lehigh Press, Inc.

For permission to use copyrighted material, grateful acknowledgment is made to the copyright holders on p. 202, which is hereby made part of this copyright page.

Cover Illustration: *Two Lanterns* by Willi Baumeister, 1955. Photo: Copyright 1995, Archive Baumeister, Stuttgart Artist's Rights Society, NY, Bild-Kunst, Bonn.

For Argument's Sake, A Guide to Writing Effective Arguments, Second Edition

Library of Congress Cataloging-in-Publication Data

Mayberry, Katherine J.
     For Argument's Sake: a guide to writing effective arguments/
         p. cm.
     Includes index.
     ISBN 0-673-52459-0
     1. English language–Rhetoric.   2. Persuasion (Rhetoric)
3. Logic.   I. Golden, Robert E.   II. Title.
PE1431.M39   1996
808'.042–dc20

95–15722
CIP

95 96 97 98   9 8 7 6 5 4 3 2 1

Contents

3

The Claim   20

4

An Argument's Support 41

5

Making Reasonable Arguments: Formal and Informal Logic 55

6

Arguing Facts   70

7

Arguing Cause   92

8

Arguing Evaluations   116

9

Arguing Recommendations   142

10

Writing and Image   163

11

Openings and Closings   175

12

Revising   188

Preface

The focus of *For Argument's Sake* is the process of creating written arguments. By subdividing argument into its four most common modes—factual arguments, causal arguments, evaluations, and recommendations—and outlining the steps involved in argument creation, from the earliest stage of invention through audience analysis to final revision, this text offers students a comprehensive guide to the creation of fair-minded and effective written arguments.

For Argument's Sake was written in response to our own experience teaching classes in argument. Frustrated by the surfeit of theory-bound argument texts on the one hand and anthology-like texts on the other, we decided to create our own book that would satisfy the *practical* needs of beginning and advanced student writers struggling to gain skill in this most crucial and common of writing tasks. In *For Argument's Sake,* we believe we have been successful in creating a guide to written argument that is relevant to students in a variety of disciplines, new in its approach to some fundamental issues, and detailed enough to be useful while avoiding unnecessary complexity.

ORGANIZATION

The text is structured around three major phases of writing: focusing, supporting, and reviewing. Chapters 1 through 5 discuss those activities required to bring a developing argument into focus, including finding and focusing a claim, identifying and adjusting to audience, and understanding the relationship between claim and support. Chapters 6 through 9 discuss the support process for factual arguments, causal arguments, evaluations, and recommendations. Chapters 10 through 12 present the reviewing activities necessary to refine and polish a draft of an argument, including a discussion of image and style, of openings and closings, and of the revising and editing processes.

We have presented these writing phases in the order students typically follow when writing arguments, but we are fully aware that there are exceptions to this order. Like most writing teachers and scholars, we recognize the recursive nature of writing, that changes in one phase or aspect of writing lead to changes throughout an argument.

SPECIAL FEATURES

The discussion of motive in *For Argument's Sake* is unique to argument texts. Asking why people create written arguments is a critical question that can lead to the creation of more meaningful and effective arguments. The question of motivation is given serious attention in Chapter 2.

The inclusion of an entire chapter on style and image (Chapter 10) enriches the traditional view of argument, which sometimes seems to suggest that effective arguments have more to do with formulas and principles than with using language fairly and effectively. It is our view that a writer's style—the image he or she projects through the writing—is a fundamental component of argument, not just a lucky accident of talent.

Our handling of the principles of formal and informal logic is also unique, in that we introduce these principles at the point in the argument process where they are most useful—the development and evaluation of support. Chapter 5 presents logic as a practical tool for creating reasonable arguments, not as a series of abstract theories bearing no obvious relationship to the writing process.

For Argument's Sake contains examples from the humanities, the social sciences, and the physical and biological sciences, as well as many examples from college life, business, and the professions. This range of applications helps students see the importance of writing effective arguments not only during college, but also in their post-baccalaureate careers.

Because improvement in writing comes only with practice, virtually all the activities throughout the text require some kind of writing. Students are asked to produce many types of written arguments, from brief paragraphs to more fully developed essays.

NEW TO THIS EDITION

The second edition of *For Argument's Sake* retains the overall structure of the first, as well as the emphasis on invention, composing, and overall practicality. Our experience in teaching the first edition has helped us recognize areas where existing strengths can be enhanced through further development and minor reorganization. The most significant changes appear in Chapters 4, 5, and 6.

To Chapter 4, "An Argument's Support," we have added an extended discussion of definition. The clear definition of an argument's key terms will inevitably strengthen the argument by making it more accessible to readers; thus definition can be viewed as an important method of support. Our expanded treatment of definition includes a discussion of stipulative definition, which can be viewed both as a method of support, and, in cases where the definition of a key term is particularly crucial or controversial, as a variation of interpretive argument.

By moving the discussion of formal and informal logic from the end of the book to Chapter 5, we introduce the traditional principles of reasoning at the point in the writing process where they will be most useful—when writers are collecting support for their arguments. Writers make use of the principles of logic—both classical and modern—to evaluate the appropriateness and reasonableness of their choice of support. A reasonable argument is one in which the claim and support are logically connected. In Chapter 5 we present an overview of logic, paying particular attention to its *practical* value in writing arguments. In the following four chapters we discuss the specific application of logic to each of the four classes of argument.

The third substantive addition to the second edition appears in Chapter 6, "Arguing Facts," where we have considerably expanded our definition of facts and the crucial role they play in all argument. Ultimately, an argument is only as good as the facts upon which it is based. But at the same time, absolute, incontrovertible factuality is a rare phenomenon. By demonstrating the relativity and contextuality of all facts, this chapter demonstrates the importance of scrutinizing so-called "facts" before building arguments upon them.

Other changes include more samples of argument in Chapters 6 through 9; a wider range of references and examples reflecting recent changes in the political, professional, and academic cultures; and greater emphasis on *writing* in the activities of all twelve chapters.

We are pleased to offer this second edition of *For Argument's Sake* as an even more useful, accessible, and manageable guide for college students at all levels who must compose written arguments.

ACKNOWLEDGMENTS

We remain grateful to the many people who initially helped us to realize this project, including George Ball, friend and one-time colleague; our colleagues Sarah Collins and Joseph Nassar; and manuscript reviewers Dr. Marti Dinger, Georgia State University; Jill Feldcamp; Christopher Gould, University of North Carolina at Wilmington; Rosanna Grassi, Syracuse University, NY; Patricia H. Graves, Georgia State University; David A. Jolliffe, DePaul University; Nevin K. Laib, University of Houston, TX; Carolyn R. Miller, North Carolina State University; Thomas A. Mozola, Macomb Community College, MI; Paul Sawyer, Bradley University, IL; and Donna Schouman. We also thank the Department of Language and Literature at the Rochester Institute of Technology for helping with copying costs; and Editorial Assistants Holly Davis and Matthew Rohrer, whose cheerful accessibility and understanding of the revision process were extremely helpful.

KATHERINE J. MAYBERRY
ROBERT E. GOLDEN

1

An Introduction to Argument

A DEFINITION

To many people, *argument* is a negative term, meaning any dispute among individuals governed by emotion rather than reason. It is synonymous with quarrel or disagreement and generally associated with unpleasantness. Baseball players argue with umpires; children argue on long, hot car trips; and married couples argue over the family budget. But this popular meaning of the term is not its primary meaning, nor is it the subject of this book. *Argument* is traditionally defined as the process of demonstrating, through the presentation of reasonable evidence, the likelihood or certainty of a given proposition (a statement that can be affirmed or denied). While writers of this kind of argument must consider its reception by readers or listeners, argument so defined does not necessarily consist of an exchange between two or more voices. Through argument, a writer converts a preliminary, tentative proposition (or *claim*) into a reasoned conclusion. More simply, argument is writing or speaking to convince, using methods of reason. More simply still, argument is making a point.

An argument is different from an opinion. An *opinion* is a comparatively soft point of view—a position based not so much on reasonable evidence as on belief, intuition, or emotion. Argument, on the other hand, is a position supported by clear thinking and reasonable evidence, with a secure connection to documented facts. While arguments rarely prove a proposition to be absolutely true, they do demonstrate the likelihood or probability of that proposition. Opinions tend to be expressions of personal taste or experience and are untested by the systematic application of reasonable principles. Your opinion may be that public education is better than private, or yellow is a prettier color than red, but these remain opinions until they are thoughtfully and fully justified.

Not only is argument a reasonable process, it is also, by our definition, an ethical one. Arguments seek to make their points openly and honestly, avoiding underhanded methods and false promises, seeking to remove ambiguity rather than exploit it. One makes an argument in order to advance a reasonable position, not to trick a reader into serving the writer's self-interest. Writers of argument recognize the influence skilled writing can exert over credulous readers, and they are committed to exercising that influence reasonably and responsibly.

Argument is not a specialized form of writing reserved for lawyers and philosophers. In fact, it operates (or should operate) in much of the writing that most of us do: business correspondence, college essay examinations, annual reports, instructional manuals, letters of application, research papers, travel brochures. All effective writers—regardless of the particular form their writing takes—are familiar with the principles and practices of argument.

For example, while most of you have written letters of application—either for a job or college admission—you may not have realized that effective letters of application are actually carefully constructed arguments. Good letters argue one central proposition: the writer of the letter is a strong candidate for the position in question. Whether or not this proposition is directly stated in the letter, every piece of information provided, as well as the letter's style, grammar, and even physical appearance, should support and develop that proposition. The chief goal in writing an application letter is to convince the reader, through appropriate supporting evidence, of the probability of this proposition. You should be able to recognize an argument within the following application letter.

Dear Ms. Miller:

In the April issue of *The Camp Innisfree Newsletter,* you advertised an opening for a senior counselor. I would like to apply for that position. My own experience as a camper and junior counselor, as well as my college minor in elementary education, convinces me that I am well qualified for the job.

Having been a camper at Innisfree for four consecutive summers (1988–91), I am familiar with the physical layout of the camp, as well as its regulations and philosophy. My experience as a junior counselor at Camp Wantabet during the summer of 1992 served as a useful introduction to the duties and responsibilities of a camp counselor. I enclose a reference letter from Mr. Jack Mead, the director of Wantabet.

My strong interest in young children led me to pursue a minor in Elementary Education at Pacific College, where I am currently a sophomore. As a requirement of this minor, I have interned as a student teacher for fifth and sixth graders this entire academic year. The knowledge I have gained through this experience of supervising eleven- and twelve-year-olds should be extremely valuable to me as a senior counselor at Innisfree.

I hope you will consider me seriously for this position. If you would like more information than that included in the enclosed résumé and reference letters, please let me know. I look forward to hearing from you.

Sincerely,
Chloë Carlson

The claim of the argument is contained in the final sentence of the opening paragraph ("I am well qualified for the job"), and the supporting evidence (relevant experience) is contained in the second and third paragraphs.

THE CLASSES OF ARGUMENT

As you will discover when you begin writing them, arguments tend to fall into different modes or classes. We have found that it is convenient to classify arguments according to the nature of the claim being made and the degree of reader agreement expected. The four most common modes (or classes) of arguments are (1) factual arguments, (2) causal arguments, (3) evaluations, and (4) recommendations.

Factual arguments seek to convince an audience that a certain proposition is factual—that a given condition or phenomenon exists or has existed. Writers of factual arguments expect their claims to be accepted as true. **Causal** arguments claim a causal link between two events or conditions—that A caused B or is likely to cause B at some future time. In the causal arguments most of us make, truth or certainty is virtually impossible; usually our goal in arguing causal claims is to establish *probable* cause or effect convincingly. **Evaluations** seek agreement about a particular value judgment made by the writer. Because evaluations tend to work from very personal value systems, they are the hardest of all arguments to make convincingly, but they *can* be made reasonably and effectively. Finally, **recommendations** attempt to establish the desirability of a particular course of action.

It is not uncommon for these classes to operate within a single argument—indeed, most arguments combine two or more of these modes. So while you may rarely have to write an exclusively factual or causal argument, you will need to know which classes are operating in a given argument and how to apply the appropriate principles to each of the argument's parts.

The following excerpt from a book by Primo Levi on the Holocaust of World War II is a good example of a passage that combines classes of argument.

> Human memory is a marvelous but fallacious instrument. This is a threadbare truth known not only to psychologists but also to anyone who has paid attention to the behavior of those who surround him, or even to his own behavior. The memories which lie within us are not carved in stone; not only do they tend to become erased as the years go by, but often they change, or even grow, by incorporating extraneous features. Judges know this very well: almost never do two eyewitnesses of the same event describe it in the same way and with the same words, even if the event is recent and if neither of them has a personal interest in distorting it. . . . Some mechanisms are known which falsify memory under particular conditions: traumas, not only cerebral ones; interference from other "competitive" memories; abnormal conditions of consciousness; repressions; blockages. Nevertheless, even under normal conditions a slow degradation is at work, an obfuscation of outlines, a so to speak physio-

logical oblivion, which few memories resist. Doubtless one may discern here one of the great powers of nature, the same that degrades order into disorder, youth into old age, and extinguishes life in death. Certainly practice . . . keeps memories fresh and alive in the same manner in which a muscle often used remains efficient, but it is also true that a memory evoked too often, and expressed in the form of a story, tends to become fixed in a stereotype, in a form tested by experience, crystallized, perfected, adorned, installing itself in the place of the raw memory and growing at its expense.

The central claim of this argument is *evaluative* and is stated in the first sentence: "Human memory is a marvelous but fallacious instrument." The rest of the passage supports and explains this judgment through *factual* examples of memory's unreliability and *factual* explanations of memory deterioration. Because Levi is arguing a phenomenon familiar to his readers, he has not included rigorous documentation of his factual support.

ARGUMENT THROUGH IMAGE

The success of an argument is dependent not only on the reasonableness of its claim and supporting evidence, but also on the particular *image* it projects. Image is the total impression a reader gets by reading your writing. It is created by a number of elements. One of these is the writing *style*, which is a product not only of your word choice and sentence length, but of the overall impression the reader gets of the writer—what we'll later refer to as *voice*. Other elements of image include attention to grammar, neatness, the spacing of text, and the presentation of visuals on the page. Together, these elements will constitute an impression of you and your work that will strongly influence a reader's final acceptance or rejection of the entire document. As a writer, you will always be well served by carefully creating a positive and suitable image through these elements. The projection of this image works as a kind of implicit argument, convincing your readers that you and your argument merit their confidence, respect, and attention.

Take the case of a new bank management trainee asked to evaluate the tellers' weekly balancing system. A wise employee would realize that this assignment is really twofold. As well as evaluating the system to the best of her ability, the trainee must demonstrate, through her writing, certain qualities her employers value. She must project an image of being thoughtful, educated, and attentive to detail. The content of her argument will help to establish these points, of course, but so too will certain quieter but equally influential elements of her writing, such as her diction, tone, sentence length, grammar, and spelling. If she projects the proper image, her employers will feel justified in having hired her; if she does not, they may reconsider their decision.

THE ARGUMENT PROCESS

In one form or another, argument informs most of the writing tasks performed by students and professionals. But recognizing the prevalence of argument is only a beginning in making your own writing more effective. As with all effective writing, successful arguments result from a cooperative process of writing and thinking that begins a long way from the ultimate polished product. While there is no set order to this process—different writers undertake it in different ways—it is possible to identify certain broad phases that every writer must work through: forming an argument, supporting the argument, and reviewing the argument. Within each of these phases, which are usually roughly sequential, a number of crucial considerations arise. This book will help you recognize these considerations and make the choices most likely to yield an effective argument. At this point, we offer a brief explanation of each phase to give you an overview of the process of creating effective arguments.

Forming the Argument

Forming your argument consists of discovering a motive for writing, identifying an audience to address, and discovering and sharpening the propositions to be argued. A successful argument is usually one that is important to its writer and is born of strong personal interest, often an interest in changing things. Whenever possible, you should inject the energy of your own interests and experience into your writing assignments. In other words, find a personal motive for writing your argument.

Identifying your audience is another important task in forming an argument. Audience is an inescapable consideration of writing, yet one that is often underestimated or misunderstood by writers. While usually a solitary act, writing is the act of writing *to* someone: friends, business associates, professors, relatives, the general public. Even writers of private diaries have an audience in mind, though the audience may be merely themselves in the future. When writing does not work, one of the most common causes is the writer's failure to understand sufficiently the needs of the audience. Without this attention to audience, even the most brilliant prose can be wasted on uncomprehending and indifferent readers. Before writing, you need to ask yourself three basic questions about your audience: Who are my readers? Why will they read my argument? What should they be able to do after reading it?

You cannot write an effective argument without a very clear understanding of the central point you are arguing. While discovering a motive for writing is very helpful, you must still discover, or at least clarify, the informing proposition of your argument. In some instances, this proposition will come to you early and easily; more frequently, you may have to labor through much reading and thinking before arriving at a reasonable and interesting proposition. In most arguments, this proposition is summarized in a one-to three-sentence statement called the *claim.* A critical element of arguments, the claim requires considerable attention: it must be absolutely clear, interesting, and representative of the argument as a whole.

Supporting the Claim

Having identified your claim and your audience, you need to determine how best to support your argument. An argument's *support* is all the material that turns a tentative claim into a justified conclusion. Support is the single most important component—the defining component—of argument. Without appropriate and sufficient support, a claim remains purely speculative and hypothetical; with the right support, it becomes a sound and credible conclusion.

How do you know that the support you have selected is the right support? While many of the basic principles of support are applicable to all four of the classes of argument identified earlier in this chapter, certain principles apply exclusively to certain classes. Starting the argument process with a preliminary working claim will allow you to identify the class of argument you are developing, thus easing your selection of appropriate supporting material.

There is more to selecting appropriate support than matching it to the class of claim you are making. You will also need to ensure that the relationship between the claim and its support is reasonable. This relationship is reasonable if it accords with certain principles of formal and informal logic. Understanding these principles and their application to your arguments will be enormously useful to you as you go about the process of selecting and evaluating support for your claim.

Reviewing Your Argument

The product of the steps previously discussed—formulation of a working claim, identification of audience, selection, evaluation, and presentation of support—will be a first draft of your argument. Once you have written this first draft, you will want to take a step back and review what you have created. This review (or revision) stage may be the point at which you want to make some self-conscious decisions about the image projected by your argument. As it can be inhibiting to make these choices when you are desperately trying to get your thoughts recorded, you may want to use the review process to consider alternative, appropriate ways of saying things, remembering that a style that uses language fairly, intelligently, and sensitively will project an image the reader will trust and respect.

Two substantive additions many writers make at the revision stage are an introduction and conclusion. Because introductions are the reader's first impression of an argument and its writer, particular care needs to be given to their composition. The same goes for conclusions, which, as your last words on the subject, need to be carefully thought out. Because it can be difficult to come up with a riveting and representative introduction before knowing the exact direction and content of your argument, it is sometimes wise to hold off writing an introduction until the revision stage. Likewise, composing a definitive, summarizing conclusion can be easier once you have had a chance to review exactly what the argument has accomplished.

In all the arguments you write, you should treat your first draft as a true *draft*, leaving yourself plenty of time to come back to your writing and *revise* it, to make whatever changes need to be made in the paper's content and organization. In the revision stage, you will review your entire argument, asking yourself basic questions about purpose, audience, style, organization, and adequacy and logic of support. Effective revising requires a willingness to make major changes if necessary; it should not be confused with *editing,* the review of your argument for correct spelling, grammar, usage, and format. Revision can mean redesign; editing should be the final spit and polish on a nearly finished report.

CONCLUSION

Recognizing the prevalence of argument in all writing will help you sharpen the focus and purpose of the writing you do for professors and employers. Whether you are writing an essay examination, a letter of application, or a laboratory report, you can apply the principles and methods of argument contained in this book to make a compelling and convincing case for the claims you advance. Your writing will be tighter and more pointed, and thus more interesting to any reader. It will also be convincing and responsible, raising it high above the level of much of the writing most of us are required to read daily.

SUMMARY

An Introduction to Argument

- Argument is the attempt by the writer to convince the reader of a point of view, using methods of reason. Most effective writing contains some kind of argument.

- Argument can be divided into four classes: factual, causal, evaluations, and recommendations.

- *Argument by image* helps convince the reader through the impression the writer creates. This image is created through style, correct spelling, punctuation, grammar, and physical appearance.

- While the process of creating arguments varies from writer to writer, the following three phases should be worked through: (1) forming an argument, which can consist of discovering a motive for writing and identifying an audience to address, discovering and sharpening a position, and developing an appropriate style; (2) supporting the argument; and (3) reviewing the argument, which can include considering the image your argument projects, adding an introduction and conclusion, and revising the entire argument.

SUGGESTIONS FOR WRITING (1.1)

1. Write a job application letter that is an effective argument. Your first paragraph should state the position desired and announce your primary qualification for the position. The second paragraph should expand on this primary qualification, while the third paragraph—and other paragraphs if needed—should develop your other qualifications. Your concluding paragraph should state your willingness to answer additional questions or to be available for an interview.

2. Analyze an editorial in your local newspaper. What is the editorial's proposition and what kind of support is given for this proposition? Do you find this support convincing? Why or why not? Write a two- to three-page essay on these questions.

3. Review an essay examination you have written recently. Is the central claim clearly stated? Are supporting facts carefully presented? Does the essay consider the expectations of its reader? Rewrite the essay so that all of these considerations are met.

2

Where Writing Begins: Motives and Audience

Most of us are accustomed to writing from sheer compulsion, because authority or policy or necessity requires a written document from us. A student writes a research paper because a professor has assigned it; a sales representative writes a monthly report because a supervisor requires it; a mother writes a note about her child's absence because a school's policy insists upon it. Yet we all know or suspect that the best writing springs from some source other than mere necessity and that even when necessity is present, in good writing there are other motives at work. Shakespeare wrote *Hamlet* to earn a living, but earning a living was hardly his sole motive for writing.

MOTIVES FOR WRITING

What are these other motives for writing? They can vary enormously, from a desire to create a record for posterity, to a desire to express love or joy, to a yearning to get a strong feeling out of our system. One very common motive for writing, especially for writing arguments, is an attempt to resolve dissonance in our lives. *Dissonance* is a musical term meaning an inharmonious arrangement of tones containing a tension that seeks resolution. More generally, dissonance means lack of agreement or disparity. It is a good way to describe the mismatch between the way we want life to be and the way it is. Dissonance energized Socrates' questioning of the conventional wisdom of his time, the angry voice of the prophets in the Old Testament, and the writing of the Declaration of Independence and the *Communist Manifesto*. It also drives much that is written in private diaries, editorials, and general-interest essays.

The Value of Dissonance

The principle of dissonance can be a useful starting point for students who are at a loss to discover an argument worth making. If you are required to write a composition for which you have no ideas, you might begin by asking yourself the following questions: What bothers you? What do you wish were different? What changes would improve the situation? The cause of the dissonance could be anything from parking problems on campus, to the status of women in large corporations, to the chemistry experiment that went awry. The field could be English composition or campus politics or economics or medical ethics.

Identifying a starting point of dissonance can suggest not only a subject to write about, but also a position to take regarding that subject. Because this position originates in your own interests and experience, the process of creating an argument around it will be far more meaningful to you than writing on a topic to which you are comparatively indifferent. In turn, the argument will almost certainly be more effective, as we tend to write more compellingly about those subjects genuinely important to us.

Let's assume that in an English Composition class you are asked to write about the impact of technology on education. It would be simple enough to take the position that technological developments like the computer, educational software, and CD-ROMs enhance the learning process for children and young adults. You could certainly formulate a creditable argument from this position. But before proceeding in this rather predictable direction, take some time to probe for dissonance. What discomforts or uneasiness have you experienced as a result of educational technology? What are the reasons for this uneasiness? Do you have material for an argument here? Perhaps, as you consider the amazing educational software that has been available to you as a high school and college student, you begin to recognize the losses that have accompanied these developments—say the loss of working with tangible texts, with pages that can be turned and fingered, books that can become friends. Reading encyclopedia entries from a computer screen just isn't the same as reading it from the volume taken down from your living room shelves. This could be the beginning of an interesting argument about the losses incurred when screens replace pages, when electronic texts render tangibility and portability obsolete.

This approach has many advantages, one of which is its uniqueness: most students assigned this topic would concentrate on the benefits of educational technology. In writing, an unusual approach, as long as it is intelligent and not merely eccentric, is often effective. Second, working from dissonance gives you the opportunity to think through a vague or reflexively held opinion, to justify your discomfort by discovering *reasons* for it. Turning an opinion into an argument is an excellent way to trust and challenge your unexamined views. Finally, focusing on problems is more useful and productive than ignoring them; neither you nor your readers can improve a situation until you have identified its problems.

We don't advocate your turning every writing assignment into an occasion for pointless complaining; such an approach is rarely effective. Searching for dissonance does not mean becoming a professional cynic; you can be critical without being negative, discerning without being a whiner. The student who writes about the disadvantages of educational technology would be wise to acknowledge the indisputably positive impact of this technology. To ignore altogether the benefits suggests to the reader a certain nearsightedness on the part of the writer, thus undermining the overall effectiveness of the argument. Of course, sometimes balance and fairness are not appropriate (the Declaration of Independence would be much less effective if it presented a balanced view of the British government), but extreme situations calling for one-sided appeals are relatively rare.

Writing Arguments That Are Meaningful to You

It will not always be possible or desirable for you to write from dissonance or even from your own emotions and opinions. Nevertheless, you will find that it is much easier to write about a subject that bears some relationship to what you find important. Even when the assignment you are given is narrowly defined, offering little room for you to maneuver, the following suggestions may help you make the adjustments necessary to bring the topic closer to your own experience:

1. Search for the most interesting facets of the assignment. If your assignment requires you to write on a topic in which you have little interest—the Civil War, for instance—try to find the one aspect of the Civil War that is at least potentially more meaningful to you than any other. This may require some research, but the time spent will be rewarded by your more positive attitude toward the topic. If you are interested in medicine, for example, you may be able to write about the medical treatment of the wounded during the war, comparing and contrasting it with contemporary practice.

2. Don't lie. Express only those opinions you can honestly believe in. If you are unsure of your claim despite your best efforts to become comfortable with it, don't hesitate to use qualifiers such as "perhaps," "probably," "usually," or "likely." Never be lukewarm when you can be hot or cold, but don't take a position simply for the sake of taking it. That ground is too slippery. A qualified claim, such as "Athletes who train with professional coaches will usually perform better than athletes who do not," is preferable to the unqualified statement "Athletes who train with professional coaches will perform better than athletes who do not" because there will be some exceptions to this rule. On the other hand, try to avoid the risk—common in much student writing—of overqualifying your claim to the point that it is virtually meaningless. A claim such as "Some athletes who train with professional coaches may perform better than athletes who do not" is too qualified to be useful or interesting.

3. Don't be pompous. Much ineffective writing is composed by students trying to write like their professors, and some of the worst writing in business comes from people who believe they have to leave their humanity behind when they write at work. Pomposity is partly in the eyes of the beholder, of course, and there is no

foolproof way to guard against it, but ask yourself one key question about your writing: "Does it sound as though *I* wrote it?" A title such as "An Examination of Personality Traits of the Central Character in Jane Austen's *Emma*" is stuffy and vague. A title like "Emma's Pride in Jane Austen's *Emma*" is more direct and certainly less pretentious.

These suggestions apply not only to college assignments, but to any assigned writing: a monthly sales report, a memo on improvements in office procedures, a technical report on which brand of copier to buy. You may not have chosen to do the writing in the first place, but to the degree you can, you need to make the project your own, not simply a task assigned you by someone else.

ACTIVITIES (2.1)

1. Look at the last four things you have written: letters, reports, essays, memos, and so on. What were your reasons for writing them? Were any of them written merely because you had to write them? Would any of them have been improved if you had tried to write about what is important to you? Write a one- to two-page essay addressing these questions. Adjust the topic of one of these so as to make it meaningful to you and then rewrite it following the suggestions presented in the preceding part of this chapter.

2. List four aspects of your life or of the world around you that you wish were different. From these four aspects derive tentative topics for essays.

THE IMPORTANCE OF AUDIENCE

Writing assignments for college professors is in many ways excellent preparation for the writing you will do as part of your job once you leave college. Good professors give you constructive feedback and opportunities to practice what you learn. But while college writing assignments sharpen many skills and increase your knowledge of the subject matter, they often give you little practice in the critical skills of assessing and addressing a particular *audience*. When you write in college, you are usually writing for a professor who is a specialist in the subject of the paper, who knows very well the purpose of the paper, and who is obliged to read it through to its end. In advanced courses, not only are you writing *to* a specialist, you are also encouraged to write *as* a specialist, demonstrating your facility with the concepts and terminology of a particular field or discipline.

But in most of the writing you will do outside an academic setting, you won't have this luxury of addressing a specified and attentive reader. This does not mean you can afford to ignore the question of audience. Writing is a transitive act. It assumes a relationship between a writer and a reader: the writer speaks and the reader listens and reacts. Your most basic goal as a writer is to engage your audience—to obtain their attention and, ultimately, their favorable response to what you have written—whether it is a report or short story or letter to the editor. If you take the time before you write to consider your audience, you will be much more likely to avoid boring or alienating or confusing them. Further, having an audience in mind gives your writing focus and a sense of purpose—you write with "a reader over your shoulder," as Robert Graves put it, which is vastly preferable to addressing blank faces. Good writers keep the image of a reader constantly before them.

Careful consideration of audience is particularly crucial in writing arguments. Argument is a method of convincing others of something—of demonstrating *to* someone the reasonableness of a given claim. Thus, writers of argument must think through the question of audience very thoroughly, considering the probable disposition of the audience toward the argument, the nature and extent of support needed to convince them, the implications for them of their acceptance of the argument.

Developing an accurate sense of audience depends in part on experience, but you can sharpen this sensitivity by considering the following questions each time you prepare to write: *Who* is the audience? *Why* will the audience read your argument? *What* should the audience be able to do after reading your argument? You should keep these three questions in mind both before you write and while you are writing.

Who Is the Audience?

Sometimes this question about the composition of the audience will be answered in terms of specific individuals you know, but more often it is answered in terms of categories or groups of readers, such as the readers of a certain newspaper or magazine, or the users of a certain product, or the students in a particular class. Most college essays are written for professors as the primary audience; most memos are written to members of the same department or unit as that of the writer. But whoever the audience may be, you must identify them *before* you begin to write.

Once you have identified your audience, you need to consider their degree of familiarity with the subject matter. Readers usually know much less than writers about the subject in question; even readers in the same organization with similar education and experience may be unfamiliar with the content of your report. You should take care to provide any necessary background information and to explain all specialized vocabulary, basic concepts, and assumptions that may be unfamiliar to even *part* of your audience. The most cogent and convincing of arguments will be ineffective if it baffles its readers; if they have any choice at all, they will stop reading a difficult argument before they will struggle with its unfamiliar language and concepts. If you don't know what level of sophistication is most appropriate to your audience, or if your audience comes from a mixed background, you are better off providing too much explanation than too little. It is better to make your audience feel superior than inadequate.

In the writing of arguments, the most important facet of audience identification is consideration of your readers' probable disposition to your claim. Knowing whether your readers are likely to be receptive to your claim will affect the way your argument proceeds, making you particularly cautious about how you frame your claim and how you engage your audience's attention. For example, if you expect your audience to be hostile to your claim, you would do well to give them credit for their views at the outset. In recommending an expensive federal crime prevention program to an audience already frustrated by the cost of crime to taxpayers, acknowledging and legitimizing that frustration could be an effective way of neutralizing their hostility: "There is something wildly unjust about living in fear of crime *and* having to pay for that crime as well." From this concession to the audience's probable reluctance to absorb more cost for crime prevention, you could proceed to argue for a new crime bill that, while temporarily costly, offers an excellent chance of substantially reducing crime and its costs to the taxpayer. Telling the audience that they are selfish, or pigheaded, or shortsighted will not gain you much agreement, but expressing a genuine understanding of their frustration will demonstrate that your motives and theirs are essentially the same.

When you know that some in your audience hold a view contrary to your own, or when an opposing view is well known, you will often have to include a *refutation* of the opposing argument. (We discuss refutations in Chapter 4, under Addressing the Counterargument.) Even if you don't directly refute this opposing argument, you will at least have to acknowledge its existence, thus letting your readers know that you are sensitive to their knowledge and beliefs.

Knowing your audience shares your views is no occasion for complacency. Flaccid, cliché-ridden sermons, political speeches, and essays are the result of a writer telling the already converted what they already know in language with which they are already too familiar. In such cases, when the challenge of converting your audience seems minimal, you need to guard against triteness and predictability—perhaps by playing devil's advocate, perhaps by expressing your central claim outrageously, perhaps by reminding your audience of the dangers of knee-jerk, reflexive responses.

In the absence of information about probable audience response to your specific claim, it helps enormously to have some sense of your readers' general beliefs and values so that you can, if appropriate, appeal to them in the course of your argument. Some arguments—particularly evaluations and recommendations—depend on successful appeals to readers' values and beliefs. An argument written for the *New Left Journal* recommending the recitation of the Pledge of Allegiance in public schools could only succeed if it appealed to a value held by the *Journal's* readers. These readers would not be moved by a "Your country: love it or leave it" approach. But if you rested your claim on the principle of free choice, arguing that every student should have the choice of saying the pledge, your argument might succeed.

Writers of argument consider these questions of audience familiarity, disposition, and needs and values so that they can meet their readers halfway; that is, they provide whatever is necessary to put their readers in a position of neutrality or open-mindedness vis-à-vis the argument's claim. This is *not* the same thing as manipulating readers—gaining their agreement through underhanded, unreasonable methods. Understanding the psychology of readers is important in argument because it gives reason the best possible chance, but reason must never be replaced by exploitation of audience psychology.

ACTIVITIES (2.2)

1. Examine a copy of *four* of the following and try to identify the probable audience for each. Estimate the level of education and the kinds of occupations each audience would probably have.
Example: *Publications of the Modern Language Association* (PMLA). Level of education: usually at least some graduate education. Occupations: primarily graduate students in English or foreign language and literature and college-level instructors in these subjects.
   a. The *Wall Street Journal*
   b. *Time* magazine
   c. *Cosmopolitan*
   d. *People* magazine
   e. The *New England Journal of Medicine*
   f. *Popular Mechanics*
   g. *Soldier of Fortune* magazine
   h. Instructor's Manual for the Apple Macintosh Computer (or some other personal computer)
   i. *Mad* magazine
   j. The *New York Times*

2. The following passage is from a brochure on how employees can use statistics to improve the quality of their organization's products. The intended audience for this brochure is company employees with a seventh-grade reading level and with no previous knowledge of statistics. How well does this passage communicate with its intended audience? If you believe the passage would be difficult for its intended audience, can you suggest ways to change it to make it more accessible to them? Write a one- to two-page essay addressing these questions.

   Quality can be best maintained by preventive action in advance of complete tool wear or predictable machine maintenance. If we check characteristics of parts on a sampling basis as they are produced, it is better than sorting through a bin of hundreds of parts looking for the defective parts and then trying to determine which parts can be salvaged.

   Collecting and analyzing data on current operations is essential in supplier and company plants. By studying the data, the causes of defects for each main quality characteristic can be investigated and determined. Appropriate solutions, including redesign or reprocessing, can be developed. Once problems are identified, a decision can be made whether to analyze past data, to collect new information, or a combination of both.

Why Will the Audience Read the Argument?

Writers rarely ask themselves *why* readers will want to read their work, often assuming that the reader has the same interest in the subject as they do. Unfortunately, the level of interest is usually not as high; the reader's interest must be captured and held. Even in business, where the reader often must read a report as a part of work, the report competes with all the other reports that must be read and with other responsibilities. Because a reader at work is a busy person, the report should contain something that will get the reader's attention and hold it. A good introduction and compelling claim help to win over the reader, but before you can write these you must understand what is interesting and important to the reader.

In a sales report, for example, what is the one item that is going to be most important to the district sales manager, who is the primary reader of the report? What is the one way to phrase the claim that will catch this reader? If sales in the district seem to be going well because they were up 10 percent last month compared to a year ago, but the situation is actually far less promising because sales of the most profitable items were down 15 percent, the writer must be precise in word choice. An opening such as "Although overall sales for August were up 10 percent when compared to a year ago, the district must address the problem of a 15-percent decline in the sales of our most profitable merchandise" would alert the district manager to the basic facts and the crucial problem that needs to be solved. The opening shows an awareness of the particular audience and its needs and interests.

These same issues are even more pressing in writing outside a professional context, because then the readers are under no compulsion to read what is written. Writers who write daily or weekly columns in newspapers are under continual pressure to find a "hook" that will catch the readers' attention. These writers need to find, in a subject important to them, the topic or angle that will also interest their readers. What aspect of the American crime crisis will interest readers who have been reading and perhaps having nightmares about the subject for years? If readers are tired of hearing about the personal devastation created by crime, perhaps they will be interested in an essay on the cost of crime to the taxpayer. Or if readers' interest in the subject seems to be exhausted, but you feel compelled to bring the issue to their attention once more, what about a "hook" such as "The taxpayer as criminal"?

You need to be constantly aware of what is likely to catch your readers' attention by asking yourself such questions as, What will appeal to the readers' self-interest? What are people talking about right now? What don't the readers know about this subject that they should? Or even, What is currently unfashionable or unpopular that I can make people look at in an entirely new way? You can address these questions while still writing about what is important to you; good writing is always a successful marriage of the writer's commitment and the reader's interest.

Our hypothetical essay about crime points out the importance of the audience's attitude toward the subject. In the case of crime, you can assume that no one believes it is a good or desirable thing, that everyone would like to see it disappear. But you also may suspect that most people are tired of hearing about the topic. If you write about crime, you may have to tread carefully between your readers' fear of crime and their fatigue about hearing about an issue that has been intensely discussed for years to little effect.

ACTIVITIES (2.3)

The following audiences are likely either to be uninterested in or hostile to the following claims. Rewrite the claims and add whatever additional sentences are called for to engage audience attention. In a brief essay, explain why the rewrite is likely to be more effective than the original.

1. Parents of a college student—recommendation for increased tuition.
2. A sales manager for a large corporation—monthly sales for her district must increase.
3. An African American woman—affirmative action results in reverse discrimination.
4. An inner city high school principal—discipline in public high schools is too strict.
5. A software specialist—our society looks at too many screens.

What Should the Audience Be Able to Do After Reading the Argument?

All arguments seek something from their readers. At the very least, they seek to convince their readers that the proposed claim and its supporting material constitute a reasonable position, even though readers may not fully agree with it. Most arguments aspire to the more difficult goal of gaining their readers' full agreement, which in many cases means changing readers' minds. The most ambitious of arguments seeks not only to gain this agreement, but to convince readers to take some action based on their agreement. The material you include in your argument as well as the tone you use will vary depending on the expectations you have of your audience.

For example, if you were trying to convince an audience that fraternity term-paper files on your campus are a problem, you would need to argue why, and to what extent they are a problem. But if you wanted your audience not simply to agree with your claim but to take action to solve the problem you identify, you would need to include specific steps to be taken, such as applying pressure on fraternity councils, setting up a more rigorous honor code for students, and encouraging faculty to change term paper assignments on a yearly basis. You would also need to convince your readers that these actions are likely to be effective: fraternity councils will monitor the problem more carefully if they are in danger of losing campus support; term paper files will be useless if assignments are not repeated from year to year. Arguments that end with a request for action on the part of the reader should be specific about the proposed action, show the connection between the argument and the proposed action, and convince the reader that the action will lead, or at least probably will lead, to the desired changes.

Your expectations of the readers largely determine the tone of your writing. If you intend to convince gently, the tone can be mild: "The citizens of this community need to consider an alternative to the property tax as a way of raising money for education." If you intend to exhort, the tone should be more forceful, as in Winston Churchill's famous address to the British people in their darkest days of World War II: ". . . we shall fight on the beaches, we shall fight on the landing grounds, we shall fight in the fields and in the streets, we shall fight in the hills." If you intend to command, you can be very blunt: "No smoking is allowed in the computer room. Those caught smoking there will be asked to leave and will have their right to use the room suspended for two weeks."

ACTIVITIES (2.4)

For each of the situations below, prepare an outline of an argument, indicating when delineation and support of action steps are necessary and why.

1. **Claim:** subsidized housing ruins neighborhoods, lowering property values and weakening community pride.
   Audience: readers of the Letters to the Editor section of a local newspaper.

2. **Claim:** the new mandatory bicycle helmet law is an infringement of personal liberty, depriving the citizen of his or her right of self-determination.
   Audience: listeners of a local call-in talk show.

3. **Claim:** bicycle helmets should be made mandatory in this state, just like motorcycle helmets.
   Audience: your state legislature representative.

4. **Claim:** my years of experience as PTA chair, parent, school volunteer, and community activist qualify me to serve as a school board member.
   Audience: voters in a town election.

5. **Claim:** while I have had some academic difficulties over the past year, my commitment to receiving a college degree and my newfound understanding of study strategies will contribute to my eventual academic success, if only you will agree to waive my suspension.
   Audience: dean of your college.

SUMMARY

Where Writing Begins

- Dissonance—the mismatch between the way we want life to be and the way it is—can be a motive for effective arguments.

- When you write, try to write about what is important to you, expressing only those opinions you honestly believe in and avoiding pomposity.

- Before you write, consider these three questions:

  Who is the audience?

  Why will the audience read the argument?

  What should the audience be able to do after reading the argument?

SUGGESTIONS FOR WRITING (2.5)

1. From your list of topics from Activity (2.1) at the end of the first section of this chapter, Motives for Writing, select one of the topics and write a two- to three-page essay proposing a solution to the problem that bothers you.

2. Write a two- to three-page essay trying to convince a hostile audience of the appropriateness of a certain action. Two possibilities are writing to college students about an increase in tuition or writing to homeowners telling them that the road in front of their homes is going to be widened. You may think of some other possibility.

3. Examine the last report or essay you wrote and write a two- to three-page essay on who your audience was, why they would have read what you wrote, and what you expected them to do after they had finished reading. How well does that report or essay, when looked at in light of these questions, communicate with its intended audience? Are there any changes you would make in it now that you have looked carefully at these questions about audience?

4. Write a one-page essay to students in one of your classes, evaluating the effectiveness of that class's instructor. Then write a one-page essay to the instructor about the same topic. Make a list of the differences in the two essays. (One possible structure for each essay is to begin with a claim and then support it with two brief paragraphs.)

5. Write a two- to three-page evaluation of a speech you have heard given by a politician or other public official. Who is the audience for the speech? Why would the audience listen to the speech? How does the speaker appeal to this audience? What does the speaker want the audience to do after hearing the speech? How effective do you believe the speaker was in achieving this goal? If it is possible to obtain a printed transcript of the speech, give your instructor a copy of it.

3

The Claim

Having discovered a subject and motive for your argument, and having identified the composition of your audience, you are ready to begin focusing your argument. Every step in the writing process—from discovering a motive to revising a final draft—will sharpen your argument's focus. The first part of this chapter covers an early stage of the focusing process: formulating, modifying, and positioning your argument's claim.

Some writers do not write a word before devising their claims; others let their claims evolve during an exploratory first draft, focusing and modifying as they write. Whether you come to your claim early or late in the writing process, your argument is not sufficiently focused until you can succinctly summarize its principal proposition.

HOW CLAIMS WORK

The claim of an argument is a short summary of the argument's central proposition. All arguments have at least one claim, and some longer arguments more than one. Usually, the claim is stated directly, but occasionally it is only implied by the material chosen to support it. Regardless of its placement within the argument, regardless even of whether it appears at all, the claim informs and propels the argument, giving it energy and structure.

Claims can be short and highly condensed, as in the statement "America's youth is becoming insular and self-absorbed," or they can be long and intricate, reflecting the structure of the entire argument: "Because a capitalist system rewards aggressiveness, competitiveness and intelligence, offering little recompense to the timid and the weak, it is an almost perfect economic extension of Darwinism. In a capitalist society, the 'fittest' get rich, the unfit stay poor."

Because it summarizes the argument's central point, a clear statement of your argument's claim is extremely useful to readers. Whatever their levels of interest, knowledge, and intelligence, all readers approach an unfamiliar manuscript ignorant of its content and direction. An unequivocal, succinct statement of a document's chief point or points alerts readers to the goal of the argument and equips them to understand the relationship of the parts to the whole.

A good claim also helps readers evaluate an argument. Knowing exactly what central point a writer has intended to make, readers can judge whether the point has been made successfully. A claim such as "The United States should not attempt to protect dying industries with high tariffs" provides a benchmark against which readers can judge the supporting argument, but a claim such as "Free trade has a role in international commerce" is too vague, too unfocused, to serve as a meaningful benchmark.

While claims can be discovered or changed at virtually any point in the first draft, formulating a tentative, working claim early in the process can help you generate ideas, focus your writing, and direct your structure. A preliminary claim will determine the kinds of evidence you will need to support your argument, and it will serve as guide and reminder about the content of the argument, its organization, and its ultimate direction.

Generating a Claim

For inexperienced writers, the most critical question about the claim is "Where does it come from?" Writers who do not feel they have a wealth of ideas and experiences to draw from are often very insecure about coming up with an arguable position. Unfortunately, claims rarely spring fully polished from the brain at the touch of some magical switch; more frequently they evolve gradually from writers' early reading and thinking about the subject or from their own vague discomfort with a particular situation or issue.

Sometimes the invention process can be short-circuited. In some situations, claims are actually assigned. Students in beginning college writing courses are often assigned a particular claim to develop ("Write a two-page essay supporting your view of the effectiveness of student orientation at this college"). Essay examinations can offer students at least the germ of a full-blown claim. For example, the question "Was the dropping of the atom bomb in August of 1945 on Hiroshima and Nagasaki necessary to achieve Japan's surrender? Support your answer with specific reasons" dictates the rough form, though not the content, of the claim that will begin the answer: "The dropping of the bomb was/was not necessary, for the following reasons."

Some writers, moved to argue a position they strongly believe in, come to their work with their main point already firmly set in their minds. Yet the passion of their initial conviction can prevent them from reasonably examining the evidence for and against their position. In Chapter 2 we noted the value of dissonance in giving writers a starting point for their writing, but strong feelings about a subject do have a certain risk. Writers who begin an argument in the white heat of commitment to some unscrutinized position can blind themselves to its weaknesses or to the strength of its opposition. They would be wise to treat such a ready-made claim as tentative, as a guide to their preliminary research and thinking. Such a tentative claim, or hypothesis, serves as a starting point, a basis for further investigation; it is flexible, even expendable in the face of contradictory material.

On the other hand, many arguments originate in a vague topic and little direction about the specific conclusion to be reached. A literature student asked to write a fifteen-page analysis of the early poetry of William Wordsworth is almost certainly going to begin with little focus or sense of purpose. A new employee asked to evaluate the product quality and cost effectiveness of one of a company's suppliers would probably be equally adrift.

In cases such as these, how do writers move from a vague assignment to a working claim that will give the evolving argument some direction and discipline? There are many answers to this question, because generating a claim or position—indeed, the entire writing process—is a highly idiosyncratic process. Some writers logically deduce a claim from the evidence in Sherlock Holmes fashion, while others have their claims come to them unexpectedly while daydreaming, or jogging, or listening to music. Claims can be slowly and painfully dredged from the earth or they can come like lightning from the sky. Either kind of claim can be sound, provided it can be convincingly and reasonably supported.

For those times when you have difficulty arriving at a claim, we offer these three suggestions:

1. Don't press to arrive at a claim prematurely. More time is wasted following up a forced, dead-end claim that eventually has to be scrapped than thinking, reading, and taking notes as preparation for deciding exactly what your position is going to be.

2. Instead of rushing the claim during the preliminary research phase (and research can mean nothing more than tapping the contents of your own brain without ever opening a book), concentrate instead on gradually narrowing your topic. For example, if you're preparing to write the paper on the poetry of Wordsworth, your reading and thinking might lead you originally (and accidentally) in the direction of thematic content, then to the narrower concern of images of nature, then still more narrowly to the recollection of nature as an inspiration to poetry. By the time you have gathered material on this focused subject, you will not be far from imposing a particular point of view on the subject. This point of view on a focused topic will be your claim, which might be something like "Wordsworth as a poet was inspired by nature, but nature sifted through memory, not nature as it is immediately perceived." While you may have accumulated a lot of seemingly useless notes along the way, you should be saved the agony of distorting your paper to fit an unworkable claim you have discovered with too little consideration. As you are closing in on a claim, keep in mind that good claims are rarely too narrow, and poor ones often too broad.

3. In the early stages of writing, don't spend too much time polishing and refining your claim. At this stage a claim needs a narrow topic and the expression of

a definite attitude toward that topic. A good working claim could be no more than "Smoking in public places is harmful to everyone." Later, after the first draft, you can refine and shine, adding a summary of supporting reasons if necessary.

Keeping Your Working Claim Flexible

As you proceed with a rough draft that works from a tentative, working claim, you may discover that the preliminary claim needs modification. Perhaps the thinking and research you have done on the subject have made you realize that your claim does not apply as widely as you thought, that there are significant exceptions to your position. Be flexible enough to accept these discoveries and change your claim accordingly. Writing is not simply the recording of previously established thoughts but also a way of clarifying your thoughts, of discovering if what you meant to say can be said in a coherent and defensible way. Take advantage of the guiding service offered by a thoughtful claim, while remaining open to those discoveries to which writing and thinking can lead you.

Let's say you begin the composition process with a claim that arises easily out of your own strong opinions about the issue of affirmative action. Your preliminary or working claim is "Jobs should be given to the most qualified applicant, not to the most qualified minority applicant. To reject the best candidate on the grounds of his or her majority status is unjust and inequitable." This claim statement not only summarizes your position toward affirmative action, but also points to the main support for that position—that affirmative action is unjust and inequitable. In order to argue this evaluative claim convincingly, to convince your audience that one's minority or majority status is irrelevant to considerations of merit, you will need to demonstrate the injustices of affirmative action.

So far, so good. Even though you aren't personally aware of a wide range of cases, it should be easy to come up with examples of the basic unfairness of affirmative action. In the course of your reading, however, you keep coming up against the stubborn argument that majority candidates are often more qualified for jobs and educational opportunities because they have had far more educational and economic privilege than members of minority groups. To reward the most qualified, this argument continues, is to perpetuate this tradition of unequal opportunity. You find this position persuasive and reasonable, though it doesn't change your central view that qualifications, not race, should determine one's success in the job market. Gradually, you realize that this is a more complicated issue than you had recognized; a hardline position is not completely defensible.

You consider ignoring the counterargument and sticking to your original claim, but you conclude that your argument will actually be stronger if it reflects the ethical complexity of the issue and your awareness of the unfair advantage long given to the majority group. So you rewrite your working claim to read "Although affirmative action laws were designed to redress the tradition of unequal educational and economic opportunities, they are not the ideal answer to the problem. Hiring on the basis of race and gender with secondary consideration to qualifications is unfair; only the victims of inequity have changed." This new working claim is richer and more balanced than the first, reflecting your new understanding of the issue as well as your continuing disagreement with affirmative action laws.

The primary lesson to be learned from this example is that working claims should be seen as starting points, not as immutable conclusions; the thinking and writing processes will inevitably influence the starting point of an argument, shaping and modifying and in some cases even reversing the original position. Your final argument will benefit if you remain flexible about the original claim, being prepared to alter it in the face of contrary evidence or new ideas.

ACTIVITIES (3.1)

For five of the following topics, first narrow the topic to one that could be dealt with in a seven- to ten-page essay; then from that topic derive a working claim for such a paper. Your working claim is the claim with which you would begin to write your essay, though it may be refined or changed as you write.
Example topic: the risks of cigarette smoking.
Narrower topic: the health effects of cigarette smoking in public places.
Working claim: Cigarette smoking in public places is harmful to everyone.

1. Japanese automobiles
2. Jogging
3. Women's rights
4. College education
5. Television
6. Unemployment
7. Presidential elections
8. New York City
9. Careers
10. Popular music

POSITIONING THE CLAIM

Another crucial decision you will have to make about your claim is where to place it in your argument. This decision can be made at any time—before you write a paragraph or after the first draft is completed and the exact claim determined. It is a decision that should be thoughtfully made, because the position of your claim can influence your audience's reaction to the entire argument.

Claims appear most commonly in the early part of arguments, but there are perfectly legitimate reasons for placing them elsewhere. A claim placed at the beginning of the argument can have a very different effect from one delayed until the conclusion. The points to consider as you are determining the best placement for your claim are the function of the claim and your audience's probable attitude toward your argument. In the following paragraphs, we offer some guidelines (not to be mistaken for inflexible rules) for placing your claim.

Claim Stated Up Front

Claims are often presented within the first few paragraphs, usually for the sake of clarity. If your argument is likely to be difficult for your readers—complicated or highly specialized—placing the claim early in the argument will help them follow the paths of your reasoning. Claims are also commonly stated early on when the proposition is one with which readers will be comfortable, one that will not alienate them from the argument at the outset. A claim that will seem especially curious or intriguing to readers, as long as it is not immediately objectionable, can be placed early in the writing to lure them into the argument.

In the following essay on fund-raising in higher education, Janny Scott states her argument's major claim—an intriguing redefinition of the traditional activity of fund-raising—immediately after two short introductory paragraphs:

> As the last mortarboards are flung like Frisbees into the air and the last speaker winds up a peroration on endings and beginnings, at least one campus office marches on into summer on an unending mission: raising money.
>
> The task is ancient but the tools get more modern all the time. Colleges and universities, long seen as aloof from the commercial crush of life, are increasingly willing to pull out all the stops in getting alumni to give.
>
> **It's still called fund-raising—or development or even institutional advancement. But it's getting to look a lot like marketing [emphasis added].** ("Some Schools Won't Take No for an Answer," Janny Scott, the *New York Times,* June 19, 1994, section e, p. 3.)

Claim Stated at the End of Argument

Delaying the claim until the end of the argument can be effective, particularly when readers are likely to find the claim objectionable. If readers are presented with strong support for a position before they realize exactly what that position is, they may be less likely to reject the claim once it is stated; they will have been exposed to the evidence before their defenses are raised. An argument recommending a course of action unwelcome to readers might first present all of the current problems, concluding with the recommendation for change (the claim). Convinced of the seriousness of the problems, readers will be more likely to accept a writer's recommendation, even though unwelcome.

When the evidence for your argument builds directly and inevitably toward your claim with no detours or missed steps, you might consider letting your claim statement serve as the argument's conclusion. A causal argument identifying the chronological chain of causes producing a given effect might reveal the chain link by link, starting with the effect and moving backward, or starting with the first identifiable link and moving forward. Only after the final link has been identified would the claim appear. It might read:

Mid-life psychological crises do not erupt from nowhere. As our hypothetical case reveals, they result from a long series of inefficient steps an
individual takes to avoid pain or loss suffered in early childhood. But with
each attempt to avoid a reenactment of early loss, the individual only per-
petuates that loss, until finally the coping system breaks down and the
original pain must be faced and accepted.

In Chapter 5, which contains a discussion of the central principles of traditional logic, we will introduce the sequential steps of reasoning required for deductive and inductive reasoning. In both *deductive* logic (moving from premises
to necessary conclusions) and *inductive* logic (moving from particular facts to
general conclusions), conclusions *follow* from preliminary assertions; they do not
precede these assertions. If you are writing an argument that recognizably fits
these patterns of reasoning (for example, in induction, a + a + a + a + a = b), you
can present the argument according to that pattern, with the conclusion (or
claim) at the end.

Other Placements of the Claim

A claim can be placed virtually anywhere in an argument, provided you have a
good reason for that placement, one that is based on your readers' probable reception of the claim and of the argument as a whole. If your argument requires you to
provide considerable background information to your readers—a long history of
the problem of toxic waste, for example—you might delay your claim until you
have provided all of the necessary background information. Or, in another argument, you might choose to lead up to your claim with your most convincing and
logical support, then move from the claim to a discussion of its significance
(which, in fact, would constitute a *secondary argument*—an interpretation of
your position).

Unstated Claim in an Argument

On rare occasions, you can strengthen your argument by omitting your claim altogether. If a bold statement of your position would be so shocking or unacceptable to your readers that they would refuse to consider any of your evidence, then
you would be wise to leave it out, supplying instead clear statements of the individual pieces of evidence that might gently lead your readers into the vicinity of
your unstated proposition. If you wished to convince homeowners of the need for
increased commercial zoning in their quiet residential town, you might focus on
the current financial difficulties of that town, discussing the advantage to homeowners of an increased tax base. It is likely that they would agree with such a position, but would see red at the mention of rezoning.

A word of caution about omitted claims: make sure you have a very good reason for using this tactic. Arguments lacking an identifiable position statement are
often ineffective because they seem to lack a point and structure.

ACTIVITIES (3.2)

For two of the following, consider where in the argument the claim statement could be effectively placed. Then write a paragraph justifying your choice.

1. **Claim:** dog owners should receive tax credits for neutering their dogs.
   Audience: subscribers to *Dog World* magazine.

2. **Claim:** despite his enormous popularity with students, Coach Stern's consistently poor record warrants his immediate dismissal.
   Audience: students with whom Coach Stern is enormously popular.

3. **Claim:** as the evidence demonstrates, ant colonies are supremely well-organized systems in which the good of the whole always takes precedence over the good of the individual.
   Audience: undergraduate biology students.

4. **Claim:** John Locke, like his predecessor Thomas Hobbes, understood human knowledge, however complex, to derive from the basic knowledge originating in experience, in sensation.
   Audience: undergraduate philosophy students. (From Art Berman, *From the New Criticism to Deconstruction.* University of Illinois Press, 1988, p. 13.)

5. **Claim:** because all the women I know are more interested in personal relationships than any of the men I know, I conclude that women in general attach greater importance to relationships than do men.
   Audience: male readers.

CLASSIFYING YOUR CLAIM

Once you have formulated even a tentative claim statement, you should spend some time identifying the class of argument to which it belongs. Knowing at the outset that you are working with a factual, or causal, or evaluative claim will greatly ease the processes of gathering and presenting support, as each class of claim requires different kinds and arrangements of support. But in order to recognize the class to which your claim belongs, you need to have a full understanding of the characteristics and functions of the different categories of claims. In the following section of this chapter we offer a full discussion of these different categories, and representative samples of claims from each.

Factual Claims

Factual claims seek to convince an audience that a certain proposition is factual—that a given condition or phenomenon exists or has existed. The fact can be as basic as "Despite appearances, the sun is the center of our solar system, not the earth," or as little known as "Bats find their way in the dark by using their own radar system." Writers of arguments introduced by factual claims would expect their audience to accept their claims as true, although perhaps not as true forever and under all circumstances (in the Middle Ages it was a "fact" that the earth was the center of the solar system).

The concept of arguing a fact may seem a contradiction in terms. You probably think of facts as true and immutable statements about reality, not as provisional propositions requiring support and verification. If it's a fact, why argue it? But a fact only becomes a fact if it is adequately verified, if evidence is presented that proves its existence. Because facts become the cornerstones of so much of what we know and expect about the world, we must subject factual propositions to rigorous scrutiny. We cannot afford to accept on faith statements paraded as facts. In more cases than you realize, facts require verification—sometimes brief, sometimes extensive.

Facts are crucial to argument; indeed, an argument cannot succeed without some reference to fact. In the arguments you will write, facts will play three roles. Sometimes they will appear as the central claim of an argument, as in a laboratory write-up reporting that "The addition of sulfur to the compound created sulfuric acid,"or in an annual sales report claiming that sales have increased 125 percent in the last year.

More frequently, facts will function as support for other claims, as secondary claims for a claim of the same or different class. A general claim such as "All of the teachers in the Wildwinds Day Care Center have experience working with preschool children" would be supported by facts about the particular experience of each teacher. In this supporting role, facts are subject to the same principles of verification that apply to facts as central claims.

Facts are also extremely useful as examples or illustrations of difficult, unfamiliar, or abstract concepts. In this role, they do not so much prove a point as clarify it. A writer might explain or illustrate the concept that modern physics views time as relative to space and the motion of an object through space by offering the fact that a clock in a rapidly moving spaceship will have recorded the same passage of time more slowly than a clock on the earth. Concrete facts such as this give a reader a great psychological boost, because they create a comfortable, familiar footing. As with the other uses of facts, illustrative facts must be verified or at least verifiable.

The four types of facts that will figure most commonly in your arguments are (1) common knowledge facts, (2) personally experienced facts, (3) facts reported by others, and (4) factual generalizations.

Common knowledge facts are so universally acknowledged as true that they require no support or proof beyond mere statement. "Men cannot bear children" is such a universally accepted fact, as is the statement "The winter season in Florida is milder than in Vermont."

Personally experienced facts are the events, observations, and conditions cited in your argument that you have personally experienced and thus have verified through that experience. In his essay "Ali: Still Magic," Peter Tauber supports his claim that former world heavyweight boxing champion Muhammad Ali remains strong and vigorous through such personal observations as the following:

Walking down the driveway he slipped on a patch of ice and almost fell. But he didn't fall. Instead, without taking his hands out of his jacket pockets, he did a kind of modified Ali Shuffle, a quick two-step, and after a small hop, kicked one foot off a flower bed's retaining wall until he was on dry paving. He turned around without breaking stride, to warn me . . . "Careful—ice."

Often it is necessary to bring into an argument facts that do not arise out of your own experience but that do not qualify as commonly acknowledged facts. Such material, *facts reported by others,* is obtained from second- or third-party sources. A second-party source would be the person who ascertained the fact—for example, your manager telling you that sales had declined 5 percent in the last quarter, or a written report containing that information. A third-party source would be a person or document containing facts ascertained by someone else—for example, a biology textbook describing some little-known facts about Darwin's work on the *Beagle.*

Factual generalizations are broad claims made about a large group or time-span. Any class of claim can be stated as a generalization. A factual generalization claims that a certain condition is true for a large number of subjects or over a long period of time. Factual generalizations are not separate from the three types of facts just identified; any of these could be stated as a generalization, as in the personally experienced generalization "Most of my friends are interested in sports." In formal written argument, generalizations must be supported, whether they are the central claims or reinforcements for a claim.

Factual claims are stated as unequivocal assertions, containing no elements of personal opinion, speculation, or prediction. The following are typical examples of factual claims:

1. New York City is the banking center of the United States. (The claim makes a quantifiable assertion that could be verified by a survey of the number of banks and banking transactions taking place in major American cities.)
2. Our solar system is approximately five billion years old. (While no individual could verify this claim through firsthand experience or knowledge, it is a statement of the consensus of experts on the subject and could thus be documented.)
3. Steel radial tires last longer than tires made with nylon. (Again, this claim can be verified, though the process of verification might be tedious and time-consuming.)
4. Most of my friends are involved in intramural sports. (A statement of fact that can be supported, if necessary, by listing the number of friends that are involved and not involved in intramural sports.)

ACTIVITIES (3.3)

1. For each of the factual propositions listed below, identify the category or categories of fact (common knowledge, personal experience, second- or third-

party, generalization) in which the proposition belongs.

Example: The Cuban Missile Crisis occurred in October of 1962. Second or third party for most students; personal experience for older people.

a. The disappearance of former Teamster's Union leader Jimmy Hoffa is still unexplained.

b. The risk of getting cancer is decreased by a high-fiber diet.

c. My Communications professor routinely missed her 8:00 class.

d. Alaska is the largest state in the United States.

e. An apple a day keeps the doctor away.

f. I get better grades on the papers I take the time to revise.

g. Severe air pollution is dangerous for people suffering from lung disease.

h. Women under age 30 have better driving records than men under age 30.

i. In Italy, people take more time to enjoy life than we do in the United States.

2. Write a claim for a factual argument on *three* of the following topics; then develop each claim into a paragraph:

Example claim: "If you don't know much about the Chicago skyline, you would probably guess that the world's tallest building is in New York. While the Empire State Building and the World Trade Center are the most well known examples of skyscrapers, the world's tallest building is actually in Chicago. The Empire State Building is 1,250 feet high, the World Trade Center, 1,350 feet high, but the Sears Tower in Chicago, at 1,454 feet, is the tallest of the three."

a. Comparative standards of living among the countries of the world

b. The popularity of soccer in the United States

c. The decline of the railroads as a means of passenger transportation in the United States in the last forty years

d. Career expectations of female college students

e. Skyscrapers

Causal Claims

Causal claims propose a causal link between two events or conditions. They can argue that A caused B or, more speculatively, that A could cause B at some future time. Statements such as "Excessive layers of management have caused the decline of several large American corporations" or "High consumer spending will lead to greater inflation" are examples of this kind of argument.

Most of us are drawn naturally to the activity of assigning cause. We witness the careers of prominent public figures and wonder what factors account for their phenomenal successes. We reflect on a great tragedy like the Holocaust of World War II and want to know how such a thing could happen. We seek the reasons behind events because we want assurance that the world is governed by certain principles, not simply by random chance. Identifying cause is also almost always instructive. If we know why a certain phenomenon came about, we have a reasonable hope of preventing that effect (if it was an unfortunate one) or of reproducing it (if it was a desirable one) in the future. Airline officials would want to know what caused a plane crash in order to prevent similar crashes; a sales manager would want to know what circumstances contributed to a dramatic growth in quarterly sales so the success could be reproduced in succeeding quarters.

In arguing an effect, that A could cause B at some future time, we predict a future occurrence on the basis of certain current or intended circumstances. Stockbrokers must be skillful in this form of argument, as they try to enhance and protect the interests of their clients by predicting market activity. Doctors focusing on *preventive* medicine regularly identify probable effects to their patients: "If you don't eliminate fatty food from your diet, you have a greater risk of heart attack." In business and industry, the long-term health of a corporation often depends on the prediction of future trends and their impact on the business. Eastman Kodak, for example, with its enormously successful traditional business of photographic products, must determine the probable future of photography in the face of competition from electronic imaging products like the camcorder, the VCR, and computer software.

Under carefully controlled scientific conditions, it is possible to identify cause and even to predict effect with such a high degree of certainty that the causality can be established as *factual*. Researchers have determined that smoking increases the risk of lung cancer and that lobar pneumonia is caused by the pneumococcus bacteria. But in the causal arguments that most of us make, arguments that revolve around human behavior—our actions, our successes and failures, our relations with others—certainty is virtually impossible. In these more speculative arguments, the best we can hope for is to establish *probable* cause or effect convincingly.

But because a claim cannot be proven with certainty does not mean it isn't worth arguing. Probable, reasonable positions are extremely sound bases for decisions and actions and are the goal of most of the arguments we write. If we allowed ourselves to be moved by certainty alone, our progress would be slow. Probability is not easy to achieve; in many cases, it requires more skill than establishing certainty in factual arguments.

Causal claims are easy to spot because they (1) often contain words indicating causality—cause, produce, effect, consequence—and/or (2) posit a relationship between two phenomena occurring at different points in time. Some representative causal claims are:

1. The decline of Great Britain as an economic power after World War II was primarily caused by a lack of entrepreneurial spirit in British business leaders. (The word *caused* is always a dead giveaway of a causal argument.)
2. If Sally had written a better résumé she might have been given the job. (A causal relationship is advanced between two events happening [or potentially happening] at two different times.)
3. A balanced budget promises a stable government. (Again, the claim posits a close causal relationship between a balanced budget and a stable government. The verb *promises* can be understood as a verb signifying cause.)
4. Increasing numbers of two-career families have contributed to the rising divorce rate. ("Contributed to" suggests a causal relationship between the two phenomena.)

ACTIVITIES (3.4)

1. Write a paragraph about five of the following claims, explaining why you believe the claim anticipates a speculative causal argument or a factual causal argument.
   a. If Abraham Lincoln had not been assassinated, he could have lessened the bitterness between the North and the South after the war.
   b. The widespread use of computers in business and industry will increase total employment, not decrease it.
   c. If it had not snowed, Ohio State could have defeated Michigan in that football game.
   d. For most automobiles, failure to change the oil at regular intervals will damage the engine.
   e. The decline in the percentage of the population attending organized religious activities has caused the rise in the crime rate in the past 40 years.
   f. The use of seat belts decreases the number of fatalities in automobile accidents.
   g. If newlyweds had more realistic expectations about marriage, there would be a decline in the divorce rate.
   h. The children of the affluent would be happier if they had to do more for themselves.
   i. Some cold medicines can cause drowsiness.
   j. The existence of nuclear weapons has prevented the outbreak of World War III.
2. Write a claim for a causal argument for one of the following; then make a list of all the reasons you can think of that would convince a reader of the cause or effect you identify. Describe these reasons in a paragraph.
   a. The cause of a particular war
   b. A team's victory or loss in a certain game
   c. A change in some aspect of the government's social or economic policy
   d. A change in exercise or dietary behavior
   e. The cause of a person's career success or failure
   Example of (3): "There would be fewer homeless people if the federal government increased its aid to cities."
   Reasons: Money could be used for low-income housing. Money could be used for training programs that would give the poor a means of self-support. Other countries that give substantial aid to cities do not have the problem with the homeless that we do.

Evaluations

Evaluative claims seek agreement about a particular value judgment made by the writer. When we are arguing an evaluation, we are proposing our own personal judgment about a work of art, a policy, a person, an action, even another evaluation. Informal pronouncements of personal taste—"Your tie is ugly," "That restaurant serves the best chicken wings in town," "I enjoy playing basketball more than tennis"—come under the category of value judgments, though they are so purely subjective, so clearly a matter of personal taste, that there is little point in trying to argue them reasonably. We are all inclined to pass judgment on the world's passing show, and frequently we do not much care whether these judgments are taken seriously.

But when we do care about the impact of these judgments, when we want our opinions to influence others, we must understand how to argue judgments of value. In fact, many value judgments, while perhaps originating as unconsidered personal opinion, *can* be effectively and convincingly argued. Such assertions as "Pornography is an offense to all women" or "The government made major mistakes in trying to trade weapons for hostages," if they are serious, carefully considered judgments, could become useful and important arguments.

Because evaluations tend to work from very personal value systems, they are probably the hardest of all arguments to argue convincingly. It is extremely difficult to change someone's mind about an opinion or judgment. But if your concluding judgment is reached by a responsible and reasonable presentation of evidence and if that judgment gains the sympathy of your audience, you will have argued the value judgment successfully, even if it does not change everyone's mind.

An important variant of the evaluative claim is the *interpretive* claim. Interpretations are explanatory evaluations of a person, event, or object: "The key to Hamlet's character is his Oedipal fixation on his mother"; "Richard Nixon's presidency was destroyed by his inferiority complex." Neither of these examples is simply factual or descriptive; each gives us a particular explanation of what happened beneath the surface. Interpretive claims can surpass mere opinion only by being supported by facts and reasoned argument. Reasonable, intelligent people can vary in their interpretation of a certain situation, such as the key to Hamlet's behavior in Shakespeare's play, but not all interpretations are equally plausible or illuminating. To argue, for example, that gout explains much of Hamlet's behavior when there is no evidence to support that view is an example of very poor interpretation.

The following claims would introduce evaluative arguments:

1. Many people do not realize that Herman Melville, the author of *Moby Dick,* was also an accomplished poet. (Evaluative claims often contain descriptive modifiers, like *accomplished* in this example.)
2. Former President Jimmy Carter may not have been a great president, but he was an honorable one.
3. Mary's constant chatter is an attempt to keep people from abandoning her. (An interpretive claim, in that it offers a beneath-the-surface explanation of Mary's behavior. Like all other interpretive claims, this one contains causal elements, but what distinguishes it as primarily interpretive is the identification of the roots of a certain phenomenon—in this case, a certain behavior.)
4. For my money, soccer players are the most gifted of all athletes. (*Gifted* is a subjective term: it not only means different things to different people, but it also cannot be conclusively applied. Claims that include superlative or comparative judgments are likely to be evaluative claims.)

5. Human memory is a marvelous but fallacious instrument. (Taken from the Primo Levi excerpt in Chapter 1, this claim makes two judgments about memory. Although the supporting material includes clinical and scientific facts, the claim itself asserts one person's descriptive judgment about the function of memory.)

ACTIVITIES (3.5)

1. Write claims for evaluative arguments for three of the following subjects.
    Example subject: theft of library books.
    Example claim: "The theft of library books is a serious offense not only because stealing is wrong but because the theft of books dramatically increases library costs and deprives other readers of material that is often difficult or impossible to replace."
    a. Military retaliation against terrorism
    b. Computer games
    c. Pass-fail grading for courses
    d. Television shows
    e. The legal drinking age
    f. Electrically powered automobiles
    g. Teenage pregnancy
    h. The performance of your student government president
2. Give an example of an interpretive statement for two of the following topics.
    Example of topic (a): "The popularity of the film *Platoon* means that Americans are finally coming to grips with both the heroism and the tragedy of America's involvement in Vietnam."
    a. The significance of a play, movie, or short story
    b. The importance of some contemporary political figure
    c. The meaning of a current trend in music or fashion
    d. The attitude of students at a particular college or university toward their future careers
    e. The attitude of young Americans toward religion

Recommendations

A common goal of argument is to convince an audience of the need for a particular change in existing circumstances. Some *recommendations* seek only to gain an audience's agreement with an idea or a decision, but others have a more practical purpose: they attempt to move an audience to a particular course of action or, more modestly, to convince an audience that a particular course of action should be taken by another person or group. A student in an English Composition course might write a paper calling for the lowering of the legal drinking age, or the same argument might be made in a letter to the editor of a newspaper or to one's congressional representative. A lab technician might write a memo to the supervisor suggesting the purchase of new, more efficient laboratory equipment. An academic department chairperson might request from the dean an adjustment in the salaries of certain junior faculty. All of these arguments are recommendations; they recommend that certain actions be taken or that certain new policies or alterations in existing policies be instituted.

All recommendations are to some extent concerned with the future, with what should be done at a later time, but implied in an argument of this type is also a judgment about present conditions. Writers almost always propose change because of dissatisfaction with a current situation. In arguing a recommendation, you must determine whether you want to concentrate on the current problem, or the improvements resulting from your recommendation, or whether you want to give present and future equal emphasis.

The main goal of recommendations emphasizing *present* conditions is to demonstrate that a current situation is problematic or unacceptable. Because their purpose is more to demonstrate *that* something needs to be done than *what* exactly that something is, they usually do not discuss a proposed change in any detail.

In writing recommendations emphasizing the probable *future* effects of the proposed change, you must do more than identify current problems: you must come up with a new plan, arguing convincingly that your recommendation is feasible and that it will produce desirable effects. Recommendations with *equal* emphasis on present and future consider at some length what currently exists, what could exist, and what the results of the changes are likely to be.

Recommendations are hybrid claims, including evaluative or causal elements, or a combination of the two. When proposing that an existing situation be changed, you are at least implying a negative judgment of the existing situation. Implied in your particular recommendation for change is a positive evaluation of the new system. Furthermore, you will support the recommendation itself through an argument of effect—demonstrating the positive future effects of the change.

Because arguments of recommendation argue for an action not currently in effect, words such as *should, would, must, ought, needs to be, will,* or *might* typically introduce these arguments. The following are some sample claims for arguments of recommendations:

1. We need more emphasis on science and math in our schools to prepare the next generation for a world of international economic competition. (The claim proposes a *change* in the current curriculum.)
2. In order to attract more nontraditional students, this university must review and revise its course offerings. (Again, this claim calls for a change in an existing situation—a change that will have positive effects in the future.)
3. If this company is to regain financial health, it must divest itself of all divisions not directly connected to its traditional core business. (The words

must divest identify this claim as a recommendation—a suggestion for a
particular action is being made.)

4. Take back the night. (A trenchant recommendation expressed in the im-
   perative mode. In the word *back*, the command implies making a change
   in an existing situation.)

ACTIVITIES (3.6)

For two of the following situations, write two claims of recommendation, one
focusing on current conditions and one on the results of recommended
improvements.

Example: taking a typing course.

Claim with a focus on current conditions: "I need to take a typing course because
I can't use the word processor required in my English Composition course."

Claim with focus on future improvements: "I need to take a typing course so that I
will be ready for the day when every office has its own word processor."

1. Replacing a television
2. Requesting a new strict policy on noise in a dormitory
3. Advocating a freeze on the research for and manufacturing of nuclear
   weapons
4. Purchasing a new car to replace your or your family's current one
5. Increasing the number of police in the most dangerous sections of a city

Combination Claims

Professional writing is full of arguments that do not appear to resemble any of the
examples we have presented. As a writer of arguments, you may suspect that there
is only a distant relationship between our neat classification of claims according to
function and the cluttered situation you find yourself in when writing. While you
may find yourself basing an argument on a claim statement that bears no resem-
blance to any of our examples, the more you write, the more you will become
aware that most claims fulfill one or more of these four functions.

Claims that at first do not appear to fit in any category can be recast so that
their place among these four is evident. For example, the famous claim "The only
thing we have to fear is fear itself," which is a perfectly good, lively sentence needing no revision, can be translated to mean "we should beware of the dangers of
fear"—a recommendation based on an argument implying the probable negative
effects of fear. You do not have to rewrite the claim, but if you can discover this
clearer, less graceful statement in your original claim, you will be well on your way
to supporting it appropriately.

Often, as this example demonstrates, the context of your claim will help you
categorize it. This quotation about fear is taken from President Franklin Delano
Roosevelt's first inaugural address in 1933, in the heart of the Depression, when
fear about the future pervaded America. In a less urgent context, "the only thing

we have to fear is fear itself" might be an interpretive statement meaning "fear itself is a debilitating emotion apart from any real dangers that may have created the fear in the first place." In the context of Roosevelt's address, however, the remark is part of a broad recommendation to the American people to regain their confidence and to begin to plan for the future with new hope.

Reality often escapes our categorizations of it, and claims are no exception. You need to know the different kinds of claims and what they usually look like, but you must also be flexible and prepared for the unexpected. If you are arguing a claim that doesn't seem to fit into any of the categories discussed here, and you can't seem to recast it mentally, as we did with the Roosevelt example, ask yourself some questions about the function of the argument to be based on the claim. For example, is the claim verifiable? If not, it is not factual. Does it make an unverifiable judgment about something or someone? If so, you probably have an evaluative claim. Does it propose a course of action? If so, it is a recommendation. Does it in any way account for or predict a particular phenomenon? If so, it is a causal argument.

Some claim statements actually contain two claims, as in the sentence "Acts of terrorism are serious offenses against human freedom and should meet with deadly retaliation." The first claim is the *evaluation* that acts of terrorism are serious offenses, and the second is the *recommendation* that they should meet with deadly retaliation. In supporting these claims, you would first have to defend your value judgment that terrorism is a serious offense against human freedom before moving on to the second assertion. The second claim is a recommendation—terrorism should meet with deadly retaliation—supported by another value judgment: namely, that retaliation is not only effective but morally just. Ideally, both claims should be defended, though frequently writers assume that their audience agrees with them on the most basic points—for example, terrorism is a flagrant offense and retaliation against it is just—and concentrate on one or two more arguable points, such as whether retaliation is effective in preventing future acts of terrorism.

Cutting corners in this fashion is frequently desirable because of limitations of space or the necessity of concentrating on just one aspect of a topic, but it can also lead to assuming too much, or to thinking only what the crowd thinks. Writers who deal with such controversial topics as terrorism should at least *consider* such basic issues as whether retaliation is morally just, even if they do not write about it in their essays. Reviewing what will be assumed in an essay is one way writers can keep themselves honest.

Frequently, a factual claim is combined with one of the other three kinds of claims. When this is the case, as in the statement "The rise in the divorce rate in the last twenty years may increase the divorce rate in the next generation," you must establish the accuracy of your facts (that the divorce rate has risen) before you go on to speculate about possible effects of this phenomenon. So too with the statement "Increased credit spending by consumers is bad for the nation's political stability." First, the increased credit spending must be established as a fact, and then the value judgment can be argued.

The following are examples of combination claims:

1. The recent rise in interest rates may contribute to higher inflation. (This combines a factual assertion about rising interest rates, which could very quickly be supported, with a causal argument predicting the effect of the higher rates. This second claim would be the focus of your argument.)
2. No nation is truly free that does not offer its citizens equal opportunity in education and employment. (This combines a causal argument—lack of equal opportunity results in an unfree nation—with an evaluation judging the degree of a nation's freedom.)
3. If the candidate wants to win votes, he must convince constituents that his reputation for moral laxness is undeserved. (This combines a recommendation that the candidate make his case to his constituents and a causal argument that making this case will win him their votes.)
4. While men seem to be driven to success by a fear of failure, women are made comfortable with failure by their fear of success. (This breathtaking generalization combines interpretation—identifying hidden motives for behavior—with elements of a factual argument. The writer will have to present *many* instances of these gender-linked phenomena in order to warrant the generality of the claim.)

ACTIVITIES (3.7)

Into which of the four main argument types or combination of types do two of the following belong? Be prepared to support your answer.
Example: Automobiles should be designed so that they get a minimum of 30 miles per gallon of gasoline.
Type of argument: recommendation.

1. Excessive consumption of alcohol can lead to many illnesses.
2. Honesty is the best policy.
3. Cutting defense spending will create a safer world.
4. Tariffs on imports merely raise prices for domestic consumers.
5. Alley cats are a public nuisance in this neighborhood.
6. Politics is the art of the possible.
7. An improved sewer system would solve these flood drainage problems.
8. America should protect its domestic industries with tariffs and quotas.
9. Without a belief in God, life has no meaning.
10. Obesity can help cause heart disease.

SUMMARY

The Claim

- Claims help readers understand and evaluate arguments, and they help you, the writer, generate the direction and content of your arguments.
- If you have difficulty coming up with a working claim, you probably need to do more thinking and reading about your topic. When you are knowledgeable enough, a claim should come to you.
- Always be prepared to modify a working claim to fit with new ideas and information.
- Claims can be placed virtually anywhere in an argument. The most effective placement depends on the nature of your argument and its probable reception by readers.
- *Factual claims* seek to convince an audience that a given object or condition exists or has existed. The four kinds of facts are common knowledge facts, facts experienced by you, facts reported by others, and factual generalizations.
- *Causal claims* assert that one event or condition produces or helps to produce another event or condition. In claiming *cause,* we look for what produced a past or current event or condition. In claiming *effect,* we predict a future occurrence on the basis of certain current or intended circumstances.
- *Evaluations* make a value judgment of a person, activity, or object.
- *Recommendations* argue for a particular course of action in order to change existing circumstances. Recommendations can focus on present conditions, future effects, or a combination of both.
- Some arguments work from claims that combine elements of the four classes.

SUGGESTIONS FOR WRITING (3.8)

1. Take one of the following vague or overused claims and turn it into an interesting claim with fresh and precise language. Then write a two- to three-page essay to support this new claim. As you develop support for your argument, you may have to modify the claim so that it will fit your support.

   a. Waste not, want not.
   b. Children are not as respectful of their elders as they should be.
   c. America must remain the strongest power in the world.
   d. A little learning is a dangerous thing.
   e. Meryl Streep (or someone else) is a talented actress.

2. Read an argumentative essay in a magazine like the *Atlantic Monthly* or the *New York Times Magazine* and write a one- to two-page essay on what kind of argument it is and why. Be sure to give your instructor a copy of the argumentative essay you are analyzing.

3. Select a familiar document such as Martin Luther King Jr.'s "I Have a Dream" speech, Lincoln's "Gettysburg Address," the Declaration of Independence, or a famous Shakespearean soliloquy, and identify the class or classes of argument it represents. In a one- to two-page essay, support your identification and discuss the effectiveness of the argument. Be sure to give your instructor a copy of the document you are analyzing.

4

An Argument's Support

We are accustomed to hearing the term *hypothesis* used in connection with scientific research. A hypothesis is an "unproved theory, proposition, supposition . . . tentatively accepted to explain certain facts or . . . to provide a basis for further investigation" (Webster's *New World Dictionary*). A research scientist observing peculiar and surprising behavior in laboratory mice hypothesizes a tentative explanation for this behavior. The scientist then tests the validity of that explanation in many complicated ways, or perhaps simply has an educated hunch to test against a variety of controlled situations. If the tentative explanation or hunch stands up during the experiments, the hypothesis has been proven.

A writer with a working claim is in much the same situation as the scientist with an educated hunch. Like the scientist, the writer must discover convincing evidence (or *support*) for a hypothesis. Broadly defined, an argument's support is all the material that transforms a working claim, or hypothesis, into a justified, reasonable conclusion. To argue a claim successfully, a writer must know what kind of support is appropriate to the claim being proposed, how much support will be sufficient, and which arrangement of supporting material will make the argument most effective.

In most cases, once you come up with a claim you wish to argue, you will also have in mind, if only dimly, certain material that supports or proves that claim. Sometimes you will have plenty of supporting material before you have a claim. The more your claim emerges from your experience of dissonance and your own interests, the more likely it is that you will have ready at hand some solid support for your argument. (Claims that have no connection with your own experiences, interests, or knowledge are usually difficult to support.)

For example, if your observations of an unhappy grandparent move you to write an argument about age discrimination, you will have at hand some examples of discriminatory practices and their effects. Some of these examples would

certainly be useful in a claim arguing "American society, for all its public attention to human rights, is guilty of systematically depriving its senior citizens of
countless 'inalienable' rights." But in order to argue convincingly such a wide-
ranging claim as this, you would need to provide more support than your own
personal observations.

Knowing the class of argument to which your working claim belongs will help
you select the most appropriate support, because each class tends to require certain kinds of support. In Chapters 6 through 9 we will discuss these specific requirements. In this chapter, we will introduce the general varieties of support that
can be applied to all arguments, and we will offer some guidelines for determining
the amount of support an argument requires and the most effective way to arrange
it within an argument.

SOME VARIETIES OF SUPPORT

We find it useful to view this concept of supporting material as discrete units (or
building blocks) that strengthen a claim in different ways, with different degrees of
effectiveness. We offer below a discussion of some of the generic varieties of support commonly used to strengthen arguments.

Secondary Claims

Virtually all claims, regardless of their class, are supported by further claims,
which will require their own support. In some cases, these secondary claims will
belong to the same class as the central claim; in other cases, they will belong to a
different class. If you were arguing the factual claim "Students in my major are
more interested in learning marketable skills than in educating themselves," you
would need to support your fairly general claim with individual instances of this
preference. You probably would cite conversations in which individual students
had expressed this preference to you, and/or perhaps a survey asking students in
your major to rank their educational priorities. In both cases, you are supporting
your central claim with a secondary factual claim, which will itself need to be supported or authorized.

An argument of recommendation claiming that "This university should offer a
pass-fail grading option to its students" could cite as support the secondary *causal*
claim that "Removing the traditional evaluative system of letter grades will facili-
tate learning by reducing pressure." While not your argument's chief point, this
secondary causal claim would require its own support. One way to support this
secondary causal claim is through a third, factual claim. Perhaps you have access
to a survey taken at another university that offers the pass-fail option, and this survey demonstrates a positive student response to the policy. Or perhaps you have
friends at other schools who have expressed a similar positive response. Whether
gathered through a large survey or individual conversations, these responses, if responsibly obtained and accurately reported, are facts that will strengthen your
claim.

As these two examples demonstrate, eventually all central claims will come to rest on supported factual claims. While some arguments depend more heavily on facts than others, no argument is likely to be convincing if it does not at some point refer to supporting factual claims. The example factual claim about student learning goals is immediately supported by secondary factual arguments: the expressed preferences of other students in your major and/or a more widespread survey of student learning goals. In the second example, a recommendation ultimately comes to rest on a secondary factual claim: positive student response to the pass-fail option. As you will see in Chapter 6, these secondary factual claims would be supported by your assurance that they have been gathered, interpreted, and reported responsibly.

ACTIVITIES (4.1)

Supply and identify secondary claims that would support the following central claims of arguments:

1. The *Bates GRE Study Guide* is an excellent tutorial for students preparing to take the GRE.
2. Television newscasting influences the way Americans think about social and political issues.
3. In my high school, food abuse was a far bigger problem than alcohol or drug abuse.
4. Dostoyevski's *Crime and Punishment* is a ponderous novel of sin and redemption.
5. If we really want to eradicate racism, we must institute within the primary grades curricula that honor diversity.

Comparisons

Some claims can be supported by citing a comparable claim that has already gained wide acceptance. This tactic will only work if the two claims are substantially comparable, not just vaguely similar. In an argument predicting financial difficulties for a particular company, for example, you might support your claim by citing the documented financial problems encountered by a comparable company in comparable circumstances. Or if you were arguing against proposed cuts in state money for scholarships, you might cite what another state had done in order to avoid reducing its education budget. Such a comparison would only work if the fiscal situation of the state you refer to is truly comparable to that of your state. In order to know this, you would have to get a fair amount of information on each, and probably present that information in the argument itself.

Appeals to Authority

Any claim can be supported by referring to a similar position held by a recognized authority in the field. An evaluative argument claiming that Charles Barkley is the most talented professional basketball player in the game today could be supported by citing a similar judgment made by Michael Jordan—obviously an authority on the subject of basketball talent. When using this strategy of support, you must be sure that the person whose judgment you cite *is* an established expert in the subject of your argument. Even though Michael Jordan is a sports celebrity, his fame does not make him an expert on investment strategies or health care. Fame does not automatically confer expertise.

Appeals to Audience Needs and Values

As we said in Chapter 2, writers of argument must carefully consider the readers they are addressing—the extent of their familiarity with the subject, their predisposition toward the claim, their needs, and their values. Obviously, audiences will be favorably disposed toward arguments they see as likely to satisfy their needs or affirm their values. Many arguments presume the needs and values of their audience without explicitly referring to them. But some arguments can be strengthened by directly addressing these considerations, particularly when the match between claim and audience needs or values is not immediately apparent. In a recommendation addressed to the administration of your college that proposes changing from a trimester to semester calendar, you would be wise to identify precisely how the change would benefit the interests represented by the administration. Perhaps you could demonstrate the probability of increased enrollment, higher student satisfaction, or long-term savings.

ACTIVITIES (4.2)

In a one- to two-page essay, discuss which methods of support (comparison, appeal to authority, appeal to audience needs and values) could be effectively applied to two of the claims that follow.

1. The costs of statewide and national political campaigns will discourage all but the rich from running for office.
2. The study of homosexuality is (is not) appropriate in a college course.
3. Regardless of what your mother used to tell you, you cannot catch a cold by going outside with wet hair.
4. Parents should recognize how they risk their children's intellectual development by parking them in front of a television.
5. The widespread use of antidepressant drugs has revolutionized the psychotherapeutic community.

Addressing the Counterargument

Any argument worth making will suggest a counterargument—a position different from and often directly opposed to your argument's claim. Awareness of this counterargument, and, in many cases, direct reference to it within your argument, will strengthen your own claim considerably. Familiarity with your subject and with your audience should allow you to identify what the most compelling counterargument is likely to be. Having identified the most convincing objection or objections, you need to consider the extent to which you should address them within your own argument.

Sometimes you may choose to omit direct reference altogether—perhaps because the counterargument is a weak one, or because it is not likely to be widely held. But omission does not mean ignorance: to some extent, that counterargument should shape or inform your own argument.

In some arguments, the most effective strategy can be to acknowledge the counterargument without directly refuting it. Acknowledging the counterargument shows a reader that you are aware of the complexity of the issue and the legitimacy of other positions; it contributes to the impression that you are reasonable and broad-minded. The following example demonstrates this strategy. Toward the end of her essay on the advantages of competitive athletics for girls, Margaret Whitney includes a brief acknowledgment of some predictable objections to her argument.

> I am not suggesting that participation in sports is the answer for all young women. It is not easy—the losing, jealousy, raw competition and intense personal criticism of performance.
>
> And I don't wish to imply that the sports scene is a morality play either. Girls' sports can be funny. You can't forget that out on that field are a bunch of people who know the meaning of the word cute. During one game, I noticed that Ann had a blue ribbon tied on her ponytail, and it dawned on me that every girl on the team had an identical bow. Somehow I can't picture the Celtics gathered in the locker room of the Boston Garden agreeing to wear the same color sweatbands.

By pointing out that her views are not universally applicable, the writer actually strengthens the point she is making.

On other occasions, direct refutation of an opposing position is called for. If, for example, you know your readers agree with a position substantially different from yours, you should identify that position and point out its flaws in reasoning, facts, or relevance. Or if you know that a credible, often-cited countercase or exception exists, regardless of whether your audience subscribes to that position, you should address it. And finally, if for some reason it is particularly important for you to project a broad-minded, well-balanced image, you should include a refutation in your argument.

As an example of direct refutation, we cite this paragraph from Martin Luther King, Jr.'s 1963 "Letter from Birmingham Jail," where King responds to criticism from Alabama clergymen about his program of nonviolent resistance to racial segregation.

> You may well ask, "Why direct action? Why sit-ins, marches, and so forth? Isn't negotiation a better path?" You are quite right in calling for negotiation. Indeed, this is the very purpose of direct action. Nonviolent direct action seeks to create such a crisis and foster such a tension that a

community which has constantly refused to negotiate is forced to confront the issue. It seeks so to dramatize the issue that it can no longer be ignored. My citing the creation of tension as part of the work of the nonviolent resister may sound rather shocking. But I must confess I am not afraid of the word "tension." I have earnestly opposed violent tension, but there is a type of constructive, nonviolent tension which is necessary for growth. Just as Socrates felt that it was necessary to create a tension in the mind so that individuals could rise from the bondage of myths and half truths to the unfettered realm of creative analysis and objective appraisal, so must we see the need for nonviolent gadflies to create the kind of tension in society that will help men rise from the dark depths of prejudice and racism to the majestic heights of understanding and brotherhood.

Note how King specifies the opposition's position and even concedes them a point (they're correct in calling for negotiations) before he then refutes their position and moves to an idealistic statement of his own. This pattern of statement–concession–refutation is typical of effective refutations, though the concession should be included only when it is appropriate.

Direct refutations need to be strategically placed within arguments. If you have a very recalcitrant audience dedicated to an opposing position, you aren't likely to convince them of the weakness of their views at the outset. Readers without strongly held views are less likely to be swayed by a counterargument if it follows an impressive array of support for your claim. If you include your refutation as the final piece of support, remember that it may linger in your reader's mind for some time, so make it as strong and convincing as possible. Remember also what we said in Chapter 2: some very powerful arguments are no more than refutations of opposing arguments, gaining precision from knowing exactly what they are against and intensity from the energy of this opposition.

ARRANGING YOUR ARGUMENT'S SUPPORT

Not only is the identification of appropriate support crucial to an argument's success, but also the arrangement of that support. You can make strong support more convincing by organizing it effectively, especially by considering the impact your organization is likely to have on your readers.

In most arguments, a number of good organizational strategies exist, but the best organization for any given argument is the one that best suits its particular audience. If you take the time to consider your readers' familiarity with your subject, their ability to follow the course of your argument, and their probable disposition toward your claim, you should be able to organize your support effectively.

When considering the organization of an argument's support, think of the support as separate units that can be moved around within your essay. In an argument claiming that "Bay City should construct a convention center to attract visitors to the city," the units of support could be listed as follows:

1. Bay City attracts 30,000 fewer visitors per year than Rock City, a similar city with a convention center.
2. A convention center would add a minimum of $15 million a year to the local economy, which would benefit all citizens of Bay City, not just those in the food, hotel, and tourist industries.
3. The convention center could be financed by long-term bonds, which would spread the cost over a long period of time.
4. Bay City already has the air, train, and bus facilities to handle more visitors.
5. Experts in the convention business point out that there is a high correlation between convention centers and attracting new industries to a city.
6. Most of Bay City's citizens share a belief in industrial and economic progress, which is the basic value being appealed to here.

A good general principle is that the *strongest* support should be presented first, so that you gain at least provisional agreement from your readers early on. If at all possible, you should save at least one very effective supporting point for the end of the argument, thus leaving your readers with a final impression of your argument's strength. In the previous list, for example, the strongest argument probably is the comparison with Rock City, because Rock City really is comparable to Bay City, and the success of its convention center is well known among Bay City's citizens. The last argument—the appeal to shared values—is also strong because this belief in progress is one of the strongest shared values of Bay City's citizens.

What constitutes strong support? To some extent this will depend on your audience. A credulous, inexperienced group and a cynical or expert audience will be convinced by different points. However, relevant factual support—figures, examples, and statistics, as in the previous list's supporting points 1 and 2—usually is very strong. Less convincing to a sophisticated audience is more speculative material—an identification of the possible effects of a certain condition. For example, a knowledgeable audience might be skeptical of point 5's claim that a convention center in itself would attract new industry; the claim may be true, yet many readers would hesitate to believe it without further study of the issue. Comparisons, as in point 1's comparison of Bay City with Rock City, can be convincing as long as you can establish true comparability. Citing expert opinion is usually effective, provided your expert is truly an expert. With point 5, for example, who are the "experts in the convention business" cited in the claim? Do they have a strong bias toward convention centers? What is the basis of their claim? Have they considered other factors, such as the possibility that cities with convention centers usually have strong transportation systems that attract new industry, whereas cities without centers usually do not?

Of course, sometimes you must arrange your support in a certain order. Scientific experiments dictate a certain arrangement. So do causal chains, where cause A must be discussed before cause B, cause B before cause C, and so on. In these cases, you must make sure that all of your support is as strong as possible and that it fits tightly together. With these kinds of arguments, one weak piece can destroy the effectiveness of the entire argument.

ACTIVITIES (4.3)

The following evaluative argument, written by student Sharon Bidwell, contains a number of varieties of supporting material. In a two-page paper, identify which methods are used and discuss the effectiveness of their arrangement.

The administration's decision not to allow Dr. Fasciano and his white supremacist group to participate in a roundtable discussion with the students on our campus is clearly an act of censorship and should not be tolerated in a country that prides itself on free thought and expression. Censorship, as defined by the Encyclopaedia Britannica, is "the suppression or prohibition of speech or writing that is condemned as subversive to the common good." It is obvious that the administration is making a selective decision of what the "common good" is for the students of this campus.

There is no doubt that the administration has legitimate concerns that need to be addressed. First of all, Mr. Fasciano's visit will raise some eyebrows among those who make regular contributions to the university. Second, Mr. Fasciano's visit is likely to set off active protests which have the capacity to seriously disrupt the campus and even threaten the safety and security of the students.

Despite these very real risks, the administration must make it known that this university supports the Constitution of the United States, namely the First Amendment, and does not bow to pressure when it comes to suppressing free speech. To paraphrase John Milton in his "Areopagitica" of 1644: we must allow that free and open encounter in which truth may indeed prevail over error.

The argument against censorship has been made by many who fought hard against it--against anything, in fact, that interferes with self-development and self-fulfillment. For example, in his first inaugural address, Thomas Jefferson addressed the necessity of free dissent: "If there be any among us who would wish to dissolve this Union or to change its republican form, let them stand undisturbed as monuments of the safety with which error of opinion may be tolerated where reason is left free to combat it."

The administration must give the students the freedom
to be the best guarantors of quality and fairness. We rely
on these institutions of higher learning to teach future
generations by allowing them to choose freely and make difficult decisions. For those who oppose Mr. Fasciano and his
views, let there be an open forum with a free exchange of
ideas. Our forefathers fought for this privilege. Let's not
let them down.

DEFINITIONS

In order to convince readers of the reasonableness of its claim or claims, an argument must be absolutely clear. Obviously, readers cannot agree with what they
don't understand. Since an argument's claim usually contains terminology and
concepts that are central to and generative of the developed argument, the claim
statement must contain no possibility for misunderstanding. Not only must the
sentence structure and grammar help to express its meaning clearly, but also the
word choice. Terms in the claim statement that are the slightest bit vague, specialized, or ambiguous need to have their meanings carefully denoted before the
argument proceeds. Within the argument itself, the careful definition of potentially troublesome terms is also a requirement.

Because the clear definition of key terms will inevitably strengthen your argument by making it more accessible to your readers, we see the definition process
as an important method of support for virtually all arguments. In some arguments, definition of a key term is so crucial and controversial that it becomes a
central claim in itself.

When to Provide Clarification Through Definition

The following types of language, whether in your claim statement or in the body of
your argument, need clarification through definition:

1. *Unfamiliar terminology.* Any specialized or unusual terms that could be
unfamiliar to your readers must be explained. If, for example, it is unlikely that
your readers have heard of "Maxwell's Demon," or a "net revenue model," or "dys-
thymic disorder," provide a clear definition.

Unfamiliar terminology includes jargon. Though generally speaking, jargon
should be avoided, there are times when it is the best language for the job. But if
you must use phrases like "the dialogic principle of feminist discourse," don't assume that everyone in your audience will know precisely what you mean; provide
a definition.

2. *Nonspecific language.* In general, avoid vague, fuzzy terms, particularly in
statements of evaluation and measurement. If you claim that "Ajax Motors is the

world's largest corporation," consider how little that statement tells the reader. In what way or ways is Ajax the largest? Does it have the most employees? Earn the most income? Have the highest profits? A more specific statement, such as "Few people realize it, but Ajax Motors now employs more people than any other corporation in the world," is far more useful to the reader. When you do use such nonspecific words as *poor, excellent, large, grand,* or *minimal,* make sure you explain the meaning of your modifier as precisely as possible.

3. *Abstract terms.* While your writing should strive to be as concrete as possible, sometimes you cannot avoid using abstractions in argument, particularly in evaluative arguments. The problem with abstractions is that they can be understood in different ways: they can be *ambiguous.* If you must use a term like *talent,* or *equality,* or *conservatism,* make sure you indicate your understanding of the term. While your readers may not agree with your definition, at least they will understand how you intend to use it and will judge the success of your argument within those parameters.

4. *Controversial terms.* Some terms have been at the center of heated public debate for so long that they are emotionally and politically loaded. Not only is their meaning potentially ambiguous, that ambiguity is a source of controversy. *Euthanasia* and *socialism* are examples of these controversial terms; how one defines them often determines one's position toward them. When you use such terms in your arguments, you will almost certainly need to clarify your understanding or use of them. Sometimes such terms are so controversial that your definition, because it implies a position on the subject, becomes the point of the argument.

Types of Definitions

Terms requiring clarification can be defined briefly or extensively, depending on the needs of your audience and the importance of a particular term to your argument. The four types of definition you will use most commonly are the shorthand definition, the sentence definition, the extended definition, and the stipulative definition.

Writers often resort to *shorthand* definitions when the term in question requires only a quick explanation. A shorthand definition substitutes a familiar term for an unfamiliar one, as in the following example: "Acetylsalicylic acid (aspirin) is an effective medicine for most headaches."

A *sentence* definition, similar to a dictionary definition but written as a grammatical sentence, consists of the term to be defined (the *species*), the general category to which it belongs (the *genus*), and those characteristics that distinguish it from all other members of that general category (the *differentiae*). A sentence definition has the following structure:

SPECIES = GENUS + DIFFERENTIAE

An example of this form of definition is "A heifer [species] is a young cow [genus] that has not borne a calf [differentiae]."

An *extended* definition includes this basic sentence definition *and* any additional material that would help a reader understand the term being defined. The following are strategies for extending a sentence definition:

Evolution of Definition.   Sometimes an understanding of the historical development of a word's usage will illuminate its richness for readers. The word *queer,* for example, means strange or out of the ordinary. Thus it was eventually coined as a derogatory term for a male homosexual. Recently, homosexuals have embraced the term, converting it from a slur to a compliment. There is now an academic field called Queer Studies.

Comparison.   Readers can gain a better understanding of a term if it is compared to something with which they are familiar. An argument that needs to define the term *docudrama* might explain that a docudrama is similar to a movie, except the events depicted are based in fact.

Example.   Offering specific examples of unfamiliar terms is an excellent way to explain them. To define what a *haiku* is, for example, you would almost certainly present an example or two.

Definition by Negation.   Sometimes a term can be explained by telling your reader what it is not, what it should not be confused with. For example, at the beginning of this textbook, we defined the term *argument* by distinguishing it from *opinion,* a term often mistaken as synonymous with argument.

Etymological Definition.   Providing the etymology of a word—the meanings of its original roots—can also help to explain its meaning. The word *misogynist,* for example, derives from the Greek "miso," meaning "hate," and "gyny," meaning woman.

Definition by Description.   Unfamiliar or abstract terms can often be explained or introduced by a physical or figurative description. If you were defining a Phillip's-head screw, you might explain what the screw looks like. Or, in defining contrapuntal music, you could describe the sound—the listener hears two distinct melodies going on at exactly the same time.

The following extended definition of "poetry," from Laurence Perrine's *Sound and Sense,* contains many of these strategies of extended definition:

> Between poetry and other forms of imaginative literature there is no sharp distinction. You may have been taught to believe that poetry can be recognized by the arrangement of its lines on the page or by its use of rime [*sic*] and meter. Such superficial tests are almost worthless. The Book of Job in the Bible and Melville's *Moby Dick* are highly poetical, but the familiar verse that begins: "Thirty days hath September, / April, June, and November . . . " is not. The difference between poetry and other literature is one only of degree. Poetry is the most condensed and concentrated form of literature, saying most in the fewest number of words. It is language whose individual lines, either because of their own brilliance or because they focus so powerfully on what has gone before, have a higher

voltage than most language has. It is language that grows frequently in-candescent, giving off both light and heat.

This definition employs a sentence definition ("Poetry is the most condensed and concentrated form of literature"), a definition by negation (by indicating what po-etry is **not**—"poetry has little to do with line arrangement or rhyme or meter"), comparison ("Between poetry and other forms of imaginative literature there is no sharp distinction"), and figurative description ("It is language that grows fre-quently incandescent, giving off both light and heat").

When working with an ambiguous or controversial term, you may need to write a *stipulative* definition. A stipulative definition restricts the meaning of the term to a particular meaning for the sake of the argument. Some stipulative defin-itions are made for convenience and clarity: "When we use the term *argument,* we are referring only to its primary meaning of demonstrating the reasonableness of a proposition." But writers sometimes stipulate particular definitions in order to argue a position, as well as to clarify their use of the term. The manner in which you choose to define complex terms such as *discrimination, censorship,* or *re-sponsibility* can indicate the stand you take on these particular issues. In some cases, the stipulative definition constitutes the body of the argument. Within our division of argument, such substantially developed definitions would fall under the heading of interpretations. In proposing a restricted, possibly unusual, definition of a concept, you are arguing a particular interpretation or understanding that is suggested and supported by the context of the argument.

Stipulative definitions can be developed through the same methods suggested for extended definitions. When your intention is to imply or state an argument through your proposed definition, you might also want to introduce an argument of effect as a way of supporting your definition. Readers will be more likely to ac-cept your stipulated definition if you can demonstrate that this acceptance will have positive consequences. For example, if you were proposing a new definition of the word *minor* as a way of making a case for lowering the legal drinking age ("The traditional definition of *minor* as someone under the age of twenty-one leaves out those eighteen- to twenty-year-olds who are considered old enough to die for their country, to get married, and to terminate their educations"), you might introduce a supporting argument of effect that points to the money that could be saved by lifting police enforcement of the current drinking age.

Chapter 10 of this book, "Writing and Image," begins with a stipulative defin-ition of the word *image* as we apply it to written argument. This definition serves more of a clarifying than an argumentative purpose, but it does make the claim that despite the popular understanding of the term, a writer's "image" is important and meaningful.

ACTIVITIES (4.4)

1. Examine an extended definition in an encyclopedia, reference guide, or text-book, and write a one- to two-page essay that describes what elements (sen-

tence definition, examples, history of the object or concept being defined, comparison or contrast, and so on) have been included in the definition and speculate on why they have been included. Are there other elements you believe should have been included to help the definition? Are there any elements that could have been omitted?

2. Write a paragraph giving a stipulative definition of one of the following: "love," "friendship," "science," "classical." Then write a formal sentence definition that encapsulates your stipulative definition.

SUMMARY

An Argument's Support

- An argument's support is all the material that transforms your working claim into a reasonable conclusion. Knowing the class of argument you are making will help you determine the appropriate support, but there are some generic varieties of support that can be used to strengthen any class of argument. These are:

secondary claims

comparisons

appeals to authority

appeals to audience needs and values

addressing the counterargument

defining key terms

- When possible, arrange your support to have the greatest impact on your readers, with strong support placed at the beginning and end of your argument.
- Any terms in your claim or the body of your argument likely to be unfamiliar to your readers should be defined by a sentence definition, an extended definition, or a shorthand definition.
- Stipulative definitions, which restrict the meaning of a term to one of the term's possible meanings, can be used to clarify an argument or to make an interpretive argument.

SUGGESTIONS FOR WRITING (4.5)

1. Write a claim that comes out of a position or belief you hold strongly (about a political issue, a policy at your university, or your relationship to your family, for example). Identify the category of claim and make a list of all the reasons

you can think of to support your claim. In a two-page essay, discuss whether the support you have identified would be sufficient for a general audience, or whether you might need to discover further reasons. Briefly describe where you might look for further support.

2. Write a two- to three-page essay that is an extended definition of some concept or object, making sure your definition includes a formal sentence definition. Your instructor may have suggestions for this assignment, but we also suggest one of the following: academic freedom, entropy, feminism, or eugenics.

5

Making Reasonable Arguments: Formal and Informal Logic

In Chapters 5 through 8, we will match each class of claim with its most appropriate supporting methods. Before you begin working at the specific level of claim and support, you should have some understanding of the principles of *logic* that inform all successful arguments. A successful argument requires more than a well-stated claim and appropriate support; it also requires that the claim and support stand in a certain relationship to each other, that they be linked according to certain established principles. These established principles are those of formal and informal logic. Knowing how to make use of them in written argument will do much to ensure that your arguments are reasonable.

FORMAL LOGIC

The principles of formal logic were originated by the Greek philosopher Aristotle (384–322 B.C.). Today, almost 2,500 years later, these principles continue to define what we mean by **reasonable** thinking. Just as little children learn to speak their native languages with no awareness of their underlying linguistic and grammatical principles, so people learn to think reasonably with little understanding of those complex principles that inform reasonable thought. At some point in their educations, children must eventually be exposed to the rules of grammar and punctuation in order to refine their language skills; similarly, educated people, and certainly writers of argument, must become familiar with the principles and function of logic in order to become skilled and reasonable thinkers.

The two basic varieties of formal logic are induction and deduction. *Induction,* or inductive reasoning, involves reasoning from observed evidence (the support) to a general statement (the claim or conclusion). *Deduction,* or deductive reasoning, involves reasoning from premises (explicit or implicit supporting statements of a condition or activity) to a conclusion (or claim).

Induction:

Observed Evidence: In the twenty years I've lived in New York State, warm weather has begun every year between March and May.

General Statement: In New York State, warm weather begins between March and May.

Deduction:

Premise: All human beings are mortal.
Premise: Jane is a human being.
Conclusion: Jane is mortal.

Notice in our first example that we conclude from specific examples that a situation is generally true or will remain true. Yet we cannot be absolutely sure that this situation will continue: it is not *necessarily* true but only *probably* true that warm weather habitually arrives between March and May. In our deductive example, on the other hand, the statement that Jane is mortal is necessarily true if the premises that precede it are true. Deductive arguments involve specific processes that lead to necessary conclusions.

Some of the principles of formal logic (and their modern variants) are more useful to certain kinds of arguments than others. As we focus on the individual argument categories in Chapters 6 through 9, we will indicate how to make use of those logical principles most relevant to each category. At this point, we offer a general introduction to the principles themselves.

Induction

Induction is the process of formulating generalizations based on individual instances. If, over the course of your college career, you observe repeated instances of male students dominating class discussion, you might reach the conclusion that at your institution, male students contribute to class discussion more than female students. Your conclusion is useful, not because it represents the absolute truth, which of course it doesn't—there are exceptions to any generalization—but because it summarizes a set of similar tendencies you have observed. Inductive reasoning is natural to all of us, whether we are highly trained in Aristotelian logic or don't know the difference between a reasoned argument and a shouting match.

While the process is natural and the concepts comparatively simple, inductive reasoning does carry risks. If practiced irresponsibly, induction can lead not to useful generalizations, but to harmful misconceptions. There is a world of difference between the conclusion "Male political science majors at Miller College tend to dominate class discussion" and one claiming "Men are more skillful speakers than women." When working from specific examples to general conclusions, you must provide a sufficient number of examples to warrant the conclusion, state the context of the examples (i.e., political science students at Miller College), and qualify the conclusion appropriately ("male students *tend* to dominate class discussion").

A further risk of inductive reasoning concerns the use to which we put our inductive claims. For the most part, the inductive process should be used *descrip-*

tively—as a way of summarizing a set of highly similar observations or facts. If used *predictively*—for example, to predict or assume behavior based on earlier observations—induction can lead to harmful stereotypes. While you may be perfectly accurate in your observation that more men in your major contribute to class discussion than do women, you may be in for some big surprises if you expect all the women you work with to follow this pattern.

Sound inductive reasoning depends in large measure on the abilities to recognize and to argue factual propositions, since induction involves supporting a general claim with reference to individual factual instances. For this reason, we include a full discussion of the principles of induction in Chapter 6, "Arguing Facts." Since deductive reasoning and its variants, which you will find useful in some of the later categories of argument, usually move from general propositions (support) to specific claims, it is important that you understand how to reach those general propositions early in the game.

Deduction

The basic form of the deductive argument is the *syllogism*—a three-part argument consisting of a *major premise,* a *minor premise,* and a *conclusion.* We have already given one example of a syllogism in our previous sample deductive argument.

Major Premise: All human beings are mortal.
Minor Premise: Jane is a human being.
Conclusion: Jane is mortal.

This syllogism is an example of thinking in terms of classes. The major premise establishes two classes, a larger one of mortal beings and a smaller one of human beings, and it asserts that the smaller class belongs in the larger. The minor premise establishes that a still smaller class, in this case one individual (Jane), belongs in the smaller class of the major premise. From there it necessarily follows that Jane will also be a member of the largest class, mortal beings. The syllogism can also be displayed visually.

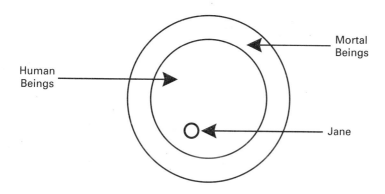

Thinking in terms of classes can be misleading if the process is done incorrectly. Examine the following syllogism:

Major Premise: All Catholics believe in the sanctity of human life.
Minor Premise: Jane believes in the sanctity of human life.
Conclusion: Jane is a Catholic.

At first glance this argument may seem plausible, but as the following diagram shows, the argument is seriously flawed because the minor premise puts Jane in the larger group of those who believe in the sanctity of life but not in the smaller group of those who are Catholics. All the argument can really tell us is that Jane and Catholics share this one trait. They may differ in everything else.

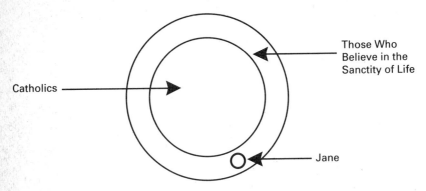

This sample syllogism is *invalid* because the process of reasoning it uses is flawed, while the first sample syllogism is *valid* because the process of reasoning used there is correct. Validity, however, should not be confused with *truth,* or invalidity with falseness, because truth is a matter of a statement's correspondence with the facts, not merely a question of the process of reasoning. To cite the example, even if Jane were a Catholic, and thus the conclusion of the syllogism were true, the syllogism would still be invalid because of the flawed process.

On the other hand, an argument can be valid but untrue because at least one of the premises is false. Much faulty syllogistic reasoning miscarries with the major premise, which is itself a generalization—a conclusion derived from inductive reasoning. In the following syllogism, the major premise is a false generalization:

All women are feminists.

Jane is a woman.

Jane is a feminist.

Clearly, the generalization that *all* women are feminists is untrue; thus, though the relationship between premises (support) and conclusion (claim) is valid, the conclusion is untrue because it works from a false premise.

Deductive arguments that are both true and valid are *sound.* Deductive arguments that are untrue, invalid, or both are *unsound.* As a reader and analyzer of others' arguments, you need to be on guard against the seductions of the valid argument built on false premises, or the invalid argument luring us with the truth of its premises or conclusion.

In addition to the syllogism involving classes, is the "if–then" syllogism. The "if–then" syllogism takes the following form:

If John drops the glass on the sidewalk, then the glass will break.

John will drop the glass on the sidewalk.

The glass will break.

This syllogism is valid, and if its premises are true, it is also sound.

With "if–then" syllogisms, however, you need to watch out for a very common error, usually called "affirming the consequent," where the "then" clause of the major premise is turned into an affirmative statement in the minor premise.

If John drops the glass on the sidewalk, then the glass will break.

The glass will break.

John will drop the glass on the sidewalk.

The argument is invalid because the major premise merely claims that John's dropping the glass will make it break; it does not exclude other ways of breaking the glass, such as hitting it with a hammer. Given this major premise, we cannot conclude that John will have dropped the glass merely from the glass's being broken.

A third type of syllogism is the "either–or" syllogism, which takes the following form:

Either the doctor gave the patient oxygen or the patient died.

The patient did not die.

The doctor gave the patient oxygen.

Note that this argument is invalid if the alternative is affirmed rather than denied.

Either the doctor gave the patient oxygen or the patient died.

The patient died.

The doctor did not give the patient oxygen.

The major premise merely asserts that we can assume the first alternative from the nonoccurrence of the second; it does not claim that the patient's dying necessarily means that the first alternative (the doctor's giving the patient oxygen) failed to occur.

Another potential problem with "either–or" arguments is our frequent use of these terms in a nonexclusive sense, where "or" really means "and/or." When someone says that "Sarah is either a genius or a saint," she often does not mean that being a genius and a saint are mutually exclusive—she allows for the possibility that Sarah is both. She is not wrong in using "either–or" in this way, as long as she is aware that she is using it in this nonexclusive sense.

Applying Deductive Logic to Written Arguments.   It is far easier to distinguish between a sound and unsound syllogism when we see them set up in the classical form than it is to ferret out and evaluate the syllogistic reasoning embedded in our everyday thinking and our written arguments. Nevertheless, trying to recast your arguments into the syllogistic formula can be an extremely valuable way of testing the reasonableness of your claim and support. Is it possible, for example, to fill in a chain of premises that might lead to the claim "New York State should raise the highway speed limit from 55 mph to 65 mph"? Let's say that you plan to support this claim by citing the following facts: (1) studies have shown that 85 percent of drivers on the New York Thruway drive over the speed limit; (2) there has not been a marked decrease in highway fatalities since the speed limit was reduced in the 1970s; and (3) since returning its speed limit to 65 mph, the state of Indiana has experienced no increase in speed-related accidents. In order to apply the principles of deduction to your claim and support, you must work with each piece of support separately, trying to determine in what position it should be placed in order to lead necessarily to the conclusion (claim).

Where in a formal syllogism would the statement "Studies have shown that 85 percent of New York drivers exceed the speed limit" be placed? Since this is a fairly specific piece of evidence, we can guess that this support would be the minor premise, because minor premises of syllogisms are usually much more specific than major premises. We now have an incomplete syllogism that looks like this:

Major Premise: ?
Minor Premise: Studies have shown that 85 percent of New York drivers exceed the speed limit.
Conclusion: Therefore, New York State should raise its speed limit.

The syllogistic formula requires that the major premise establish a larger class of which the class in the minor premise is a subset. In this case, the major premise would read something like "States in which a high percentage of drivers exceed the legal speed limit should raise that limit." Now the syllogism looks like this:

Major Premise: States in which a high percentage of drivers exceed the legal speed limit should raise that limit.
Minor Premise: 85 percent of New York drivers exceed the speed limit.
Conclusion: Therefore, New York State should raise its speed limit.

Even though you may not have intended to state this major premise in your argument, the exercise helps you to recognize the assumption on which your argument would be implicitly based and to determine whether that assumption—and its relationship to the rest of the argument—is reasonable.

With the syllogistic formula in mind, you must now consider the validity and soundness of the syllogism. The syllogism is valid: the internal relationship among premises and conclusion is deductively proper. But is it sound—that is, are the premises true? We can assume that the minor premise (the support in question) is true, because it is information taken from unbiased and recent studies. But what about the major premise? Though it is only implied in the argument, the conclusion rests on it, so it must be acceptable to readers as true. Clearly, the major premise is *not* inarguable—it asks readers to accept a link between custom (driving over the speed limit) and policy (changing the law) that many would question. Indeed, the premise seems to work from a highly questionable "follow the leader" principle—behavior in which the majority of people engage should dictate policy. In this case, supplying the syllogism embedded in the argument tells the writer that this particular piece of support will not be effective unless the implied major premise can itself be successfully argued as a secondary claim.

The incomplete syllogism discussed above is an *enthymeme*—a form of syllogism common to spoken and written arguments, where presenting all components of the syllogism can be tedious for the audience. An enthymeme is a rhetorical syllogism that implicitly relies on an audience's existing beliefs to support the conclusion. Enthymemes are not inferior syllogisms; as rhetoricians have noted, the very incompleteness of enthymemes helps to convince because it allows the audience to help complete the argument, thus making the audience more likely to identify with the argument and accept it. But as in the case above, the writer must have good reason to believe that the audience will accept the premise it provides.

As you will see in Chapters 8 and 9, this process of uncovering the syllogism or enthymeme of an argument can be particularly useful when arguing evaluations and recommendations.

ACTIVITIES (5.1)

1. Identify the syllogistic reasoning within the following claims, as in the following example.
   Claim: The novelist Herman Melville was an accomplished poet.
   Major premise: An accomplished poet is one who writes poetry that reveals something interesting about the human condition, employs fresh language, and has a certain degree of order or coherence.
   Minor premise: Herman Melville's poetry satisfies this definition.
   Conclusion: Herman Melville was an accomplished poet.
   a. Mack did not get the job because his résumé was poorly written.
   b. Although we lost the playoff game, our team played a clean, fair game.
   c. The professor's tendency to interrupt his students demonstrates his lack of respect for those he teaches.
   d. If we wish our young people to succeed, we must teach them to value family and community.
   e. If Abraham Lincoln had not been assassinated, he could have lessened the bitterness between the North and the South after the Civil War.
   f. Since I cannot possibly complete all the work in this class, I will have to withdraw.
   g. Bill Clinton's ability to compromise makes him a good statesman.
   h. The only way for the U.S. automotive industry to survive is to levy import tariffs on cars manufactured outside the United States.

2. Examine an essay you wrote recently and present its major argument as a syllogism. What are the argument's major premise, minor premise, and conclusion? Are any of these parts of a syllogism implicit rather than explicit in

your essay? Is the syllogism a sound one? Or is it untrue or invalid? Write a one- to two-page essay presenting the syllogism and your analysis of it.

THE TOULMIN MODEL:
A MODERN VARIANT OF FORMAL LOGIC

Formal deductive reasoning yields necessary or certain conclusions, yet written arguments about our complex, provisional, and messy world rarely presume to discover absolute truth. It is in this mismatch between the goals of formal reasoning and those of written argument that the limitations of deduction are exposed. The fact is that most of the arguments we judge to be worth making are worth making *because* they are arguable, because they admit the possibility of more than one reasonable position.

Recognizing the limitations of Aristotelian logic for practical rhetoric, the twentieth-century philosopher Stephen Toulmin identified and formalized a slightly different relationship between an argument's claim and its support. Toulmin's model can be a useful way to judge the reasonableness of many of the arguments you construct.

According to the Toulmin model, a claim is linked to its support through what is called a *warrant*. A claim's warrant indicates how one gets from factual support (which Toulmin calls *data*) to the claim. In many ways, the warrant resembles the supplied major premise of the speed limit example above: it is the general belief, convention, or principle that permits the data to support the claim. Suppose you were proposing that your college major institute a junior year abroad program. You have a number of supporting reasons for this claim: the program will attract students to the major; it will be an invaluable educational experience for students; it will allow the department to establish important international connections. The Toulmin model requires that each supporting reason be linked to the claim through some assumption or principle acceptable to the audience. Using the last support cited, a diagram of this argument would look like this:

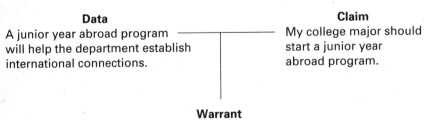

Data
A junior year abroad program will help the department establish international connections.

Claim
My college major should start a junior year abroad program.

Warrant
International connections would be valuable to my college.

We can identify an argument's warrant (which is not always stated explicitly in the argument itself) by asking, "What is it about the data that allows me to reach the claim?" In this case, it is the *value* of international connections that makes the claim desirable. Just as major premises are sometimes left unstated in real arguments, warrants are sometimes only implied. If you have any reason to suspect that your audience will not accept the warrant as generally true or at least reasonable, you will have to support it with what Toulmin calls *backing*. In this case, one backing for the warrant might be identification of the benefits of international connections in a world where more and more college graduates will be working for international organizations.

A fifth element of the Toulmin model, which makes the concept particularly useful to written argument, is the *qualifier*. The qualifier is a word or words that modify the certitude with which the claim is made. In our example, that qualifier is the word *should,* a word that makes the recommendation less strong than "must," but more strong than "might want to consider." Unlike the syllogism, the Toulmin paradigm gives the writer room to entertain claims that are less than necessary or certain. Adding the backing and the qualifier to our example, we come up with the following diagram:

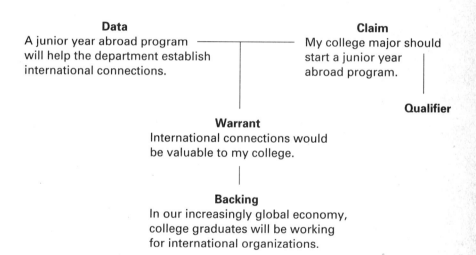

Data
A junior year abroad program
will help the department establish
international connections.

Claim
My college major should
start a junior year
abroad program.

Qualifier

Warrant
International connections would
be valuable to my college.

Backing
In our increasingly global economy,
college graduates will be working
for international organizations.

Applying Toulmin's model to your own arguments can help you to flush out the assumptions that generate your claim and to evaluate their reasonableness. We find that this model is most useful in making recommendations (as in the example above) and causal arguments. The most useful point in the composition process at which to apply both the Toulmin and Aristotelian models is after you have formulated a claim and collected some support. Fitting these elements into one or the other paradigm will help tell you what is missing, what needs further support, and what is patently unreasonable. We do not suggest that you *begin* the argument process by trying to fit ideas into the models; this will only frustrate your thinking and limit your inventiveness.

ACTIVITIES (5.2)

1. Identify the unstated warrants for each of the following pairs of claim and support.
   a. **Claim:** cigarette smoking should be prohibited in all public places.
      Support: secondary smoke is harmful.
   b. **Claim:** celebrities who stand trial for capital crimes are not likely to get fair trials.
      Support: the media focus unrelentingly on celebrity suspects.
   c. **Claim:** if you have the flu, you should stay at home.
      Support: this year's strain of the flu is highly contagious.
   d. **Claim:** Ted has nothing but his own laziness to blame for his academic suspension.
      Support: he sleeps every morning until noon, watches TV every night until midnight, and rarely does his homework.
   e. **Claim:** writing is a dying art.
      Support: my freshman students don't know the difference between an independent clause and Santa Claus.
2. Which of the warrants supplied above would require some backing in order to be acceptable to readers? What kind of backing might you supply?

INFORMAL FALLACIES

Unfortunately, even when we pay careful attention to the logical principles previously discussed, our reasoning can still go awry through committing any of a number of *informal fallacies*. Like the principles of formal logic, informal fallacies usually involve a faulty relationship between an argument's claim and its support. Familiarity with these flaws in reasoning can be especially useful during the revision phase, when you scrutinize the relationship between your claim and its support with these fallacies in mind. Since an inclusive list of these fallacies is a very long one—as inexhaustible as human inventiveness—we include here only those fallacies that students commit most frequently in their writing. For each fallacy, we also indicate the category or categories of argument in which it is most likely to occur.

Ad Hominem Argument

An *ad hominem* argument is against the arguer (Latin *ad hominem*—"to the man") rather than against the argument: "Smith's argument against increasing taxes on the rich is worthless because he himself is rich." This fallacy, which substitutes irrelevant judgments of an individual for reasonable evaluations of an issue, is most likely to occur in evaluative arguments.

Ad Populum Argument

Ad populum is Latin for "to the people." One commits the *ad populum* fallacy when supporting a claim by referring to popular opinion or behavior to justify it. A teenager trying to convince her parents to remove her curfew because "everybody else's parents have done it" is attempting to convince her parents through an appeal to popular behavior rather than to reason. This fallacy is a corruption of the legitimate tactic of appealing to established authorities to strengthen a claim.

Circular Argument

A circular argument is one in which the claim is already contained in the support: "John did not succeed on the track team [the claim] because he did not do well in track events [the support]." This is also known as **begging the question**. This fallacy most frequently occurs in evaluations and interpretations ("This film is immoral because it contains immoral scenes") or in causal analysis, such as the explanation for John's failure on the track team. When revising your arguments, be on the lookout for supporting claims that restate key terms from your premise: this repetition often signals a circular argument.

Distraction

Distraction is bringing in irrelevant points to distract attention from the issue being argued: "Sure I cheated on my income taxes, but I've never broken any other laws." It is also known as the **red herring**, from the practice of dragging a dead herring across a trail to distract hunting dogs from the scent of their prey. Distraction is frequently used to deflect unfavorable evaluations.

Either–Or Argument

This is setting up two extreme positions as the only alternatives and denying any possible middle ground: "The painting is either a masterpiece or trash." The painting could be something in between. Also known as *bifurcation* or the *fallacy of the excluded middle,* this fallacy can occur in any category of argument, though it is probably most frequent in evaluations (as in the claim about the painting) or in recommendations, where sometimes extreme solutions are seen as the only options: "Either we build a new computer facility or we give up on using computers at this school."

Emotive Language

This tactic involves making a case through slanted, value-laden language rather than through reasonable support, as in the statement "Smelling blood, the media will attack and destroy any candidate with a newsworthy weak spot." This claim, with its implicit identification of the media with carnivorous beasts, presumes a value judgment about the media that it does not justify. Writers of argument should try to refrain from using prejudicial language, at least until their claims have been made reasonably. Emotive or slanted language can be used in any kind of argument, but is most common in evaluative arguments.

False Analogy

This is supporting a claim by comparing its subject to something not *essentially* similar: "Offering courses in gay and lesbian theory is no more defensible than teaching pedophilia or necrophilia." While both sides of the comparison refer to noncustomary sexual preference, there are more *differences* between gay theory and pedophilia than there are similarities, and comparing them attempts to prejudice the reader against gay and lesbian theory. As we point out in Chapter 10, analogies can be useful in generating and illuminating arguments, but they can never prove a point. Just as legitimate comparison can be used to support any kind of argument (see Chapter 4), analogies can be misused in all of the four classes of argument. If you find that you have introduced an analogy to *support* rather than explain or illuminate a claim, you have probably committed this fallacy.

Hasty Generalization

Basically a misuse of the inductive method, hasty generalization consists of a general claim based on an insufficient sample: "Young professional people tend to be self-centered and materialistic. My friends Eric and Melanie certainly are." This fallacy typically occurs in factual arguments and in the supposedly factual support for evaluative statements about entire groups of people: "Women are sentimental"; "Asian-American students are good in mathematics."

Non Sequitur

This is claiming a logical relationship between a conclusion and a premise where none exists: "Henry should make a good governor because he is tall and handsome." *Non sequitur* in Latin means "it does not follow"; non sequitur reasoning is behind almost all fallacies. The term is really a generic one that has been specifically applied to cases where the relationship between a premise and a conclusion is seriously askew. The term is also used to cover some fallacies in causal analysis: "I performed poorly on that speech because I wore my green tie rather than my red one." This is an example of our next fallacy—*post hoc ergo propter hoc*. Non sequitur reasoning can occur in any category of argument.

Post Hoc Ergo Propter Hoc

This is claiming that because one event preceded another it must have caused the subsequent event to occur: "I performed poorly on that speech because I wore my green tie rather than my red one." *Post hoc ergo propter hoc* is Latin, meaning "after this, therefore because of this." This fallacy is at the root of much superstition, as in the case of a pitcher who carries a red handkerchief with him whenever he pitches because he had one with him the day of his no-hitter. It is a serious risk in any causal analysis and can be guarded against by following the principles of causal reasoning presented in Chapter 7.

Slippery Slope

Designating a first and a last step in a causal chain, when the intervening steps have not occurred, constitutes the slippery slope fallacy. "I didn't get the first job I interviewed for, so I guess I'd better forget about a career as an engineer." In this simple example, the speaker creates a worst-case scenario (forgetting about engineering) based on a series of events that has not yet occurred and will not necessarily occur—that is, repeated failure to be hired in engineering jobs. This fallacy appears most commonly in arguments of effect, usually when the writer wishes to prove that the consequences of a particular action are likely to be negative.

Strawperson Argument

A strawperson argument involves attacking a view similar to but not identical with that of an opponent: "How long will America tolerate softheaded opponents of gun control who want only criminals to have guns?" Advocates of gun control vary in their views, but they do not want only criminals to have guns. The adjective "softheaded" is an example of emotive language; in this sentence it is designed to arouse a particular emotional response. Negative loaded terms are frequent in strawperson arguments. This fallacy is a common but misguided tactic of evaluative arguments.

You can improve your ability to analyze your own and others' arguments by familiarizing yourself with the kinds of fallacies previously defined, but you need to remember that what is considered "correct" thinking depends on your context. What may be incorrect in one context may be perfectly acceptable in another: *ad hominem* arguments are frowned on in academic writing (though they do occur), but they are perfectly acceptable in a court of law, where questioning and at least implicitly attacking witnesses' backgrounds and motives are frequently practiced. In addition, some of these fallacies are only a slight step off the path of correct reasoning. For example, there is nothing inherently fallacious about "either–or" reasoning, but this kind of reasoning goes wrong when "either–or" alternatives lead to excluding other, real possibilities.

ACTIVITIES (5.3)

Identify the informal fallacies committed in the sentences that follow. Select from the following list:

ad hominem argument	false analogy
ad populum argument	hasty generalization
circular argument	non sequitur
distraction	*post hoc ergo propter hoc*
either–or	slippery slope
emotive language	strawperson argument

1. Legalized abortion puts us only a step away from legalizing murders of anyone we deem undesirable or inconvenient.

2. "If you can't beat them, join them."

3. I strongly disagree with your proposal to allow women to join fraternities. Fraternities are "men only" clubs.

4. Those traitorous, draft-dodging youths who preferred deserting their country to serving it should never have been granted amnesty.

5. Discrimination should be fought on every front—whether it's practiced against members of a certain race, a certain sex, or those who bear arms.

6. I spent two weeks at a military academy and realized that private school is just not for me.

7. It is unfair to penalize Eastman Kodak for harming the environment when they have been such a strong supporter of the local economy.

8. *Supercop* had the highest ratings of any television movie. Clearly, it was a superior film.

9. Tom Hanks is a brilliant comedian; he should leave heavy drama alone.

10. Opponents of the Equal Rights Amendment believe that women should stay barefoot and pregnant.

SUMMARY

Making Reasonable Arguments: Formal and Informal Logic

- Understanding the principles of formal logic will help you link claim and support reasonably.

- The principles of inductive logic—moving from specific instances to general conclusions—are important to all writers of argument and particularly applicable to factual arguments.

- The syllogistic formula, common to most deductive reasoning, can be applied to an argument's claim and support as a way of determining the reasonableness of their connection.

- The Toulmin model of claim/warrant/backing is particularly useful to writers of argument, as it does not make absolute certainty a requirement of the claim.

- Informal fallacies are any of those errors in reasoning that can undermine the credibility of a claim. The best time to consider the possibility of informal fallacies is during the revision process.

SUGGESTIONS FOR WRITING (5.4)

1. Pay attention to the informal conversations and discussions of your friends. Start a list of all the generalizations you hear them make. Then write a one- to two-page letter to your friends telling them what information and evidence they would need in order to support their generalizations reasonably.

2. Focus on three advertisements you see repeatedly on television or in print. Write a one-page essay on each advertisement, discussing your application of the syllogistic and Toulmin models. How would the advertisement look within the format of each model? What premises or warrants are only implied? Are those claims true? What would have to be argued in order to make the advertisement more reasonable? Finally, rewrite the ad so that it conforms to the principles of deduction and the Toulmin model.

6

Arguing Facts

In order to appreciate the crucial role that facts play in all arguments, you need to have a clear understanding of the general structure of argument. As you know, arguments make, develop, and support a writer's position (the claim) on a particular issue. The argument's central claim or claims can be supported in a number of ways, as we shall see in the following chapters. As we indicated in Chapter 4, one common piece of support for a claim is another claim or assertion. If you were arguing the factual claim that students graduating from your major have had trouble finding jobs, you could support that claim with job placement figures about a number of students, and/or with anecdotes about the employment woes of your acquaintances. In both cases, you would be supporting your central factual claim with further factual statements.

But let's take a slightly more complicated example. In arguing the central claim that "First-time DWI offenders should have their driver's licenses revoked" (a claim of recommendation), you cite as support the secondary claim that "The threat of license revocation would deter many from driving while intoxicated." This secondary assertion is causal (predicting the *effect* of the change) and would itself require the kind of support appropriate to causal arguments. Among others, one piece of support you might ultimately use for this secondary claim is a factual assertion about the effectiveness of similar laws in other states.

There are two points to be taken from these examples: first, as you already know, arguments almost always consist of a central claim supported by secondary claims, which themselves must be argued appropriately; second, **sooner or later, all argumentative claims will come to rest on factual assertions.** The arguments you make will only be as good as the facts on which they are built. If your facts are shaky, your argument will inevitably suffer. In composing your arguments, you must be extremely discriminating in your selection of facts, ensuring as much as

70

possible that they are accurate and up to date, drawn from objective, authoritative sources.

Because facts are the building blocks of argument, skill in selecting, presenting, and supporting them is necessary when you are writing *any* kind of argument. Thus, everything we say in this chapter about making factual arguments applies to any situation in which you make use of factual assertions to support or develop other kinds of claims.

WHAT IS A FACT?

The New College Edition of *The American Heritage Dictionary* gives the following primary definition of *fact:* "Something known with certainty." According to this definition, a fact is a proposition about which there can be no debate or doubt—it is known to be absolutely true. Assertions like "My physics teacher is a woman," "George Washington was the first president of the United States," and "Human beings are mortal" would fall under this primary definition—they are inarguable, proven facts that in most writing would require no support beyond their simple assertion. Often these facts emerge from your own experience or have been confirmed by your own experience; sometimes they fall under the heading of "common knowledge." In any event, these are assertions that can be accepted as indisputable.

But what about statements like "Beta-carotene is a carcinogen," "Secondary smoke is not harmful," or "The FDA-established minimum daily requirements are inadequate"? While these claims are stated as if they are known with certainty, we might hesitate to call them indisputable, conclusively proven. For one thing, these assertions derive from fields in which most of us are comparatively ignorant; we lack the expertise to judge their accuracy. Second, anyone who reads the newspaper regularly knows that these are the kinds of "facts" that seem always to be retired or revised when new evidence or new research methods emerge. Indeed, each of these statements is a correction of an earlier assertion that claimed to prove the contrary: beta-carotene was for years thought to be a cancer-preventive dietary agent; the "known" dangers of secondary cigarette smoke have just recently been scientifically moderated; and healthy eaters have based their diets for years on the minimum daily requirements endorsed by the FDA.

Assertions like these fall more properly under the dictionary's secondary definition of *fact:* "Something asserted as certain." Such statements are made in good faith, based on the best available evidence, and stated with conviction, but they are the findings of incomplete and ongoing research in comparatively dynamic fields and thus are always subject to revision and correction as newer, more inclusive, more reliable evidence is gathered. In other words, such factual assertions are *believed* to be certain, but not *known* with certainty; they are more like state-of-the-art educated guesses.

Then there is the assertion that is stated with certainty, dressed up as factual, and credited to a seemingly impeccable source, but that is nonetheless utterly preposterous. Some of these "pretend" facts are easy to identify: we can be virtually certain of the falsity of headlines from the *National Enquirer.* Unfortunately, we are also surrounded by preposterous factual claims that look perfectly plausible because they appear in reputable sources and because we have no way of actually testing their truth. We are particularly susceptible to accepting false facts (and circulating them) if they will strengthen our own argument. If you were arguing for a pass-fail option at your college and came across figures linking this option to high student retention at other institutions, you might be tempted to make use of these figures, however skeptical you might be, simply because they support your position. You will need to learn to resist such temptations, subjecting any factual assertion to the principles of selection that follow.

SUPPORTING FACTS REPORTED BY SECOND- AND THIRD-PARTY SOURCES

Most of the arguments you will write will depend on facts you find in your reading and research. Sometimes these facts will be reported by what we call second-party sources, sometimes by third-party sources. A second-party source is the individual or group that ascertained the fact in the first place; for example, a manager reporting that sales declined 5 percent in the last quarter, or a write-up in a medical journal by a research oncologist summarizing the findings of her study on cancer remissions. A third-party source is the person or document reporting facts ascertained by someone else; for example, a biology textbook describing some little-known facts about Darwin's work on the *Beagle,* or a recent history of the eighteenth- and nineteenth-century slave trade between Africa and America.

Given the importance of facts to argument *and* the dubiousness of many of the statements paraded as facts, you need to be extremely discriminating about selecting facts obtained from second- and third-party sources, recognizing that whenever you include a fact in your argument, you are tacitly saying to your audience, "I believe this to be a trustworthy statement." While you will often lack the knowledge or opportunity to verify the fact, there are certain steps you can, and should, take to assure yourself—and thus your audience—that the facts you are presenting are reliable.

Determining the Reliability of Your Source

First, you must satisfy yourself that the source of the fact—whether second- or third-party—is trustworthy. The most obviously trustworthy sources are those individuals who are acknowledged experts in the field, people with a proven track record in the area. You can probably trust the facts given out by your college career counselor on postgraduate career opportunities, or facts about astronomy contained in an article by the noted astronomer Carl Sagan, because both of these people have established professional reputations. But you should be wary of advice on the stock market obtained from your sixteen-year-old sister. Information obtained from nonexperts—from eyewitness observers or amateurs, for example—can be reliable, but you should be more skeptical about these sources than about acknowledged experts.

If you can determine nothing about the reliability of the individual presenting the fact, or if the fact appears in an unsigned article in a periodical or in an unsigned entry in a larger volume, you can consider the reputation of the periodical or volume. Reputable journals in a particular field (for example, the *Journal of the American Bar Association* and the *New England Journal of Medicine,* have reputations for reliability, though their inclusion of a given article by no means guarantees its truthfulness. Newspapers like the *Wall Street Journal,* the *Christian Science Monitor,* and the *New York Times* are generally recognized for reporting news events fully and accurately, but again, even these publications can and do make mistakes. Certainly a report found in the *Wall Street Journal* is more credible than one found in *Star* magazine or the *National Enquirer.* Reference books like the *CRC Handbook of Chemistry and Physics* or the *Oxford English Dictionary* have long-established reputations for reliability; whenever possible, you should go to works such as these for the facts you need.

In evaluating your sources, you must also consider the possibility of bias in your source. Some bias is almost inevitable in human affairs. Even the most dispassionate and objective scholar is probably biased in favor of the results of his or her own research as opposed to research that contradicts it. In advertising and politics, bias is the norm. When you use a source in an argument, you can assume that it reflects some bias, but you need to determine if the bias is so extreme that it negates the value of what is being claimed. One safeguard here is to see if your source gives you enough particular evidence to make the case credible. An article claiming the danger of eating vegetables because of pesticide contamination that cites specific scientific tests is probably credible or at least worth taking seriously, even if the author is biased in favor of this theory. But an advertisement that claims a twenty-pound weight loss for dieters in three days but offers no independent verification of this claim is almost certainly not credible.

Finally, the facts reported in your source should be as current as possible. Accepted "facts" are constantly being superseded by newer, more accurate information. In our dizzying age of expanding technology and research methods, the average life span of many facts is brief. Especially in science and technology, but in many other fields as well, a fact is of little value if it has not been recently verified. The definition of *recent* depends on the field from which the fact is drawn. A 1984 publication on computer software technology would be of questionable value in 1994 because the technology has developed so rapidly. Yet in the less dramatically changing field of psychiatry, information presented in 1984 would be considered comparatively recent. As you collect facts for your argument, you must determine if they reflect the most recent research available.

Citing the Source in Your Text

Another way to support the second- and third-party facts you present is to cite their source within your argument. Providing the source is a courtesy to readers who might want to examine the subject in more depth. More important, including the source assures your readers that your argument is a responsible one—that your facts are not fabricated for the sake of argument but come from legitimate sources. Failure to cite the sources of the facts on which your claim rests will weaken your argument considerably.

In most cases, your citation of source will take the form of a footnote, an endnote, or, increasingly, inclusion of the work in a Works Cited list at the end of your argument. The subject matter of your argument will determine which citation form you should follow, and you can find models of these forms in most college writing handbooks. In addition to a footnote or bibliographical reference, you can also include a brief reference to your source within the text of your argument. For example, "According to the *Oxford English Dictionary,* the word *flick* at one time meant 'thief.' " In this case, the source would also appear in a Works Cited or Bibliography section at the end of the argument.

If your readers are not likely to be familiar with your source, you might want to provide credentials briefly within your text. For example, "In his book *The Mismeasure of Man,* Stephen Jay Gould, the noted Harvard paleontologist and popularizer of science, argues that the results of standardized intelligence tests can be misleading and also misused by those in power."

ACTIVITIES (6.1)

Write a one-page paper analyzing the credibility of two of the following passages. Consider the issues of expertise, bias, and currency of facts. You may need to do some research on the credentials of the author or of the publication in which the passage appeared.

1. Mailer had the most developed sense of image; if not, he would have been a figure of deficiency, for people had been regarding him by his public image since he was twenty-five years old. He had in fact learned to live in the sarcophagus of his image—at night, in his sleep, he might dart out, and paint improvements on the sarcophagus. During the day, while he was helpless, newspapermen and other assorted bravos of the media and literary world would carve ugly pictures on the living tomb of his legend. Of necessity, part of Mailer's remaining funds of sensitivity went right into the war of supporting his image and working for it. (Norman Mailer, *The Armies of the Night.* New York: Signet Books, 1968, pp. 15–16.)

2. **chow chow,** powerful NON-SPORTING DOG; shoulder height, 18–20 in. (45.7–50.8 cm); weight, 50–60 lb (22.7–27.2 kg). Its coat has a soft, wooly underlayer and a dense, straight topcoat that stands out from the body. It may be any solid color and is the only breed with a black tongue. A hunting dog in China 2,000 years ago, it was brought to England in the 18th cent. (The *Concise Columbia Encyclopedia.* New York: Columbia University Press, 1983, p. 168.)

3. A SPECTER is haunting Europe—the specter of communism. All the powers of the old Europe have entered into a holy alliance to exorcise this specter: Pope and Czar, Metternich and Guizot, French Radicals and German police spies. (Karl Marx and Friedrich Engels, *The Communist Manifesto*. Ed. Samuel H. Beer. New York: Appleton-Century-Crofts, 1955, p. 8. Originally published in 1848.)

4. Many devices have been used in the attempted measurement of interests. The interest inventory is the most important of these both from the standpoint of the number of counselors using them and the number of investigators working with them. The inventory approach consists of the comparison of likes and dislikes of individuals through questionnaire items. Since the individual is asked to estimate his feeling, the method may be said to be subjective. A complete discussion of interest inventories is given by Fryer [Douglas Fryer, *The Measurement of Interests*. New York: Henry Holt, 1931]. (Harry J. Older, "An Objective Test of Vocational Interests." *Journal of Applied Psychology*, 28 (1944): 99.)

5. People who have a good sense of humor *suffer less constipation, acid stomach and sensitivity to cold* than those who don't get the joke, according to a study presented at the American Psychosomatic Society annual meeting. ("Medical Flash," *Self* (July 1994): 59.)

SUPPORTING PERSONALLY EXPERIENCED FACTS

There will be times in your writing of arguments when you will need to support a fact obtained through *your* experience or observation rather than from a second- or third-party source. Personally experienced facts are supported by a credible and objective description of the experience or observation.

Describing the Experience

Let's say you were writing a report for a psychology class on phobias and you wanted to demonstrate how extreme and irrational phobic behavior can be. As evidence for this position you refer to your observations of a friend with a severe flying phobia: "I have seen a friend go into panic on a routine commercial flight." Because this statement suggests extreme abnormal behavior, it requires some support. The support in a case like this consists of a brief description of the experience—of the pallor, the tremors, the hysteria you observed in your friend. (We are not at this point talking about explaining or interpreting the fact, but about presenting it in such a way that your reader will accept that it happened.)

We have used a simple example to illustrate how to support personal experience—the most basic kind of fact—but the principle holds in more complicated contexts. A chemist reporting results of a laboratory experiment would support her findings by describing the process by which she obtained those results. That is, she would describe her experience, providing the details necessary to demonstrate that the process had not been flawed, that it had been conducted according to certain established rules, and that it really did yield certain results.

Establishing Your Own Credibility

Success of written arguments always depends on the reader's confidence in the writer. Arguments are credible if their writer seems organized, well-informed, and reasonable. The important principle of the writer's image underlies everything we have to say about argument, but it is particularly relevant here. Since *you* are usually the sole support of a personally experienced fact, you must give your readers no reason to mistrust your description of the experience. You must record your description in a manner that reflects honesty and accuracy.

If your readers have any reason to believe that your record of experience is not reliable, your argument, however modest, will fail. For example, if you referred to your 85-year-old grandmother as support for an argument against mandatory retirement, citing her daily five-mile runs, her ability to benchpress 300 pounds, and her current prize-winning research in recombinant DNA, your readers would be very suspicious of such obvious exaggeration, and your credibility as an observer would be seriously questioned.

In presenting facts derived from personal experience, you must also guard against the inevitability of your own bias. Without realizing it, we often see only what we want to see and ignore what is convenient to ignore. Ask two politicians on opposing sides of an issue their perceptions of a stormy meeting and you will almost certainly get two very different stories about what happened. They are not necessarily trying to falsify evidence, but their biases can color their perceptions. In some contexts, such as sports writing about the hometown team or essays on the opinion page of the newspaper, readers expect and even welcome a certain bias, but they tend to reject open manifestations of it in other contexts, such as front-page news, academic projects, or business reports. One way to protect your rendering of personally observed facts from excessive personal bias is to ask yourself whether a person making a different claim would have observed the same things; if the answer is no, you should aim for more neutrality in your description. Another way to guard against the possibility of bias in reporting fact is to consult other people who observed or experienced the same event to ensure that your view is essentially a shared one. If it is not, you must consider whether your own bias accounts for the difference.

SUPPORTING FACTUAL GENERALIZATIONS

Any claim, regardless of the class it falls into, can be stated as a *generalization*. For example, the factual claim "*People* magazine and *USA Today* use much the same format as television news shows" becomes a factual generalization when the communications scholar Neil Postman tells us that "the total information environment begins to mirror television." Similarly, the claim "Frank is a successful salesman because his father was also a good salesman" (introducing a limited causal argument with an element of evaluation) can be extended to the following generalization: "Successful salesmen tend to have other good salesmen in their families."

To support any generalization, you need to apply two sets of principles. First, you must demonstrate the reasonableness of the singular claim; for example, that significant similarities do exist between the television news show *20/20* and *People* magazine, or that there is a demonstrable *causal* connection between a father and a son who are both salesmen. In other words, you must rest your claim on the principles of support applicable to the category to which the singular claim belongs. Second, you must also demonstrate that your generalization, regardless of its specific category, has been properly drawn—that there are sufficient grounds for claiming the broad applicability of the specific claim. We will use factual generalizations to illustrate this concept of sufficient grounds, but you should be aware that it applies to all categories of generalization.

Applying the Principles of Induction

All generalizations, even the most informal and sweeping, begin on a specific level. We see something a few times and assume that it happens frequently or even all the time. That is, we move from specific observations to general conclusions; from the particular we infer the general. In traditional logic, this process by which we assume the widespread existence of particular instances is called *induction*. Conclusions drawn by inductive reasoning are always somewhat risky because they are based on incomplete evidence. You assume that because you have never seen or heard of a flying cat, no such creature exists, yet unless you have seen every cat that ever existed, your claim "There is no such thing as a flying cat" has made a rather staggering leap from the particular to the universal. Yet these leaps are the nature of induction.

Supporting a generalization consists of identifying a number of specific, verified instances or examples. If you claim, for example, that American films increasingly show the dangers of casual sexual relationships, you would have to cite individual films to support your claim. Or if you write "Many young American novelists find universities a supportive and economically secure place to work," you would need to point to specific examples. If the generalization is a factual generalization, the specific examples will be individual facts, which in some cases may need verification. What makes a factual generalization "factual" is not the absolute truth of the generalization, which can never be proven, but its foundation in singular factual instances.

The most credible generalizations are those with the most, and best, examples supporting them. You cannot reasonably conclude that all algebra teachers are women if your experience is limited to one or two teachers, but you can reasonably conclude that many teenagers like rap music if you have known hundreds of teenagers in many different settings, all of whom like rap. In supporting generalizations, you need to know how many examples are enough, whether they are representative of the available evidence, and which examples to include.

Unfortunately, no simple formula exists that can supply answers to these questions, but the following general rules of thumb can be helpful.

How Many Examples Are Enough?   First, the more sweeping your claim, the more examples you will need. Generalizations can be phrased at any point along a continuum of frequency: "*Some* business majors are good in math"; "*Many* business majors are good in math"; "*All* business majors are good in math." Although the word *some* does constitute a generalization, it is a very limited generalization, a safe one to make if you don't have abundant evidence. To support "some," you need only a handful of examples. "Many" requires more than a handful of examples, certainly, but is far easier to prove than "all." In fact, absolute statements using words like *all, everyone, never,* or *always,* should be avoided in written argument unless every constituent in the group referred to can be accounted for. Otherwise, the claims they make are too grandiose to be credible. The following passage supports its factual generalization with carefully chosen examples.

> A number of fraternity members on this campus contradict the broad and usually unflattering stereotypes circulated about "brothers." While I am not a fraternity member myself, I know a number of them well, and none of them fits the popular image of the beer-swilling, women-chasing party boy. For instance, my friend Judd, a dean's list electrical engineering major and obviously a dedicated student, says that fraternity living gives him the supportive environment he needs to excel in a difficult major. Two of my roommates from freshman year who have joined fraternities have become respected student leaders—Brad is vice-president of student council, and Kelly is the student representative to Faculty Council. Both Brad and Kelly are well-rounded, academically successful students. Finally, I know that the entire pledge class of one campus chapter received the Mayor's commendation for public service for their renovation of an inner city recreation center. Of course, there will always be individuals who confirm the stereotype, but my observations question its widespread applicability.

In this passage, three examples, the last involving a large group of individuals, are presented to support the claim that few fraternity members fit the campus stereotype. In a more formal academic argument, we would probably insist on more rigorous, less personally observed evidence, but we would very likely accept these examples as adequate in a short, informal essay. As a general rule, three is a good number of examples for a short essay, since one or two examples might seem to be merely exceptions, while four or more would become tedious.

The less familiar your readers are with your subject matter, the more specific examples you should supply. If your readers are very comfortable and familiar with your topic, they will often accept sensible generalizations that are only minimally supported. If you refer in an internal business report to the "widespread reliability problems with our new printer," those familiar with the problem will accept the reference and not demand that it be supported. But a reader unfamiliar with this problem may demand evidence that the problem really exists. Of course, some readers unfamiliar with your subject area will accept dubious generalizations simply because they don't know any better. If these readers are misled, however, some of them will probably eventually learn that you were wrong in your generalizations, and they will then suspect your reliability in other situations, even when you are correct in your claims.

Do Your Examples Fairly Represent the Evidence?   In selecting which evidence for your generalization to include in your argument, you should make sure that the examples you choose are representative of the ones you have omitted. If, for example, you support the statement "Local elections are controlled by the state capital" with three good examples of this control, but in the course of your research you discovered that there is much evidence contradicting your generalization, you are misrepresenting the evidence by failing to cite this material. True, you may have provided enough examples to satisfy your readers, but you are misleading them by excluding the contradictory evidence. The best way around this error is to qualify the claim in such a way that the evidence you omit is not contradictory. If you rewrote the claim as "The state capital has controlled a number of local elections in the recent past," your three examples would perfectly support the claim, and the omitted evidence would no longer be contradictory.

Which Examples Should Be Included?   Sound generalizations must be based on appropriate examples, as well as a sufficient number of them. If your generalized claim is very broad ("Art majors are the most politically liberal of all college students"), it must be based on proportionately broad examples—in this case, instances taken from a number of different colleges in different areas of the country that offer majors in art. If your claim were more limited ("Art majors at my college are the most politically liberal students"), you would be justified in citing examples taken only from your college.

But in this second case, you must still guard against generalizing on the basis of instances drawn from too narrow a context. If from a major whose students come from all over the country, you cite only those students who come from the New York City area, your support is not broad enough to justify the conclusion. You will need either to limit your claim further ("Art majors from the New York City area are the most politically liberal students at my college") or to collect examples drawn from a broader geographical group. Inductive reasoning always requires that the breadth of your conclusion matches the breadth of your supporting evidence.

ACTIVITIES (6.2)

1. The following inductively derived conclusions claim varying degrees of applicability. For each one, supply an appropriate number and range of specific examples.

    a. Most librarians are women.
    b. High school librarians tend to be women.
    c. In my experience, librarians have been pretty evenly divided between men and women.
    d. I have attended two major universities and have been struck by the number of librarians who are women.
    e. Library Science departments tend to attract more women students than men.

2. Write a generalization that is adequately supported by the examples listed for each case below.

    a. John, Susan, and Jim prefer chocolate ice cream, while Jane prefers strawberry, and Henry prefers vanilla.
    b. Last Saturday night I sat alone at a showing of the new film *Anxious Hours,* and I saw no line for the film when I walked by the theater just before show time on Sunday.
    c. It is January 15th here in Minnesota and so far this winter we have had two snowfalls that just covered the ground and then disappeared.
    d. There were twenty-five Mercedes-Benz automobiles parked in the lot the night of my high school reunion, and as I recall there were only about seventy students in my graduating class.
    e. When I returned from winter break to my classes here in Vermont, I noticed that Jack, Jeff, Mary, Matthew, Carrie, and Megan all had deep tans.

STATISTICS

Statistics are based on the practice of drawing conclusions about a large number on the basis of a limited number of instances. Statistics are factual information compiled and reported numerically. Statements like "Thirty percent of the American people believe a woman should never be president," "The unemployment rate is 11 percent," and "One quarter of all bridges in this state need repair" are statistics—they indicate the number of instances in which a given fact applies to a particular group of subjects. In our world, statistics are an inevitable and integral part of our lives. We judge the quality of our manufactured products and of many of our services through statistics; we constantly encounter statistics on the health of our economy, our educational system, our sex lives, our souls. We tend to suspect claims that lack statistical support and use statistics in virtually every field in our society, from weather forecasting to managing baseball teams. But these general conclusions inferred from a limited number of instances are only reliable if the original process of information gathering is conducted according to certain principles. Whether you are conducting your own statistical studies as support for your argument or citing statistics obtained from other sources, you must be sure of the following:

    First, the smaller group surveyed (or *sample,* as statisticians refer to it) must be *known.* If you read that eight out of ten women think they are overweight, but no reference is made to the source of the survey or who or how many were surveyed, you should not accept or use the figure. For all you know, only ten women were questioned, and they were picked from a list obtained from a weight reduction clinic. Every cited study should be identified and the sample group defined. Without such information, the figures are suspect.

Second, the sample must be *sufficient,* or sufficiently large, in order for you to accept the conclusion drawn from that sample. That both of your roommates prefer classical music to rock does not justify the conclusion that classical music is more popular with college students; you need a much larger sample.

And **third**, the sample must be *representative.* If a figure is given about the political inclinations of all Californians, the sample surveyed must represent a cross section of the population. If the 2,000 people questioned all have incomes of $40,000 and up, or if they're all over the age of 45, your sample is slanted, not representative of the variety of the population as a whole. Professional polling organizations like Gallup and Harris (groups hired to identify the preferences of large populations based on small samples) choose either a representative or a random sample. A *representative sample* is one that guarantees in advance that the sample will reflect the major characteristics of the population; for example, that the sample will have a percentage of Californians earning over $40,000 that is equal or nearly equal to the percentage of Californians earning over that figure in the total population. In a *random sample* on political attitudes in California, every adult Californian would stand an equal chance of being questioned. When chosen randomly, in 95 out of 100 cases a sample group of 1,500 people will be within 3 percentage points of duplicating the answers of the entire adult population. In evaluating the usefulness of any poll, you should know the method by which the sample was selected.

When you include in your argument statistics obtained from other sources, not only must you test them for the preceding three principles, you must also be certain they satisfy the requirements of second- or third-party facts. The source should have a reputation for expertise in the field and for objectivity, and the figures themselves should be recent. It is unwise to accept as support for your own argument any statistical data not credited to an authoritative source. If you cannot identify the instrument, individual, or organization through which these facts were obtained, chances are good that those facts are not reliable.

When using statistics in your argument, you also need to be aware of the variety of terms used to report large figures and of the way these terms can influence the impact of the figures. A study on high school literacy could report its findings on extracurricular reading habits in a number of ways. It could say that out of 500 high school seniors surveyed, **100** had read at least one unassigned novel in the last year; or the same fact could be reported as **20 percent** of the students. Of those 100 readers, one could report the **average** number (or **mean**) of novels read (the total number of novels read divided by the 100 readers), the **mode** (the number of novels most frequently read by individual students), or the **median** (the midpoint of the range of frequency of novels read). The mean, mode, and median for this sample of students follow.

Students	Novels Read	Total Novels
25	4	100
10	3	30
45	2	90
20	1	20
TOTAL 100		240

AVERAGE = 2.4 novels (total number of novels read divided by total number of students)

MODE = 2 novels (the most common number)

MEDIAN = 2 (midpoint of the list of number of novels read according to the frequency of the number. Imagine the hundred students standing in a line, starting with all of those who read four novels, then those who read three, then two, and so on. The midpoint of this line of 100 would occur in the group of students who had read two novels.)

Statistics can be powerful tools in argument, but it is crucial to realize that they cannot *prove* claims, they can only *support* their likelihood. A recent poll indicating teenage hostility toward adult society is not proof that it was a teenager who attacked your English teacher or even that the students in a particular high school have hostile feelings toward their parents. It merely indicates that out of a sample of so many teenagers, a certain percentage indicated feelings of hostility toward the adult generation. In argument, responsibly gathered statistics are not suspect, but the use to which we put these figures can be.

You should also be restrained in your use of statistics; if scattered profusely throughout a written text, they can have a deadening effect on the audience. Often, a visual display of statistics through a chart or a table can be more valuable to your audience than a verbal summary; graphic representations can help to clarify the meaning of the statistics and to reinforce their significance. With statistics it is easy to lose track not only of the "big picture" but also of any picture at all, and visual displays can give the reader the necessary picture.

ACTIVITIES (6.3)

1. For two of the following statements based on statistics, write a paragraph stating the kind of information you would need to assure yourself that the statement was reliable.
   a. Over 50 percent of the doctors surveyed in a nationwide study recommend Brand A medicine over any of the leading competitors.
   b. Brand C: the best built truck in America, according to a survey of truck owners.
   c. Over 60 percent of all Americans favor the president's plan for peace, while 85 percent oppose Senator Flag's call for more offensive weapons.
   d. Despite competition from television and VCRs, moviegoing is still popular in America. When asked how much they enjoyed going to the movies,

88 percent of moviegoers responded that they enjoyed moviegoing a great deal.

e. A survey of leading economic forecasters indicates that a mild recession will occur in the next six months.

2. Conduct a survey of some of your classmates or of some friends. Ask them one or two questions that can be summarized in statistics, such as how many hours they have studied this week. Compute the mean, mode, and median for these statistics. Write a one-page description of the results of your survey and also present this information in visual form. Also state how representative you believe this group is of some larger, similar group, such as all students who studied last week.

SUMMARY

Arguing Facts

- All arguments rely on factual claims, either as their primary claim or as a form of support for the primary claim.

- To support facts reported by others, you must be satisfied of their accuracy and provide in your argument brief reference to the source of the fact.

- To support facts founded in your own experience, you must describe the experience accurately and clearly and establish your own credibility through a responsible, objective, and accurate rendering of the experience.

- To support facts reported by others, you must be satisfied of their accuracy and provide in your argument brief reference to the source of the fact.

- To support a factual generalization, you must cite a number of the verified facts that have led you to the general conclusion. The more sweeping the generalization, the more examples you will need to cite. If your readers are likely to be unfamiliar with the subject matter, you should provide several examples as evidence. The examples cited must be typical of all the evidence discovered. The breadth of the examples cited must match the breadth of the generalization.

- Statistics can be effective support for arguments, provided they are not overused and their significance is made clear.

- When including a statistical generalization, you must be satisfied of its reliability. It is reliable if the sample cited is known, sufficient, and representative.

- You must be aware of the exact meaning of the terms used to report statistical conclusions, particularly average, median, and mode.

TWO SAMPLE FACTUAL ARGUMENTS

The following factual argument, intended for a general audience, presents what to many would be a surprising hypothesis—that the specific language we speak influences how we view the world—and then questions whether this hypothesis will ever become a commonly agreed-on fact among linguists.

THE WHORF HYPOTHESIS

One question that has drawn the attention of twentieth-century linguists is the effect of specific languages on our thoughts and perceptions. Does a speaker of English see the world differently from a speaker of German or Chinese or any other language? And if he does, what are these differences? Are they in specific ideas or in more general patterns of thought? Do speakers of different languages literally see the world differently, in the sense of noticing different objects or qualities of objects because their language has words for them?

Languages vary enormously in their sounds, grammar, and vocabulary. In vocabulary, differences are striking. As Carley H. Dodd notes in his Dynamics of Intercultural Communication, English has at least seven words for the spectrum of colors from violet to red, but the American Indian language called Shona has four, while another American Indian language, Basa, has two. For our one word "snow" Eskimo languages have as many as twenty-five words (p. 136). In grammar, differences are even more striking. The student of language Benjamin Lee Whorf observed that the American Indian language of Hopi contains no past, present, and future tense and uses instead a scheme based on distinguishing between the always true (for example, "people need food"), occurrences that are observed or could be observed, and occurrences that are not observable or at least not yet observed (Ellis and Beatie, 58-59).

Whorf's study of American Indian languages, which he carried out in the 1920s and 1930s, led to his formulation of what is variously called "the Whorf hypothesis" or "the Sapir-Whorf hypothesis" (co-named for the linguist Edward Sapir, with whom Whorf studied) or "the linguistic relativity hypothesis." Stated simply, the hypothesis claims that specific languages, especially the underlying patterns of specific languages, play a major role in determining the thought and behavior of a culture. One of Whorf's most famous formulations of this hypothesis is the essay "The Relation of Habitual Thought and Behavior to Language," where he argues that a major characteristic of Hopi behavior, the emphasis on preparation, is a result of linguistic patterns in Hopi (Whorf, 134-159). As Whorf puts it, this emphasis "includes announcing and getting ready for events well beforehand, elaborate precautions to insure persistence of desired conditions, and stress on good will as the preparer of right results" (148). Our culture, because of the different view of time implied by English and other major European languages, does not stress preparation as intensely as Hopi culture.

Is the Whorf hypothesis true? Andrew Ellis and Geoffrey Beatie, in their The Psychology of Language and Communication, report on studies indicating that humans actually see the same colors even though the number and reference of their words for colors may vary enormously (p. 61). We know that a speaker of English will observe different kinds of snow, even though there is only one "snow" in his or her vocabulary. Whorf, however, was mainly concerned with the more subtle and profound effects of language on the basic world view of a culture. Even here, though, Whorf seems to have downplayed the effect society has on language, as a study reported by Ellis and Beatie of the changing nature of Chinese shows: Chinese is becoming more abstract as it moves to accommodate modern

science and technology (61-62). Of course, we are not in a
position to observe the social conditions prevailing
during the formation of our major languages, but it seems
just as plausible to argue that these early societies
affected the nature of the language as much or more than
the languages affected the society. Certainly today we
observe rapid changes in language, at least in vocabulary,
as a result of social change.

The Whorf hypothesis does contain some useful
insights. We will probably notice different kinds of snow
if we have different words for these kinds, and different
languages may encourage different kinds of thought. But we
do not have much evidence to show that language actually
determines a culture's pattern of thought. At least for
now, the Whorf hypothesis remains a hypothesis, tantaliz-
ing in its suggestive possibilities but unproven and
apparently too one-sided in its view of how language and
society interact.

WORKS CITED

Dodd, Carley H. Dynamics of Intercultural Communication.
    Dubuque, Iowa: Brown, 1987.
Ellis, Andrew and Geoffrey Beatie. The Psychology of
    Language and Communication. London: Weidenfeld and
    Nicolson, 1986.
Whorf, Benjamin Lee. "The Relation of Habitual Thought and
    Behavior to Language." Language, Thought, and
    Reality: Selected Writings of Benjamin Lee Whorf. Ed.
    John B. Carroll. New York: Technology Press of M.I.T.
    and Wiley, 1956, pp. 134-159.

The following argument exemplifies how a primary factual claim is supported
through other facts and through appeals to authority. The argument, written by a
student majoring in statistics, also indicates why it is so important to exercise caution and restraint when we rely on statistical support. This essay is based on the
second Suggestion for Writing at the end of this chapter.

STATISTICS LIE, OR DO THEY?

Benjamin Disraeli, English statesman and writer of
the nineteenth century, once quipped, "There are three
kinds of lies: lies, damned lies, and statistics."
Disraeli was not a mathematician, but his judgment about
the reliability of statistics is one that many intelligent
people still hold today. Those not trained in the field
assume that Disraeli's stereotype is a just one.

The stereotype is not without foundation.
Advertisers, politicians, news reporters, and lawyers
misuse statistics so frequently that we, the public, have
come to have little faith in the numbers they quote to us
daily. But the fact is that it is rarely the statistics
themselves that are suspect, but the use that these people
make of them. Statistics don't lie, the people who use
them do.

Many of the statistics that we read in newspapers are
reported from retrospective, case-control studies,
particularly epidemiological studies. A retrospective
study is one in which a control group is selected that
does not currently possess the characteristic under
examination, and a study group is selected that does
exhibit the characteristic. In epidemiological studies the
purpose is to find correlation between the presence of
some disease and a small group of factors that may
influence the course of the disease (Heafey 674). For
instance, Jane Brody reports in the New York Times that
Dr. I-Min Lee, epidemiologist at the Harvard School of
Public Health, has "found a direct relationship between
weight and mortality, with heavier men at all ages being
more likely to die." Here the living are the control
group, and weight is the discriminating factor. Dr. Lee
said that she found correlation between men's weight and
their death rate. She was quoted, "So I believe the upward
trend in desirable weights is not justified" (emphasis

added). Dr. Lee did not say that excessive weight in men
was the <u>cause</u> of their higher death rate, merely that <u>she</u>
<u>believed</u> it to be so. But Brody's entire article, even the
headline, "In Midlife, the Leanest Men Survive," implies
that the <u>cause</u> of higher death rates is greater body
weight. Brody, the reporter, has interpreted for us as
cause, what the epidemiologist (biomedical statistician)
had presented only as a strong correlation.

The fact that two events are correlated does not
necessarily imply that one causes the other. In the
courtroom, statistical correlations are not admissible as
proof that <u>cause</u> exists even for correlations as high as
98.95% (Heafey 685).

A classic example of the misinterpretation of cause
versus correlation is found in the relationship between
the number of stork citings and human population
statistics in Oldenburg, Holland. Seven years of
population statistics (beginning in 1936) imply a direct
relationship between the number of stork citings and the

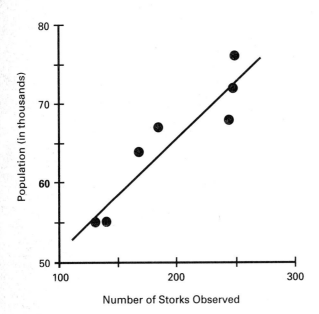

total human population of the city. The population of
Oldenburg is plotted against the number of storks observed
each year. Few people would hypothesize that the increased
number of storks caused the increase in population. Did it
really require more storks to bring all those babies?
Correlations between two variables Y and X often occur
because they are both associated with a third factor W. In
the stork example, since human population Y and the number
of storks X both increased with time W over this 7-year
period, a correlation appears when they are plotted
together as Y versus X. Maybe there is real cause and
effect in the stork versus human population correlation.
It is possible that more storks were cited just because
there were more people around to see them. But the figures
can't demonstrate cause, even if it should exist.

Statistics are also distorted by their method of
presentation. For example, the American Cancer Society
reported in 1991 that women have a 1-in-9 chance of
contracting breast cancer (Blakeslee). But 1 in 9 is the
cumulative probability that any woman will get breast
cancer sometime between birth and age 110. Women at age 40
typically have a 1 in 1,000 risk of getting breast cancer,
and that risk climbs to 1 in 500 by age 50 (Blakeslee). So
even with the hard statistical evidence at hand, the
American Cancer Society has chosen to report the numbers
in such a way as to stretch the truth, to scare women
about this terrible disease. The statistics are not
disputed; it is the users of the statistics that are to be
questioned.

The Brody article also shows how sound statistical
findings can be manipulated to mislead the reader. Jane
Brody failed to give us the actual numerical death rates
that Dr. Lee had correlated. Dr. Lee found that men in
the upper 20th percentile for body weight had death rates
two and a half times greater than men in the lowest

20 percent. But what is the actual death rate? If the rate
is 2 in 10,000 for lean men, then Dr. Lee's findings
indicate that it would be 5 in 10,000 for the heaviest
men. This is hardly a difference worth reporting (perhaps
that's why it was omitted). However, if the death rate for
thin men is 1 in 5, then the heavy men would presumably be
dying at a rate of 1 in 2. Without this essential
information, readers are led down the path again by
sensationalism, perpetrated through under-reported
statistics.

Do statistics really lie? Can statistics be used to
prove anything? A statistician will answer NO to both of
these questions. The trained statistician uses statistics
to make informed decisions in the face of uncertainty.
Statistics can only be used to show the likelihood of some
event or process; by themselves statistics prove nothing.
Properly used, statistics are a form of scientific
evidence that help us get closer to the true state of
nature. When misused by partial omission (whether
deliberate or not) or improper interpretation, statistics
can be contorted to fit anyone's aim. Liars will use
statistical half-truths to further their cause, and
statistical novices will make interpretive mistakes; but
the numbers themselves do not lie.

SUGGESTIONS FOR WRITING (6.4)

1. Write a two- to three-page essay supporting a fact that runs counter to popular
   opinion. This fact can come from your own experience, from your studies in
   college, or from your general knowledge. Examples of such surprising facts
   are: "Despite predictions to the contrary, the increasing use of computers has
   created more new jobs than it has eliminated existing ones." "In spite of their
   image as cold and unfriendly places, large cities (or a specific city you know)
   can be friendly places." This surprising fact can be about yourself, your family,
   your friends, your hometown, your college, your job, your academic field, or
   whatever else comes to mind.

2. Stereotypes are misleading factual generalizations that make the false claim
   that all members of a group have a certain trait: "The English people have stiff

upper lips in times of crisis." "American men like to watch football." Take a prevalent stereotype and analyze to what degree the stereotype is true and how the stereotype is misleading. Make sure the stereotype is one you can deal with in a three- to four-page essay, such as "Engineering students at my college don't get involved in extracurricular activities." You don't have to do a statistical survey to gather data for this essay, but you should carefully examine and present samples to support your claim.

3. Analyze either a newspaper or a television news show for examples of bias or misleading generalizations (for the television news show you may have to videotape the show so that you can view it two or three times). How objective is the reporting of the news? Are there any examples of misleading generalizations? What kind of news is *not* included? Write a two- to three-page essay addressing these questions.

7

Arguing Cause

The goal of causal argument is to establish a probable cause or effect for a given condition. Sometimes you will begin the argument process with a claim firmly in mind ("Television coverage of political campaigning has resulted in a dilution and oversimplification of complex political issues"), and other times you will begin with nothing more than an unexplained effect that you must account for ("Why are so many teenagers abusing alcohol?"). In either event, determining your causal claim (or verifying the one you begin with) is the most critical step in arguing cause, one that requires understanding the nature of causality and a good deal of common sense. The actual argument you write will consist of a report of the process you followed to determine causes or effects.

In the first part of this chapter we will concentrate on arguments of *cause*—arguments that identify and support the cause or causes of an existing circumstance or condition. The principles and processes involved are identical to those you will rely on when you write arguments of *effect*—arguments that predict the probable future effects of an existing circumstance or condition. In the last part of the chapter we will demonstrate how the principles and practices of causal argument apply to these arguments of effect.

DETERMINING CAUSE

Any single effect will be the consequence of a number of causal factors—some powerful and direct, others less influential but still contributory. Making causal arguments is usually not a matter of isolating *the* single cause of a given effect, but rather of discovering and supporting those causal factors whose identification is most useful to the context and purpose of your argument. If the point of your argument is to give as full a causal explanation as possible for the effect in question, you will want to identify and support a number of causal factors, both direct and indirect. But if the point of your argument is to assign responsibility, you would concern yourself only with immediate causes (such as who did what, regardless of why). If your argument has an instructive purpose, and if you want some action taken or avoided on the basis of the causality you demonstrate in a similar situation, you will emphasize those causes, both immediate and remote, that exist in the current situation. For example, if you wish to be as successful in math as Susan is, you might try to reproduce as many of the causes of her success as you can. You certainly can try to emulate her conscientiousness with homework, her regular class attendance, and her active class participation; a third cause of her success—her family of talented mathematicians—will not help you at all.

Developing Causal Candidates

Before you begin to discriminate among causes, you will need an extensive range of causal candidates from which to choose. Whether or not you begin with a particular causal claim in mind, we suggest that early in the process you list all those facts and conditions that seem to be causally linked to the effect your argument seeks to explain. Depending on your subject, this list could come from your own thinking and brainstorming and/or from any reading and research you might do. This list should be as inclusive as possible of every fact or condition you think is even remotely associated with the effect. You will then apply your knowledge of causal principles to this working list in order to select those causal factors that have been most influential.

Assume you are writing an argument that identifies and supports the reasons for student attrition at your college. Part of your argument will consist of a discussion of individual cases—why particular people you know decided to leave school. You know one student (we'll call her Emma) who has explained her decision by saying simply that she didn't like college, but you know it's more complicated than that. Why didn't she like college? What circumstances and conditions caused unhappiness strong enough to prompt this extreme decision? After careful thought and discussion with Emma and some of her friends, you come up with a number of possible reasons for her decision.

For one thing, Emma was not doing well academically. Although a good student in high school, she found college work extremely difficult. Because she is the kind of person who gets down on herself for failure, her poor academic performance had to have been a blow to her self-esteem; it makes sense that she would want to leave a place where she didn't feel good about herself. Also, Emma was the first person in her family to go to college. Her parents, who were not well educated, had worked very hard so that she could have the educational advantages they had lacked. Their ambition for Emma put a lot of pressure on her, which probably made it even harder for her to relax and do her best. Emma's family background worked against her in another way: it deprived her of any close role models to emulate, of any family tradition of success. Graduating from college seemed very foreign to her. Add to these factors Emma's crazy roommate and their closet-size room, and you begin to wonder how Emma lasted through the first semester.

Your examination of the situation has identified a number of possible causes for Emma's decision—some very immediate, like the fact that she did not like college; some directly influential, like her poor academic performance, her low self-esteem, and her crazy roommate; some much more remote in time, like her parents' lack of a college degree. But in one way or another, you conclude, all of these factors influenced Emma's decision. Only a thorough analysis like the one you have conducted can fully explain the reasons behind a given effect. The next step would be to determine more precisely the relative influence of each point in this cluster of causes. But in order to take this step, you must know something about the properties of the different points on your list.

ACTIVITIES (7.1)

1. For the following effects, prepare a cluster of probable causes.
   a. The popularity of John Grisham's lawyer novels
   b. The success of Japanese products in the American market
   c. The popularity of American movies throughout much of the world
   d. The rebirth of feminism in America in the last thirty years
   e. The increasing interest of college students in liberal arts programs

Necessary and Sufficient Causes

Understanding the concepts of *necessary* cause and *sufficient* cause will help you identify which of those causes from your original list are likely to have been most influential in bringing about the effect you are analyzing. To qualify as a cause for a given effect, a causal candidate *must* satisfy the conditions of a necessary *or* sufficient cause, or both. If it does not, it is not a direct cause of the effect, though it may well have contributed to the effect in some way.

A *necessary* cause is a cause without which the effect could not have taken place. One cannot get typhus without the introduction of a rickettsia, or gram-negative microorganism, into the bloodstream. This rickettsia is necessary to the contraction of the disease. Thus, you can be certain that anyone who has contracted typhus has been infected by this particular microorganism. But while introduction of the rickettsia is necessary to the contraction of typhus, it doesn't guarantee that the disease will result. People with a vigorous immune system or those who have been inoculated against typhus will be safe from the disease.

Necessary causes are usually easy to identify: if we know the effect, we know that certain causes or conditions had to be operating. To use a nonscientific example, if you had not parked your car next to a construction site, it would not have been hit by falling debris. Parking your car in that spot was necessary to the effect. In the case of Emma, the cause necessary to her withdrawing from college was her unhappiness there. Presumably, if she had been happy and had liked college, she would have stayed.

Sometimes identifying the necessary cause will not be particularly helpful in your attempt to explain an effect. Necessary causes can seem like redundant re-statements of the effect itself: the necessary cause of a company's filing for bankruptcy is that it ran out of money, but that doesn't tell us very much about the significant factors that led to the bankruptcy filing. In the case of Emma's withdrawal from college, the necessary cause—her unhappiness with college—does not shed much light on the question of student attrition. In order to understand her decision, we have to work backward from the necessary cause, identifying those factors that set it up.

Sufficient causes, on the other hand, are always helpful in causal analyses. A sufficient cause is one that by itself is capable of producing a particular effect. A person's decision to join a health club can have a number of sufficient causes: winning a year's membership in a raffle; wanting to meet new people; wanting to become physically fit. Any one of these motives would be enough to prompt an individual to join a health club, but none of them *has* to exist in order for that decision to be made; that is, they are all sufficient to the effect, but not necessary. In Emma's case, a number of sufficient causes operated: her poor self-esteem, her crazy roommate, and her distaste for dormitory life. Any one of these might have been enough to prompt her decision, but none of them was necessary to that decision.

Sometimes a single cause combines the properties of necessity and sufficiency. The example of the rickettsia demonstrates this combination. Not only *must* one be infected with that microorganism to contract typhus (the necessary cause), but this infection is by itself enough to cause the disease (the sufficient cause). For every effect, we can expect at least one necessary cause and any number of sufficient causes.

In determining which factors on your initial list have been most influential, you need to identify those that are necessary and those that are sufficient. Unless you are writing a full causal analysis, you will usually find yourself concentrating on the sufficient causes for the effect in question.

Identifying Sufficient Causes

The ability to identify a factor as causally sufficient depends on your good sense and your personal experience of causality. There is no rule or formula that we follow in isolating sufficient causes, yet most of us have little difficulty answering the question "Is this factor by itself sufficient to have caused this effect?"

When your subject involves human behavior as either cause or effect, there is a useful test you should apply to those factors you think are sufficient. Actions performed by an individual or group are linked to their causes by some universal principle or motivator of human behavior. If you argue, for example, that a sluggish economy is a cause of the increased popularity of taped movie rentals, you are accounting for a particular human behavior—the rental of taped movies. Your claim is a simple claim of cause, with a fact at the causal end and an action (also a fact) at the effect end.

sluggish economy   increase in movie rentals
(cause)   (effect)

This causal proposition is only plausible if its two sides are linked by some acceptable motive. Why would people rent more movies for home viewing in a sluggish economy? What motive or need would urge them to react to a particular condition with a particular behavior? In this case, the linking motivation is easy to identify: in tight times, people need to economize, and it is considerably cheaper to watch rented movies at home than to pay high prices in a theater. The cause and the resulting behavior can be linked by a motivation that everyone can understand and identify with:

sluggish economy . . . . increase in movie rentals
{desire to economize in tight times}

Identifying this motivation doesn't tell you whether or not this is the only sufficient cause, but it will reassure you that the link between this cause and the effect is a plausible one. If you can supply no such motivation between cause and effect, your theory is not plausible, and it's time to look for another cause.

Applying the Toulmin Model

The Toulmin model discussed in Chapter 5 is particularly useful when you are composing causal arguments. Indeed, the relationship we have just presented among possible cause, existing effect, and linking principle fits perfectly into Toulmin's data-claim-warrant formula. Here is our example about increased movie rentals translated into the Toulmin model:

Data	**Claim**
The economy has been sluggish.	Movie rentals have increased.

Warrant
Most people find ways to economize
when the economy slows down.

In this case, the warrant is that general behavioral principle that connected the cause, which we place in the data position, and effect, which we place under claim (even though the actual claim of the argument is the causal relationship between data and claim). When you are trying to identify sufficient causes for a particular effect, you may find it useful to apply the Toulmin model to your cause and effect, making sure that you can provide a warrant that would be widely acceptable to your readers. Remember that in many cases the warrant will not be acceptable without further support, or what Toulmin calls *backing*. In those cases, the warrant and its backing will need to be provided explicitly in the argument. If the warrant does seem immediately acceptable, it need not be stated outright.

ACTIVITIES (7.2)

1. For three of the samples below, write a paragraph or two describing what you believe are the necessary and sufficient causes.

a. **Effect:** John's car accident.
   Possible causes: John was driving at night on a poorly lit road; the road was wet from rain; John had taken a very difficult exam that morning; John was driving ten miles per hour over the speed limit.
b. **Effect:** the dramatic increase in the use of VCRs in the last few years.
   Possible causes: the cost of VCRs is now at an affordable level for most Americans; videotapes of films are increasingly available; viewers can choose what films they will watch with the VCR; many Americans have a large amount of leisure time available.
c. **Effect:** the decline in oil and gasoline prices in the middle 1980s.
   Possible causes: on the average, cars were more fuel efficient than they had been ten years before; there was a growing awareness that petroleum is a nonrenewable resource; the oil-exporting countries were producing more oil than the world consumed.
d. **Effect:** Louise's winning an award for the best violin recital at the music festival.
   Possible causes: Louise practices the violin three hours each day; Louise's parents found the city's best violin teacher for her when she was five; from a very early age it was obvious that Louise was talented musically; Louise prefers Mozart to any other composer.
e. **Effect:** Charles's favorite hobby is cross-country skiing.
   Possible causes: Charles wants to stay in shape, and cross-country skiing is very good for the cardiovascular system; he likes winter and being out-of-doors; he is on a tight budget and cannot afford downhill skiing this year; he was once injured while downhill skiing; in high school he won prizes in cross-country ski races.

2. For each pair below, place the cause and effect within the Toulmin model and supply a warrant that would link the data and claim acceptably. For which warrants should you also supply backing? What would that backing be?

   a. **Cause:** increased leisure time.
      Effect: more participation in sports like skiing and wind-surfing.
   b. **Cause:** an abundance of food for most Americans.
      Effect: a stress on thinness in fashions and in our ideals of beauty.
   c. **Cause:** special incentives that reduce the price of automobiles.
      Effect: higher automobile sales.
   d. **Cause:** severe economic conditions.
      Effect: a lowering of the birth rate.
   e. **Cause:** the banning of a book.
      Effect: increased demand for the book.

DISTINGUISHING AMONG SUFFICIENT CAUSES

Sometimes in analyzing causes you will discover a number of possible sufficient causes for an effect and not know which were actually operating. In these cases you will need other methods for determining probable cause. The following strategies were formulated by the nineteenth-century philosopher John Stuart Mill to determine cause in such situations. While Mill was looking for ways to establish cause with scientific certainty, his methods have proven to be very useful in situations where certainty is unreachable.

Method of Agreement

This method is useful when you are investigating the cause of *two or more* similar effects. In these instances you determine what the sets of events preceding each effect have in common; you are looking for a single sufficient cause that operated in all these similar cases.

If you were investigating the reason or reasons for the success of the five best-selling hardbound books of the year, you would list all the factors that might have contributed to the success of each book; that is, the significant characteristics of each. If all the books centered on the subject of personal relationships in the 1990s, you could safely identify subject matter as a leading cause of the books' success. Sometimes you will not discover a factor common to all your effects; perhaps the five best-sellers have no single common characteristic, which means a number of sufficient causes are operating in these instances.

Method of Difference

Mill's method of difference can be applied to determine why two essentially similar situations turned out very differently. If you want to know why one self-help book succeeded while another failed, why one calculus class with Professor Jones was interesting while another was boring, or why the Confederate army lost the battle of Gettysburg but won the battles of Bull Run, you can apply the difference method by looking for the factor present in one case but absent in the other. If the only difference between your two calculus classes with Professor Jones was that the subject matter of the second class was more advanced, that could well be the reason for your unhappiness in the second class.

This method will only work when you are examining truly similar situations that share a number of common factors. If you were trying to account for the difference between your career choice and that of one of your grandparents, the situations would be too dissimilar for the method of difference to tell you anything; your grandparents faced an entirely different range of career choices than you did.

Method of Proportional Correlations

This method is useful in determining the cause of an effect that is continuing and varied—the movement of the Dow Jones Industrial Average, the increase and occasional decrease in the gross national product, the enrollment of college students in certain kinds of majors. In trying to identify possible causes of such measurable trends, you should look for conditions preceding the trends that vary and persist proportionally. In considering the reasons for the rise in the divorce rate since the 1960s, you might discover that there has been a congruent increase in the number of two-income families over the same time period; that is, that there has been an increase in the number of married women who are economically self-sustaining.

This fact of increasing economic independence of women is a plausible explanation of the increased divorce rate if it satisfies the following three conditions: (1) if it is truly independent of the effect (not a result of the same cause); (2) if the two trends, with all their fluctuations, are truly proportional; and (3) if the cause and effect are plausibly linked by an accepted behavioral principle—in this case the principle or motive of independence or self-reliance. If these three conditions are satisfied, we would accept that the economic independence of wives is a sufficient cause of divorce.

ACTIVITIES (7.3)

1. Take a group of at least three of your classmates or friends who share a common trait, such as their academic major, a hobby, or some other favorite activity, and try to determine what sufficient cause made each member of the group have this trait. Try to find a common sufficient cause for the entire group, but be prepared to end up with different sufficient causes if a common cause does not reveal itself. Write a one- to two-page essay describing the results of your investigation.

2. Compare two classes you have taken sometime in your education, one that you liked and one that you disliked. The two classes should be as similar as possible in subject matter and level of difficulty. What made the one class likable, while the other was not? Write a one- to two-page essay addressing this question.

3. For the next week, compare fluctuations in two phenomena that you believe might be related, such as the temperature and attendance at one of your classes. Make a chart comparing the movement of these two phenomena and then see if any proportional correlation exists between the two. If there is such a correlation, ask yourself if the two are the result of the same cause and if some plausible behavioral principle links the two. Write a one- to two-page analysis of your study. Be sure to give your instructor the chart you have created.

CAUSAL CHAINS

Some effects are best understood in terms of a directly related series of causes, like links in a single chain, or a row of sequentially falling dominoes. In these cases, identifying the entire chain of causes is far more useful than isolating those causes that are most immediate to the effect, or isolating the more remote cause that originally set the chain in motion.

If someone told you that closed captioning of television shows (where subtitles can be seen on specially equipped televisions) is a result of the rubella epidemic in the United States during the 1960s, you might initially reject the connection as utterly implausible. What you have been given is the first cause and final effect in a causal chain; if the links in the causal chain are filled in, the connection is reasonable. In the 1960s, there *was* a widespread outbreak of rubella, or German measles (at the time, there was no rubella inoculation). Rubella is a relatively harmless disease except to the fetuses of pregnant women; babies whose mothers contract rubella during pregnancy often suffer birth defects, one of which is deafness. Because of the epidemic, huge numbers of babies were born deaf. In the last twenty years, as these children have grown, we have seen increased sensitivity to the needs of the hearing-impaired, one of the most notable being the media's recent provision of closed captioning for television. With all the links in the chain identified, the causal connection between a common virus and the closed captioning service is no longer implausible, though there were other factors at work, including the increasing emphasis on the rights of the handicapped in the last twenty years.

The constellation leading to Emma's withdrawal from college contains a causal chain. Beginning with her decision to withdraw, we can move straight back as far as her parents' lack of a college education. The chain works as follows: Emma withdrew from college because she didn't like it. She didn't like it because she felt low self-esteem in that setting. This low self-esteem was a result of poor grades, which at least in part were caused by the enormous pressure she was under to do well. This pressure came from her parents, who, because they had never been to college, desperately wanted Emma to be the first in the family to get a college degree. Not all of the points in the constellation we identified earlier appear in this chain. So while the chain explains much about the evolution of Emma's decision, it does not explain everything, just as the chain linking the rubella epidemic with closed captioning is not the fullest possible explanation of the situation.

CONTRIBUTING FACTORS

In analyzing causes, we occasionally find a circumstance that is neither necessary nor sufficient yet somehow relevant. This type of circumstance is labeled a *contributing factor*. If Kathy continues to jog even when she is run-down, and then catches a virus, her jogging was not a sufficient cause of her illness; the presence of the virus without sufficient antibodies to combat it is the sufficient cause. Nor is the jogging a necessary cause, since she may have gotten the virus even without jogging. Yet her pushing herself while not feeling "100 percent" certainly didn't help and may have made her more susceptible to disease. In this case we can label the jogging as a probable contributing factor.

Emma's situation contains at least one contributing factor: her lack of a close role model. Clearly, this factor was not necessary to the effect, nor was it sufficiently influential to have caused her withdrawal. Yet it made a bad situation worse, depriving Emma of any positive example from which to take heart. Contributing factors are present in most complicated situations; if your goal is a thorough analysis of cause, you need to take contributing factors into account.

ACTIVITIES (7.4)

1. For two of the following causes and remote effects, write a paragraph describing a plausible causal chain that links the cause with the remote effect.

a. **Cause:** the rise of industrialization.
   Effect: the growth of the conservation movement.
b. **Cause:** the invention of gunpowder.
   Effect: the decline of knighthood.
c. **Cause:** Jane's high absenteeism in third grade.
   Effect: Jane's difficulty with cursive writing.
d. **Cause:** the invention of printing.
   Effect: the growth of democracy in Europe and America.
e. **Cause:** Jack's love of parties.
   Effect: Jack's becoming the mayor of his city.

2. Review the clusters of causes presented in (1) in Activities (7.2), and identify possible contributing factors for each cluster.

SUMMARY

Determining Cause

- Because causality is always multifaceted, keep your mind open to all possibilities early in your causal investigations.

- The ultimate purpose of your argument (to explain, instruct, or designate responsibility) will determine which causes you will concentrate on in your argument.

- To determine the most influential causes for your effect, you need to be able to identify the necessary and sufficient causes. A *necessary cause* is a cause without which the effect could not have occurred; a *sufficient cause* is one that by itself is capable of producing the effect.

- Where human behavior is concerned, sufficient causes must be linked to their effect through an assumable motive.

- When you have a number of potential sufficient causes for an effect, use the following methods to determine the most probable cause or causes: the method of *agreement* will help you determine the cause of similar effects; the method of *difference* will help you determine why two similar situations turned out differently; the method of *proportional correlation* will help you determine the cause of an effect that varies over time.

- Some effects are best explained by identifying a chain of causes, often originating at a time remote from the effect.

- Thorough causal arguments may also identify *contributing factors* to the effect—circumstances that are neither necessary nor sufficient causes but do play a role in creating an event or condition.

SUPPORTING CAUSAL CLAIMS

Most causal claims are supported through (1) establishing the factuality of the effect(s) and cause(s) you discuss; (2) identifying, sometimes only implicitly, an acceptable motive in arguments involving human action; (3) in some cases, describing the process that helped you validate a causal candidate (method of difference, agreement, or proportional correlation); and (4) indicating the degree of certainty your argument claims.

Establishing Factuality

Facts are the foundations of causal argument. While in most causal arguments you will write, the causal relationship you propose between two events will rarely be certain and verifiable, there can be no room to doubt the certainty of the events you are linking; they *must* be true in order for your argument to be meaningful and plausible. If you misrepresent the effect through exaggeration, understatement, or inaccuracy, your identification of cause is useless; you are explaining something that didn't actually occur.

Identifying an Acceptable Motivation

When the effect you investigate comes in the form of human action, your investigation should penetrate to the level of an acceptable motive. In cases where the linking motive is obvious, your argument may not have to cite it explicitly. If, for example, you were arguing that a decrease in DWI arrests is a consequence of tougher DWI laws, you wouldn't have to identify people's unwillingness to risk the new penalties as the linking motivator between cause and effect; it is obvious and can thus go unstated. But if your argument seeks to account for the increased divorce rate since the 1960s by citing a proportional rise in two-career families, you would want to state the motive linking proposed cause and effect because it may not be immediately obvious to your readers: women who have some degree of financial independence and employment security are more likely to leave unhappy marriages than women who are financially dependent on their spouses. Furthermore, if the motive or principle you identify may not be immediately acceptable to your audience, you should provide some backing for it as well.

We have found that students writing causal arguments tend to omit mentioning the linking motivation when they should include it; that is, they find obvious what is not as obvious to their readers. If you have any doubt about whether or not you should include this explanation in your argument, we suggest you do provide it. As we've said earlier, it is better to err on the side of too much information than too little.

Reporting the Process of Determination

In arguments where John Stuart Mill's processes of determination have been useful to you, you can support your claim by reporting in your argument how the method was applied. You don't need to use the formal terms *method of agreement* and so on, but you should provide a summary, a kind of narrative of your investigation.

If your argument identified the reasons for the failure of a number of restaurants in your town, it probably would have relied on the method of agreement, because you are looking for an explanation common to all the restaurant closings. Your report of the process might read something like this:

> From 1984 to 1986, four new restaurants were opened in the small town of East Bay, Wisconsin. None of the restaurants was able to draw enough customers to keep operating; each closed within five months of its opening.
>
> The restaurants had little in common. One specialized in moderately priced Chinese foods, serving lunches and dinners six days a week; one was a diner, with inexpensive diner-style meals served at all hours, seven days a week. *Le Papillon,* an elegant French restaurant, was the most expensive of the four, but the meals were well worth the price. The fourth restaurant, a member of a popular family-restaurant franchise, while serving the least distinctive fare, was well suited to the needs of entire families.
>
> The locations of the restaurants were as varied as their fare and ambience. The Chinese restaurant was located on a busy street just outside central downtown, a street full of strollers and window shoppers throughout the year. The diner was in a converted trolley on the outskirts of a newly gentrified section of town. *Le Papillon* was one of a series of shops and restaurants in the new shopping plaza north of town, and the family restaurant was in an indoor shopping mall.
>
> Located in very different spots throughout town, catering to different classes of customers and offering food ranging in quality from passable to excellent, these restaurants seem to have nothing in common that might explain their almost concurrent failures. But this concurrency was a significant common feature. All four restaurants opened and closed within the same two-year period. All the failures were probably caused more by timing than any other factor.
>
> The years 1984 to 1986 were terrible years for East Bay. In 1984 the ball bearing plant, the town's largest employer, closed. The unemployment rate in East Bay soared to a very high rate of 30 percent. Given the bleak economic picture during this period, it is no surprise that all these restaurants failed. In 1986 the outlook for East Bay began to improve with the opening of a new factory, but this improvement came too late to help these four restaurants.

As indicated in the preceding section on determining cause, some of the methods of determination carry with them particular risks that must be avoided. The difference method, for example, is only reliable if the effects you examine are truly comparable. In addition, when using the method of proportional correlation, you must be sure that the trends you identify are independent—that is, they are neither effects of another cause nor mutually contributing (for example, bad tempers causing quarrels and quarrels exacerbating bad tempers).

In supporting your causal argument, you will be wise to point out that your use of a particular method of determination has avoided the associated risks. For example, if you use the difference method to determine why you like golf but your friend with similar athletic ability and experience in golf does not, you should demonstrate that apparent differences between you and your friend—family background, interest in other sports—are not significant in terms of your argument.

Qualifying Your Argument

Since certainty is rare in causal arguments, you must not mislead your reader and thereby undermine your own credibility by claiming more certainty for your argument than is warranted by its support. You have a wide range of words indicating degrees of causality to choose from, so make sure you use language that accurately reflects your level of certainty. If you are very certain about your causal proposition, you can use such definite words as the following:

> necessitated
>
> caused
>
> resulted in
>
> attributable to
>
> produced
>
> created
>
> brought about
>
> was responsible for

But use these words with caution. Without qualifiers like "may have," "probably," "seems to have," and so on, they claim a certainty that can be difficult to document.

The words listed in the following group also indicate causality, but a causality that is clearly qualified:

> contributed to
>
> is associated with
>
> is a function of
>
> facilitated
>
> enabled
>
> influenced
>
> increased
>
> decreased
>
> improved

You are better off using words such as these when the causality you propose is not certain. By using such terms, you are both indicating causality and admitting *some* degree of uncertainty.

ACTIVITIES (7.5)

For two of the examples below, write a paragraph on each indicating what would be needed to make the causal argument more convincing. This additional material could include establishing facts, reporting the process of determination, describing motives, demonstrating the independence of two elements in a proportional correlation, or adding qualifying language, though other steps may also be necessary to make the argument credible.

1. Bill's alleged cheating on the exam was certainly a result of his low grades early in the semester and his desire to be accepted into a reputable law school.

2. Police report the arrest of Hubert Midas, the oil and gas billionaire, for shoplifting a $35 shirt from a downtown department store. Midas must have forgotten to pay for the shirt.

3. As more women have entered the work force, the number of families without children has risen proportionally. The increasing number of women in the work force has caused this rise in childless families.

4. Without Martin Luther King, Jr.'s charismatic personality, the civil rights movement of the 1960s would not have had the impact it did.

5. The Roman Empire fell because of the moral decadence of many of its citizens.

SUMMARY

Supporting Causal Claims

- To support a cause, you must establish the factuality of cause and effect; identify an acceptable motivation in cases where human actions are at least part of the cause; usually report how you determined the causes; if necessary, qualify your assertions about the certainty of your argument.

ARGUING EFFECTS

Because arguments of effect are concerned with the future, with events that haven't yet occurred, their claim to certainty is even less absolute than arguments of cause. Even the most carefully constructed argument of effect, one firmly grounded in the principles of causality and in experience in the relevant field, can go awry. We have only to look at the accuracy rate of weather forecasters and political analysts to recognize how frequently the future refuses to cooperate with our plans for it. But if executed carefully and according to certain principles, arguments of effect *can* be reasonable and convincing, serving as useful guidelines for many courses of action.

Claims of arguments of effect can be stated in a number of ways, as in the following:

1. If John continues to drink heavily and drive, it's only a matter of time before he has a serious accident.
2. The number of high school graduates will continue to decline for the next five years, then begin to stabilize.
3. I will not see a woman president in my lifetime.
4. Consumers are so comfortable with certain companies that they will buy almost anything carrying those companies' logos.

While they may seem quite different, these four claims share certain features common to all arguments of effect. Most obviously, all predict that something will happen in the future (or in the case of the third claim, that something will not happen). Claims 1 and 4—John's heavy drinking, and brand appeal—also identify a causal relationship between a current condition and the future event. Claims 2 and 3 do not identify such a condition; to qualify as arguments of effect, the arguments introduced by these two claims must identify certain conditions that have led the writer to draw these conclusions about the future. For claim 2, those conditions could be certain demographic trends that have persisted over time; for claim 3, those conditions could be the conservative disposition of most voters, or perhaps a poll indicating strong opposition to a woman president among teenagers and young voters. These current conditions and trends set the ground for an argument of effect. An argument of effect demonstrates that the existence of these conditions and trends is enough to cause a particular future effect. Lacking identified causes, these kinds of claims are nothing more than random predictions, similar to the bizarre predictions on the covers of the sensational magazines found in supermarkets: "Psychic Foresees Economic Collapse Following Landing of Martians on White House Lawn!"

Determining and Supporting a Probable Effect

The processes of determining and supporting a probable effect overlap considerably. If you identify a future effect through sound methods, the best supporting strategy will be to report these methods, which we discuss in the following paragraphs.

Applying the Principles of Causality.   To determine whether a projected effect could be created by current or intended causes, you treat both as having occurred and then evaluate whether and how they are causally related. Are the causes that are currently operating (or that might be set in place) enough to bring about the effect? If you can identify an existing sufficient cause or causes for the effect, your prediction is probably a good one.

Let's take the case of a publishing house editor trying to decide whether to publish a book submitted to her on personal relationships. The editor will accept the book if she thinks it will sell well; her job is to decide whether current circumstances would make the book a best-seller. In other words, the projected effect is excellent sales. The circumstances operating are as follows: the market for books on this topic has been very strong; the writer has written popular books on this subject before; the book itself, in the view of this experienced editor, is interesting, original, and provocative. An analysis of these circumstances reveals that all are sufficient causes; in the absence of the other two, one cause alone would be sufficient to create the effect. The editor's experience with bookselling makes her a good judge of the sufficiency of these causes. Our editor knows how important these three circumstances are because she has seen them again and again. In projecting any effect, the arguer must understand the principles of the subject matter.

Missing from this list of current circumstances is a necessary cause, one that has to operate in order for the effect to occur. The absence of necessary cause does not make the projected effect implausible; often it is the sufficient causes that create the necessary cause. In this example, the necessary cause to high sales would simply be that people buy the book, and they will buy the book in the presence of one or more of these sufficient causes.

Causal Chains.   In some situations, you can argue a future effect by revealing a chain of causes that plausibly connects cause A with future effect D. To demonstrate the connection between a past or present cause and a future effect, you need to make a series of arguments of effect; if A is the remote cause and D the predicted effect, you will argue that A will cause B, which will cause C, which finally will cause D.

The field of economics often uses causal chains as a basis for future action. A classic example is the government's setting of interest rates on money it lends to banks, which in turn affects the interest rates banks and other financial institutions charge customers on mortgages and other loans and the interest they pay to customers for savings and other deposits. One key step a government can take to reduce consumer spending is to raise its interest rates, which means the banks will raise their rates, and customers will find that it costs more to get a mortgage on a house, finance a car loan, or buy other items on credit. Faced with these rising costs, consumers will decide to spend less. Also, because these same banks are now paying more interest for deposits, consumers have an incentive to save rather than spend—another reason why they will reduce spending. Visually, the causal chain looks like this:

(A) higher government interest rates → (B) higher bank
interest rates → (C) lower consumer spending

This causal chain could be extended, since lower consumer spending could lead to a lower inflation rate or to less importing of consumer goods from other coun-

tries. With causal chains, however, the greater the length of the chain, the less predictable become the effects.

Sometimes, causal chains simply don't work the way they are supposed to.
When Prohibition became law in 1919, its proponents predicted that alcoholic
consumption would decrease and along with it a host of evils, including crime,
broken homes, and absenteeism from work. They did not foresee a roaring four-
teen years of speakeasies, bathtub gin, and bootleg whiskey before Prohibition was
abolished in 1933. Especially when trying to predict human behavior through
elaborate causal chains, you should always keep in mind the adage about the road
to hell being paved with good intentions.

Comparable Situations.   You can also determine the probable future result of
current conditions by examining comparable situations in which this cause and
effect have already occurred. In trying to raise the educational standards of American primary and secondary schools, teachers, school administrators, and government policymakers look to the experience of other countries. The average scores
of students from some other industrialized countries are higher than the average
scores of American students on certain standardized achievement tests in areas
such as math and science. In some of these countries, notably Japan, children
spend much more of the year in school, and the schools place more emphasis on
introducing rigorous academic material earlier in the student's academic career.
Some proponents of reform argue that the same methods used here will improve
students' performance.

This comparison method will only work if the situations being compared are
significantly similar. In arguing that the United States should follow Japan's example, advocates of these changes also need to look carefully at what each country
expects from its schools and how these expectations relate to the general culture.
What seems comparable at first view may turn out to be more complicated on
closer inspection, since American and Japanese cultures have very different expectations about the role of the individual in society.

The more comparable situations you can find, the more convincing your argument of effect will be. If you can demonstrate that a certain cause has had the
same result over and over again, and that the current conditions you are considering are truly similar to these other causes, your identification of effect will be well
supported.

ACTIVITIES (7.6)

1. For two of the following activities, write a paragraph on each describing at
   least two effects they might cause; state whether the causes would be necessary or sufficient.
   Example effect: obtaining a part-time job.
   Possible causes: applying for the position (necessary); doing well at the interview (necessary); being the only person available to do the job (sufficient).
   a. Getting an "A" in a course

   b. Arranging a date with someone you don't know
   c. Reducing the danger of theft at your college or in your community
   d. Finding a good place to live
   e. Avoiding being stopped by the police for speeding
2. Write a two- to three-page essay describing a causal chain for some area or activity with which you are familiar. How confident are you that this chain will work as you have stated? Have you ever seen it work before? Can you think of any circumstances where it might not work?
3. For the five activities listed below, cite a truly comparable activity or situation that could be used to support your prediction of a resulting effect.
   Example: Extending the academic year in primary and secondary education in the United States. A comparable situation could be the long academic year in Japan, to support the prediction of higher test scores for American students.
   a. U.S. military intervention in third-world countries in the 1990s
   b. Public relations strategies for Euro-Disney
   c. Obtaining alumni support from graduates of a large state university
   d. Being governor of a state
   e. Student success in graduate school

SUMMARY

Determining and Arguing a Probable Effect

- To argue an effect, you need to identify a sufficient cause for the effect and prove that this cause exists or could exist.

- You can argue that a certain effect is likely if you can create a causal chain that demonstrates how you move from one cause to an effect that is the cause of the next effect, and so forth. The longer your chain, however, the less likely it is that the chain will perform as predicted.

- You can demonstrate that an effect is likely in a situation if you can prove that a similar situation produced a similar effect.

TWO SAMPLE CAUSAL ARGUMENTS

The following argument is a sample of causal analysis. Based on an essay written by college student Michele Statt, the essay identifies causes for a recent increase in student interest in liberal arts majors. In her essay Michele establishes the factuality of her effect and of her main cause, reports on the process of determination she used to test this cause (method of agreement), identifies an acceptable human motivation (interest in good jobs), and appropriately qualifies her claims with such phrases as "may have influenced" and "probably associated with." Michele's essay is not an elaborate and definitive causal argument, but it is a good example of a brief and tentative examination of causes.

THE NEW INTEREST IN THE LIBERAL ARTS

In 1978 only 443 students were enrolled in liberal arts majors at my college. Today, with the recent establishment of new liberal arts majors, 604 students are enrolled in these majors. (In the same period, the total enrollment at my college has decreased by 40 students.) Many other schools have also reported that interest in liberal arts majors has been increasing. According to Michael Useem, Director of Boston University's Center for Applied Social Science, across the nation "the proportion of baccalaureate degrees in the liberal arts in 1986 was the largest in four years, and the proportion of first-year college students reporting an interest in a liberal arts major in 1987 was the highest in 10 years" ("The Corporate View of Liberal Arts," p. 46).

Several causes may have influenced this increase in interest. Many students entering college are unsure of their career choice and gravitate to the liberal arts because such programs typically do not insist on early declaration of a major. Even if the undecided student then chooses to pursue a major outside the liberal arts, she will find that her liberal arts courses can be applied to her new major. However, having started in the liberal arts, she is likely to find a liberal arts major that appeals to her.

Another cause probably associated with this increase is the growing emphasis on career training within the liberal arts majors themselves. At my college the liberal arts majors include such programs as economics, school psychology, criminal justice, and communications--all of which include a significant element of career preparation that appeals to today's college students. Several of these programs at my college are relatively new. Their existence as additional options for students certainly helps to explain the growth in liberal arts enrollment here.

Liberal arts enrollment, however, has been increasing throughout the country, even at institutions that have not added many new liberal arts programs. The central cause for this growth is very likely the increasing demand for liberal arts majors in the job market. Michael Useem's article, based on research supported by the Corporate Council on the Liberal Arts and the President's Committee on the Arts and Humanities, states that since the early 1980s many business leaders have stressed the importance of the liberal arts as preparation for a career in business (46). Useem received responses to his survey from 535 large and mid-sized American corporations. The results indicated that corporations do indeed hire liberal arts graduates, with 44 percent of the respondents recruiting liberal arts graduates on campus and 47 percent hiring such students for internships and cooperative education programs. Twenty-nine percent reported other efforts to recruit liberal arts graduates, and 61 percent have created programs to train liberal arts graduates for jobs in their corporations (47).

Students are becoming aware of this demand for liberal arts graduates. I chose my field of communication both because of my interest in it and because I was aware of job possibilities after graduation. Twelve students that I talked to said that career preparation was one of the two major causes of their choosing a liberal arts major, the other being their interest in the subject. These results are hardly scientific proof, but they are another piece of evidence demonstrating the importance of the job market in rising liberal arts enrollments.

Useem's study also notes that although many companies hire liberal arts graduates, they are often looking for accomplishments in addition to a liberal arts major, including campus or community involvement and a good grade point average. Another important requirement for most of these corporations was exposure to business courses or experience in business before graduation (47-48, 50-51). The increasing emphasis on career training in at least some liberal arts majors undoubtedly enhances the attractiveness of these majors to employers.

Ten or fifteen years ago, many college students felt that they were forced to make a choice between a liberal arts major or preparing themselves for a career. Because they wanted to find a good job, some of these students chose a program outside of the liberal arts even when they really preferred a liberal arts major. Today's students are more fortunate. They know that in choosing a liberal arts major, they can also prepare themselves for their future after college.

WORKS CITED

Useem, Michael. "The Corporate View of Liberal Arts."
    Journal of Career Planning and Employment, Summer
    1988: 46-51.

The argument "I, Too, Am a Good Parent" combines elements of a causal argument and a recommendation. Dorsett Bennett, the author, claims that the continuing custom of granting child custody to the mother is a result of the prejudice of older male judges who continue to dominate the courts. This generalized causal claim identifies a sensible sufficient cause, though it would be more convincing if Mr. Bennett had included supporting facts and examples about the number of instances in which male judges in Minnesota have granted custody to the mother. The essay ends with a recommendation to the judges themselves: "Become part of the solution to this dilemma of child custody. Don't remain part of the problem."

I, TOO, AM A GOOD PARENT

Dads Should Not Be Discriminated Against

DORSETT BENNETT

Divorce is a fact of modern life. A great number of people simply decide that they do not wish to stay married to their spouse. A divorce is not a tremendously difficult situation unless there are minor children born to the couple. If there are no minor children you simply divide the assets and debts. But you cannot divide a child. The child needs to be placed with the appropriate parent.

In my own case, my former wife chose not to remain married to me. That is her right and I do not fault her decision. My problem is that I do not believe it is her right to deny me the privilege of raising our children. Some fathers want to go to the parent/teacher conferences, school plays, carnivals and to help their kids with homework. I have always looked forward to participating on a daily basis in my children's lives. I can no longer enjoy that privilege— the children live with their mother, who has moved to a northern Midwest state.

I tried so hard to gain custody of my children. I believe the evidence is uncontradicted as to what an excellent father (and more important, parent) I am. My ex-wife is a fairly good mother, but unbiased opinions unanimously agreed I was the better parent. Testimonials were videotaped from witnesses who could not attend the out-of-state custody hearing. I choose to be a father. When I was 3 years old, my own father left my family. While I've loved my father for many years, I did and still do reject his parental pattern.

A couple of centuries ago, a father and mother might have shared equally in the care and raising of children above the age of infancy. But with the coming of the Industrial Revolution the father went to work during the day, leaving the full-time care of the young to the mother, who stayed at home. It was easier to decide who should get child custody under those circumstances. That would be true today even if the mother were put into the position of working outside the home after the divorce.

Now, a majority of married mothers are in the workplace—often because the family needs the second income to survive. With the advent of the working mother, we have also seen a change in child care. Not only have we seen an increase in third-party caregivers; there is a decided difference in how fathers interact with their children. Fathers are even starting to help raise their children. I admit that in a great many families there is an uneven distribution of child-care responsibilities. But there are fathers who do as much to raise the children as the mother, and there are many examples where men are full-time parents.

But, because we have this past history of the mother being the principal child caregiver, the mother has almost always been favored in any contested child-custody case. The law of every state is replete with decisions showing that the mother is the favored custodial parent. The changes in our lifestyles are now being reflected in our laws. In most, if not all, states, the legislature has recognized the change in child-care responsibilities and enacted legislation that is gender blind. The statutes that deal with child custody now say that the children should be placed with the parent whose care and control of the child will be in the child's best interest.

This legislation is enlightened and correct. Society has changed. We no longer bring up our children as we did years ago. But it is still necessary to have someone make the choice in the child's best interest if the parents are divorcing and cannot agree on who takes care of the kids. So we have judges to make that enormous decision.

The state legislature can pass laws that say neither parent is favored because of their gender. But it is judges who make the ultimate choice. And those judges are usually *older males* who practiced law during the time when mothers were the favored guardians under the law. These same judges mostly come from a background where mothers stayed home and were the primary caregivers. By training and by personal experience they have a strong natural bias in favor of the mother in a child-custody case. That belief is regressive and fails to acknowledge the changed realities of our present way of life. Someone must be appointed to render a decision when parents cannot agree. I would ask that those judges who make these critical decisions re-examine their attitudes and prejudices against placing children with fathers.

After the videotaped testimony was completed, one of my lawyers said he had "never seen a father put together a better custody case." "But," he asked me, "can you prove she is unfit?" A father should not be placed in the position of having to prove the mother is unfit in order to gain custody. He should not have to prove that she has two heads, participates in child sacrifice or eats live snakes. The father should only have to prove that he is the more suitable parent.

Fathers should not be discriminated against as I was. It took me three years to get a trial on the merits in the Minnesota court. And Minnesota has a law directing its courts to give a high priority to child-custody cases. What was even worse was that the judge seemed to ignore the overwhelming weight of the evidence and granted custody to my ex-wife. At the trial, her argument was, "I am their mother." Other than that statement she hardly put on a case. Being the mother of the children was apparently deemed enough to outweigh evidence that all the witnesses who knew us both felt I was the better parent; that those witnesses who knew only me said what an excellent parent I was; that our children's behavior always improved dramatically after spending time with me; that my daughter wished to live with me, and that I had a better child-custody evaluation than my wife.

So I say to the trial judges who decide these cases: "Become part of the solution to this dilemma of child custody. Don't remain part of the problem." It is too late for me. If this backward way of thinking is changed, then perhaps it won't be too late for other fathers who should have custody of their children.

Source: *Newsweek*, July 4, 1994.

SUGGESTIONS FOR WRITING (7.7)

1. Write an essay describing the necessary and sufficient causes for a major event in your life. Be sure to indicate to the reader how you determined that these causes were operating. Make the essay as long as necessary to describe fully the causes of this event.

2. Analyze at least three persons or organizations that share major common traits and determine what similar causes, if any, made them the way they are. As examples, you could analyze successful or unsuccessful teams in some sport, or successful or unsuccessful television shows. Report your analysis in an essay of approximately four pages.

3. Analyze two persons or situations that shared significant traits in common but that have ended up differing in some major way. What caused this major difference? For this essay you might analyze why you and a close friend or a sibling chose different colleges or majors or why you performed differently in two similar classes. Report your analysis in an essay of approximately four pages.

4. Examine two trends that you believe might be causally related to see if there is any proportional correlation between them. An example might be the national crime rate and the national unemployment rate, or the national unemployment rate and the inflation rate. If you expect to find a correlation and you do not, speculate on why the correlation is not present. For this essay you might start with a good almanac, since it will contain many trends with statistical data, but you will probably need to consult a more detailed source such as *Statistical Abstracts of the United States*. Report your analysis in an essay of approximately four pages.

5. In the 1990s, it seems that everyone agrees that the traditional nuclear family is faltering and that most people have a theory about the reasons for this decline in the family. Write a four- to five-page argument identifying some (e.g., 2 to 4) of what you consider to be the most influential causes of these domestic transformations of our times. Your claim will identify these causes and the body of the paper will demonstrate their plausibility through a careful presentation and arrangement of the factual evidence in keeping with the principles of causal argument.

8

Arguing Evaluations

EVALUATIVE SUBJECTS AND TERMS

All evaluations include a subject to be judged and an evaluative term that is applied to the subject. In the sentence "John is a good writer," **John** is the subject and **good writer** is the evaluative term; in "Ralph Waldo Emerson was a great thinker," **Ralph Waldo Emerson** is the subject and **great thinker** the evaluative term. Some evaluative statements include only partial evaluative terms, but their context suggests the missing parts. In the claim "capital punishment is immoral," the full evaluative term is **immoral act**; and in the claim "Rembrandt was a master," the evaluative term is **master painter**.

For an evaluative assertion to be meaningful, writer and reader must agree about the definition of the evaluative term. The basis for arguing that John is a good writer is a mutually acceptable definition of the term *good writer*; John's qualifications for the evaluation cannot be measured until the qualities constituting good writing have been established. In the sentence "John is a good writer; he communicates ideas clearly and gracefully," the evaluative term is defined: the qualities or criteria of a good writer are clarity and grace in the communication of ideas.

Often, evaluative statements are expressed negatively—as in "John is a poor writer," or "The documentation for this word processing program is useless." A negative evaluation can either imply its opposite as the standard of measurement, or it can establish a definition of the negative term itself. The writer of the judgment "William Faulkner's *The Fable* is a failed novel" could work from a definition of "successful novel," showing how this novel falls short of that definition, or could establish criteria for the term *failed novel* and apply those to the subject.

Not only must readers recognize the definition of the evaluative term, they must also agree with that definition. If their identification of those qualities constituting "good writing" or "great thinker" does not agree with the writer's, the evaluative argument will be useless. Perhaps readers agree that John's writing is clear and graceful, but they find the definition of the term too limited; in their view, good writing also includes richness of ideas and originality of expression. Thus, while they might concede that John's writing possesses the qualities of clarity and grace, they could still object to the judgment that he is a good writer.

In many evaluations, then, you must first argue the definition of your evaluative term, convincing your readers that the criteria by which you define the term are reasonable and complete. Only after successfully arguing this initial proposition can you proceed to demonstrate that that term applies to your subject.

ACTIVITIES (8.1)

1. What is the evaluative term (implied or stated) in the following assertions?
   a. Mark Twain's *The Adventures of Huckleberry Finn* is an American classic.
   b. When Roger Bannister broke through the four-minute mile barrier in 1954, he accomplished one of the greatest athletic feats of this century.
   c. Calvin Coolidge was a mediocre president.
   d. Calculators are a real boon to mathematics students.
   e. The terrible losses in wars in the twentieth century show the bankruptcy of nations using war as an extension of foreign policy.
2. Write a paragraph giving a brief definition of one of the evaluative terms you identified in Activity 1.

ESTABLISHING THE DEFINITION
OF THE EVALUATIVE TERM

The amount of space and energy you devote to establishing your term's definition will depend on your audience and the nature of the term. About some terms there is so little dispute that an extensive definition would be unnecessary—a trustworthy bank teller, for example, or a reliable car. And when you are very confident about your readers' values, about what is important to them and why, you may not need to propose and argue a definition. If you were a doctor writing to other doctors about the unprofessional behavior of a certain physician, you could safely assume agreement between you and your readers about the definition of unprofessional behavior. However, when your audience consists of people with different expertise or values, when your definition is unusual or controversial, or when the term lends itself to a number of possible definitions, you should state and argue your definition of the evaluative term.

Whether or not you explicitly define the evaluative term, remember that very vague or inflated evaluations are usually harder to argue than those that are limited and precise. It would be far easier to convince an audience that "Ralph Nader has served a valuable function in advocating consumer rights" than that "Ralph Nader is a great American."

Proposing the Definition

In most cases, the actual definition of the term can be stated quite briefly, usually as part of or directly following the claim. "Alison is the ideal management trainee: she is intelligent, ambitious, congenial, and hard-working"; or "In his highly original and influential reflections on the American spirit, reflections that affected common citizens as well as fellow philosophers, Ralph Waldo Emerson proved himself to be a great thinker."

When defining an evaluative term, you are proposing a *stipulative* definition—a definition that restricts the understanding of a term to a particular meaning appropriate to your context. (See Chapter 4 for a full discussion of the topic of definition.) In the argument about John's writing skills, the definition of good writing as the clear and graceful communication of ideas is stipulative—it asks readers to accept this particular and limited definition of the term for the context of this argument. In most cases, your definition will take the shorthand, sentence form identified in Chapter 4, although if the term is very difficult you might want to provide an extended definition.

As in all definitions, the defining, explanatory terms you offer must be clear and precise. Your definition will be useless if it offers only broad or abstract generalizations. If you write "The brilliance of the film *Citizen Kane* lies in its wonderful structure," but you fail to define "wonderful," you will leave readers guessing. You should also avoid definitions that include highly subjective terms. If you define *talented soprano* as one whose voice is beautiful at all points of her vocal range, you have not done much to clarify the evaluative term. What is beautiful to one listener may be mediocre, or heavy, or thin to another; "beauty" is not a measurement that inspires agreement. *Beautiful* requires definition; it can only be useful in this context if it is defined by comparatively objective standards—fullness, or clarity, or fluidity. While these too are subjective terms, they are more precise, and less a matter of personal taste than a term like *beautiful*.

Below are some examples of definitions that truly serve their explanatory, illuminating function.

1. A good argument is one that directly identifies its central proposition, supports that proposition with reasonable, relevant, and concrete evidence, and admits the possibility of alternative points of view.
2. A dedicated mother devotes herself to her children because she knows she should; a good mother devotes herself to her children because she can't imagine doing otherwise.
3. A good education will prepare a student not only for a career but for a fulfilling life outside a career. As important as careers are in our lives, they do not and should not occupy all of our time and energy. The well-educated person is the one who can view life outside work with zest, knowing that there are many other interests aside from a career.

While the qualities included in your proposed definition should be as clear and precise as possible, the very nature of evaluations will not always allow you to avoid subjective terms. In example 3, the term *fulfilling life* is inherently subjective, yet it is not meaningless. There are certain qualities and activities we can identify that can constitute a fulfilling life, including having friends, having hobbies or other recreational interests, and being curious about the past, the future, and the world. It may not be easy to measure precisely each of these qualities or activities, but they do exist, and they can be gauged on some comparative scale.

ACTIVITIES (8.2)

Using the foregoing definitions as a model, give a brief but useful and reasonably thorough definition of two of the following:

1. A good car
2. A good teacher
3. A good politician
4. A good basketball player
5. A good movie

Arguing the Definition

If you have any reason to suspect that your readers will not agree with your definition of the evaluative term, you will have to convince them that your definition is just, that the criteria you assign to a term such as *necessary war, master craftsman,* or *inspired teacher* are reasonable and complete. In some evaluations, the process of establishing the definition of the evaluative term actually becomes the focus of the argument. You can argue the justness of your definition using any of the methods of supporting definitions we have already discussed in Chapter 4, including appeal to assumed values, identification of effect, appeal to authority, and comparison.

To illustrate the application of these methods, we'll work with the following example: as a branch manager for a local bank, you are asked to write a formal evaluation of three new management trainees. Your reader will be the bank's vice president for personnel. There is no fixed evaluation form or criteria to work from; *you* must decide which qualities constitute promising performance in a new trainee. The qualities you settle on (in unranked order) are (1) honesty, (2) the ability to foresee the consequences of decisions, (3) attention to detail, and (4) courtesy with customers. Because you have created this list, you will need to justify it, however briefly, to the vice president. Your justification for each item on the list could use the following methods of argument:

1. *Honesty:* appeal to assumed value. You wouldn't have to say much about this quality. For obvious reasons, bankers place a premium on honesty in their employees.
2. *Ability to foresee the consequences of decisions:* identification of effect. This criterion may not be as obvious as the first, but bankers must base decisions on such things as lending money, setting interest rates, and

making investments on the probable consequences of the decisions. You could point out briefly the positive results of having this ability, and the negative results of lacking it.

3. *Attention to detail:* appeal to assumed value. Like honesty, the importance of this quality doesn't have to be argued to bankers.

4. *Courtesy with customers:* identification of effect. You can easily point out that good customer relations lead to good business. For many bankers, this criterion would be an assumed value.

You could buttress these criteria with other support. To bolster the third criterion, attention to detail, you might cite recognized authorities who stress this quality and the grave risks banks run when they hire employees who lack it. To support the fourth criterion, courtesy with customers, you might use the method of comparison, pointing to the success of a competing bank that stresses good customer relations.

If you can make a reasonable argument for your definition of the evaluative term, your readers are likely to accept the qualities you cite. But they can still object to your definition on the basis of omission: your definition is acceptable as far as it goes, but you have omitted one quality critical to them. Without the inclusion of that quality, they cannot accept your evaluation of the subject. In formulating your definition, try to anticipate the reactions of your readers; if they are likely to be concerned about the omission of a certain quality, you must explain why you chose to omit it. Any of the methods previously identified will help you make this explanation. For example, you could justify your omission of knowledge of computer programming as a criterion for judging trainees by using the identification of effect, pointing out that few bank employees do any programming anyway and that it is cheaper and more efficient to hire outside programming experts when they are needed. In this case, you are pointing out that there are no bad effects caused by these trainees' lack of knowledge of programming.

Ranking the Qualities in Your Definition

In some evaluative arguments, it is not enough to establish a list of qualities constituting your evaluative term; often, you will need to indicate the relative importance of these qualities by ranking them. Ranking is almost always necessary in evaluations of multiple subjects. If you were evaluating four models of home coffee brewers, for example, you might establish the following qualities as essential: reasonable price, good-tasting coffee, a quick-brew cycle, and an automatic timer. A reader could agree with each of these qualities yet disagree with your final choice of brewer. The reason for the disagreement would be that you and your reader rank the four qualities differently. If a quick-brew cycle is most important to you but least important to your reader, he or she will not accept your final evaluation of the three machines.

In some evaluations, particularly those that are likely to directly affect your reader, you may have to justify the relative value you place on each quality. If you were evaluating dormitory life as a valuable freshman experience, you would let your readers (incoming freshmen) know which of the criteria you cite is most important and which is least important. Suppose you rank the qualities as follows: (1) quiet study atmosphere, (2) good social opportunities, (3) proximity to campus, and (4) comfortable surroundings. You could argue the importance of (1), quiet study atmosphere, by a number of familiar methods: appeals to value or authority, comparison, or identification of effect. Regardless of the method you choose, you must be able to demonstrate that without a quiet study atmosphere, one that allows students to work hard and succeed academically, all of the other qualities are meaningless. If a student flunks out of school the first year, the other three qualities will have been useless. Thus, the first quality is the most important because, in your view, it is the *essential* quality.

ACTIVITIES (8.3)

For one of the following subjects, list in order of importance the criteria by which you would judge its quality. Then, for one of the examples, write a two- to three-page essay justifying your choice and ranking of the criteria. Use whatever methods of argument seem appropriate.

1. A college or university
2. A musical concert
3. A newspaper
4. A church or synagogue
5. A college textbook

APPLYING THE DEFINITION TO YOUR SUBJECT

Once you have defined your evaluative term, you must show that the definition applies to your subject. This process constitutes the actual evaluation.

Your evaluation will be largely *factual;* by verifying data and presenting concrete examples, you will demonstrate that your subject possesses the criteria you have cited. Establishing these facts is especially important when the subject is a service—a travel agency, a long-distance phone company—or a functional object, such as a coffee brewer or a pickup truck. In such cases, where the evaluative term is defined by objectively measurable qualities (for example, speed, efficiency, accuracy, price), your job is to verify the existence of those qualities in your subject.

Suppose you were evaluating portable FM radios in terms of affordable price, physical convenience, and power of receiver. In your judgment, a good radio of this type is one that costs no more than $40.00 (your definition of affordable price), can be carried and listened to comfortably when you are walking or jogging, and holds the signals of local radio stations without interference. Using these standards, you evaluate the Euphony "Jogmate" as a **good portable radio**. Your evaluation will be convincing as long as you can establish the following three facts: the suggested retail price of the Jogmate is below $40.00; it is easy to carry; it holds local stations firmly.

These facts can be convincingly established through reference to your own experience, provided you present yourself as reliable and objective. (Other supporting sources—the experience of friends or impartial analyses of the Jogmate found in consumer guides—could be referred to as well.) You could cite the actual price of the Jogmate at three local stores to verify the first fact. The second, which is the most subjective, can be verified by your physical description of the Jogmate—its weight, dimensions, earphone style—and a description of your experience running with it: "The small, cushioned earpieces fit comfortably into my ears; there is no connecting band to slip off the head or tighten uncomfortably; the small radio clips easily onto a waistband or can be held comfortably in one hand." The third fact can also be established by reference to your own experience: "I have run distances of four to five miles with the Jogmate at least 20 times. On those occasions, it has never lost the signal of the three stations I like to listen to." As with all factual arguments, the key to success in arguing evaluations is to cite reliable and authoritative experience and observations, and to include specific, concrete examples of general statements.

Not all evaluations are as neat and objective as the preceding example. Let's look at a very different example involving more subjective measurement and see how the principles of factual argument apply. This evaluation argues that your friend Ellen knows how to be a good friend: she respects her friends, accepting and loving them for who they are, and she expects the same treatment from them. Because the definition included in the claim is not a standard definition of friendship, it requires some preliminary support (see the preceding section on "Arguing the Definition").

Once supported, the definition must be applied to the subject, your friend Ellen. The quality of respecting others—a key criterion of your evaluative term— cannot be measured as objectively or established as definitively as the price of a radio or the fuel efficiency of an automobile. Yet general agreement exists about what constitutes respectful behavior: it is attentive, considerate, accepting behavior. The best way to demonstrate the applicability of the quality to your subject is through specific examples illustrating such behavior. As in any factual argument, you must *describe* the experience faithfully and objectively. Because you want to establish that Ellen's respectful treatment of friends is habitual, not occasional, you should cite a number of examples.

Beyond citing the examples, you might also need to point out what is respectful in the examples cited, particularly if your readers might interpret the behavior differently. But in general, the more concrete and immediate your presentation of examples, the less explicit commentary you will need.

Applying the Syllogistic Model to Evaluations

You can test the reasonableness and completeness of your evaluative claim and your definition of the evaluative term by applying the syllogistic model introduced in Chapter 5, with the definition of the evaluative term constituting the major premise, the application of the term to the subject constituting the minor premise, and the claim itself constituting the conclusion. The previous example concerning Ellen's friendship would compose the following syllogism:

Major premise: A good friend respects her friends, accepts them and loves them for who they are, and expects the same treatment from them.
Minor premise: Ellen respects me, accepts me and loves me for who I am, and expects the same from me.
Conclusion: Ellen is a good friend.

The major premise establishes characteristics that constitute friendship; the minor premise applies those same characteristics to Ellen; and the conclusion makes a very specific claim derived from the relationship between the two premises. This syllogism tells us that the claim is valid, but we can accept it as true as well only if the two premises are also true. If the major premise (the definition of friendship) does not appear immediately acceptable, it will have to be argued in the ways we have suggested. Similarly, the truth (or probability) of the minor premise may have to be established through a factual argument that provides examples of Ellen's behavior toward you. While you may not be able to *prove* the absolute truth of both premises, you can strengthen them by providing appropriate support, thus moving the entire argument much closer to a position of soundness.

ACTIVITIES (8.4)

Working from the definitions you created for Activity (8.2), compose a specific claim from each. Then turn the definition and the claim into a syllogism. To what extent would the major and minor premises of each syllogism need further support?

FURTHER METHODS OF SUPPORTING EVALUATIONS

Definition and factual argument are central to evaluations, but there are other ways to support these arguments. The tactics that follow can be used along with definition and factual arguments or by themselves.

Identification of Effect

Just as you can defend your choice of a defining quality by identifying or predicting the effect of that quality, you can also support your overall judgment of the subject through pointing to its positive or negative effects. When adopting this supporting tactic, you must be sure that your identification of effect accords with the principles of causality. If the causal link you identify seems improbable, the strategy will fail.

An action, policy, or object is generally considered valuable if its effects are valuable. Freedom of speech is good because it encourages the widest exchange of ideas, which is more likely to lead to the truth or to solutions to problems. Child abuse is bad because it causes physical and mental anguish in children. Judging a subject in terms of its effects is, of course, only useful when your audience agrees with your assessment of the effect. In using this supporting method, you must be prepared to argue your evaluation of the effect if you suspect disagreement from your audience.

Appeal to Authority

Any evaluation can be supported by appealing to the similar judgment of a recognized authority. If Martina Navratilova has publicly expressed her admiration for the tennis game of Margaret Court, this statement would be effective support for your argument that Margaret Court ranks among the finest women tennis players of the last thirty years. When using this method of support for an evaluation, you must be certain that the person whose judgment you cite truly qualifies as an authority on the subject.

Comparison

You can often support your evaluation by comparing your subject with one that would be accorded a similar judgment by your audience. For example, many feminist arguments criticizing sexual discrimination have been supported by reference to racial discrimination. The two forms of discrimination are similar in many ways: both base inequitable treatment on irrelevant and immutable characteristics—on race and gender. An audience that would object to racial discrimination would, when the similarities were pointed out, be likely to object to sexual discrimination as well. As with any comparative argument, the similarities between the two subjects must be essential, not peripheral.

ACTIVITIES (8.5)

For two of the following evaluations, write a paragraph on each describing the most appropriate kind of support: factual argument, identification of effect, appeal to authority, or comparison. Why is this support the most appropriate? You may cite more than one kind of support.

1. Shakespeare is one of the world's greatest writers.
2. Mercedes-Benz makes many of the world's best cars.
3. Failure to build a water treatment plant for the city would be a serious mistake.
4. Strato Airlines has the best customer service record of any airline in America.
5. Military involvements by major powers in small countries are usually unwise in terms of lives lost, money wasted, and the increased suspicion of other small countries.

THE VARIETIES OF EVALUATIONS

By now you realize that different kinds of evaluations demand different kinds of support. Although there are no hard and fast rules in this area, if you can identify the **kind** of evaluation you are making, you should have a better sense of what you need to do to support it. Evaluations usually fall into one of three main categories: ethical, aesthetic, or functional.

Ethical Evaluations

The word *ethical* is one of those terms that we all understand in a vague way yet might be hard pressed to define precisely. To avoid confusion, we offer the following definition: *ethical* describes behavior that conforms to an ideal code of moral principles—principles of right and wrong, good and evil. That code may be derived from any number of cultures—religious, professional, national, or political.

All of us operate within many cultures—we are members of families, communities, organizations, religions, professions, and nations. Each one of these cultures has its own set of ethical standards. For example, among the many ethical principles of Judaism and Christianity are the Ten Commandments. As United States citizens, we are subject to other standards of conduct, such as those recorded in the Constitution—including the Bill of Rights—and the Declaration of Independence. Your college also operates by certain standards that it expects its members to follow: respect for school property, respect for faculty, and academic honesty. In most cultures, these standards are formally recorded, but in some instances they remain implicit.

Beyond those ethical codes dictating right or good conduct within a particular culture there exists a range of powerful standards or values not so obviously tied to any specific culture, but pervasive in most of them, including ideals such as fair play, kindness, and respect for others.

Because each of us is tied to a number of different cultures, clashes between standards are inevitable. Some pacifist groups, for example, see a clash between the religious commandment "Thou shall not kill" and the government's standard that citizens must be prepared to defend their country in time of war. Sometimes conflicts occur between standards of the same culture. Such clashes are commonplace in law. What happens, for example, when the right of free speech collides with the right of a person to be free from libel? Free speech cannot mean that someone has a right to say anything about another person, regardless of how untrue or harmful it is. On the other hand, protection from libel cannot mean protection from the truth being told about mistakes or misdeeds, particularly when they have some impact on the public. Throughout our history the courts have struggled to find a balance between these two competing claims, sometimes slightly favoring one value, sometimes the other, but denying that either value can have absolute sway over the other.

Defining the Evaluative Term in Ethical Arguments.   Whenever we evaluate a subject in terms of right or wrong conduct or behavior, we are appealing to certain ethical values or standards held by our audience. When we assert "Hitler was an evil man," or "Ms. Mead is an honorable lawyer," or "The coach used unfair tactics," we are assuming that our readers both *understand* what we mean by the evaluative term and *agree* with that meaning. In ethical and moral evaluations, it is usually pointless to argue a particular definition, because ethical standards are powerful, long-standing, and usually unquestioningly held. In other words, it is extremely difficult to change someone's understanding of what constitutes right and wrong, good and evil.

The exception to this generalization is when your readers are not members of the culture to whose standards you are appealing and when they are not likely to hold a conflicting standard. If you were arguing against the practice of public advertising by lawyers and doctors on the grounds that it is unprofessional behavior, and your audience consisted of people from neither profession, you would probably need to define the term *unprofessional behavior*. Because your audience is not likely to be committed to a particular understanding of the term, you might be able to convince them to accept a definition not widely held in the professional communities about which you are writing.

The Argument in Ethical Evaluations.   Most ethical arguments concentrate on demonstrating what is unethical or immoral about the subject being evaluated. At the center of these evaluations, then, is a factual argument. In arguing that Hitler was evil, your focus would be on documenting the behavior you identify as evil, and on demonstrating that your evaluative term fits the examples you are citing.

You can also strengthen your evaluation through other supporting methods, including comparison (Hitler was as bad as or worse than certain other dictators) or identification of effect (aside from all of the bad he did in his life, the war Hitler started led to the division of Europe into two opposing camps, or to a pervasive sense of victimization among Jews of later generations).

ACTIVITIES (8.6)

Write an essay of approximately two pages supporting one of the following ethical evaluations. If you disagree with the evaluation, you could write an essay supporting the opposite statement (perhaps you believe, for example, that playing a radio at full volume in a public place does not constitute an act of aggression).

1. Recruitment violations in collegiate athletics are contrary to the ideals of higher education.
2. Playing a radio at full volume in a public place constitutes an act of aggression.
3. Volunteer workers are the unsung heroes of American life.
4. Regardless of the product they are selling, merchants have a right to charge as high a price as they can get for their product.
5. John Glenn, the astronaut turned senator, is a perfect example of the American dream.

Aesthetic Evaluations

Writing a convincing evaluation of a work of art—a poem, an opera, a painting—
is not as futile a task as many believe, provided you understand the goals of such
an argument. Just as personal tastes in clothes or food are usually immune to reasonable argument, aesthetic preferences—liking Chopin's music and despising
Mahler's—are often too much matters of personal taste to be arguable. There is
much truth in the Latin saying *de gustibus non est disputandum:* there is no arguing about taste. Nevertheless, while changing aesthetic tastes or opinions is difficult, it is possible and often useful to convince an audience to *appreciate* the
strengths or weaknesses of a work of art by giving them a greater understanding of
it. A successful aesthetic evaluation may not convince a reader to like Rubens or to
dislike Lichtenstein, but it will at least give a reader reasons for approving of or ob-
jecting to a work.

All artistic fields have their own sets of standards for excellence, standards
about which there is surprising conformity among experts in the field. Most literary critics, for example, would agree about standards for a successful short story:
coherence of the story, careful selection of detail, avoidance of digression, an interesting style. When critics disagree, and of course they do so regularly, they usually disagree not about identified standards of excellence but about the application
of those standards. Such disagreements are often matters of personal preference
for one kind of artist over another. Even professional critics are not immune to the
influence of their personal tastes.

When you argue an aesthetic evaluation, you should work from standards currently accepted within the field, though you may not have to do more than briefly
or implicitly refer to them. Your evaluation is likely to fail if you ignore these standards, or if you try to effect an overnight revolution in them. As with ethical standards, aesthetic standards usually change gradually, though there can be periods of
revolutionary change, as occurred in artistic tastes in the early twentieth century.

Usually, then, your chief task is to demonstrate that these standards apply (or
don't apply) to your subject. This demonstration consists of careful description
and concrete examples. In the following review of the performance of Jane Torvill
and Christopher Dean, the British ice dancing couple, Anna Kisselgoff supports
her judgment that the team has achieved "technical perfection" and the status of
"the great romantic team of the 1980s" with effective description and examples:

> The music [from the dance "Paso Doble"] is taken from Rimsky-Kor-
> sakov's "Capriccio Espagnol," and as both skaters stand at the center of
> the rink, the surprise to come is kept literally under wraps. Miss Torvill
> clings to Mr. Dean's back, a hand draped over his right shoulder from be-
> hind. Dressed in a bullfighter's costume, he reaches across his chest as if
> holding a cape. Then, in a second, this is what Miss Torvill "becomes." Her
> black, winglike sleeves held out, she spins off—flung away by her partner.
>
> As both skaters move continuously in serpentine paths around each
> other, Mr. Dean whirls, twirls and twists the shape that is his partner. The

most spectacular moments are those when the matador drags his cape behind him—that is, Mr. Dean pushes forward emphatically to an insistent rhythm, as Miss Torvill is pulled along, gliding on one knee. . . .

The final moment, no matter how frequently seen, preserves its power to surprise. Mr. Dean, eyes flashing, suddenly throws his "cape" to the ice. Miss Torvill falls prone, revolves on her stomach and comes to rest. Like the grandest of all toreadors, her partner salutes the crowd, one arm raised in triumph.

Kisselgoff's graphic description and detailed language demonstrate how Torvill and Dean achieve the standards of "technical perfection" and being a "great romantic team"—two standards Kisselgoff explicitly mentions elsewhere in her article. The description also points to other implicit standards as well, including originality of artistic conception and close artistic cooperation between the two partners.

If you wish to convince an audience of the excellence of a work of art, you would be wise to consider carefully how much that audience knows about the work in particular or the field in general. If you suspect inexperience or ignorance on the part of the audience, you should offer a lucid and deferential *explanation* of the standards you are applying and of the work in question. The principle behind this suggestion is that people often fail to appreciate what they don't understand; if your evaluation can teach them about excellence in the field, it may have a better chance at convincing them that your subject represents that excellence.

Another useful tactic when arguing a positive evaluation to an inexperienced audience is to relate your subject to one with which they are more familiar. If, for example, you wanted to convince an audience familiar with and appreciative of modern abstract art that the art of ancient Egypt is also interesting, you might point out the similarities between the two: "Although they are widely separated in time, modern abstract art and ancient Egyptian art both concentrate on the essence of a person or object, not the surface appearance." In taking this approach, you are borrowing from your readers' appreciation of modern abstract art, shining its positive light onto the subject of your evaluation.

ACTIVITIES (8.7)

For each of the following forms of art or entertainment, list at least three standards by which you would judge the quality of a specific work of this type. Then, for one of the categories, write a two- to three-page essay demonstrating how a specific work of that type does or does not fit your standards of excellence. (You should make these standards explicit in your essay.)

1. A film
2. A detective novel
3. An album (or tape, or compact disc) of popular music

4. A photograph
5. A painting

Functional Evaluations

Functional evaluations stand a better chance of changing readers' minds than do ethical and aesthetic evaluations. It is easier to convince a reader that her views about turbo engine cars are inaccurate than that her views about abortion are wrong. While people do form sentimental attachments to objects and machines, they can usually be convinced that however powerful that attachment, it has nothing to do with the subject's actual performance; an audience's preconceptions about performance quality are less matters of cultural values and personal tastes than of practical experience, assumptions, or hearsay.

Functional evaluations always work from a definition of ideal standards: you cannot demonstrate that Sony makes a superior compact disc player in the absence of standards against which to measure the Sony player's performance. You must use your judgment to determine which arguments require an explicit presentation of standards and which can assume audience recognition of the standards. Certainly, if your list of standards is for some reason unusual or innovative, you will need to state it directly in the argument and to argue its relevance and completeness (using any of the methods discussed earlier in this chapter).

When writing a functional evaluation, you must consider ranking the standards from which you work. Functional evaluations typically work from a number of different standards that are rarely viewed as equally important. A reference book's function could be evaluated in terms of its thoroughness, its physical format, and its accuracy, but the three are not equally important. In order to justify your final judgment, you must first explain and support the relative weights you have assigned to each standard.

Most successful functional evaluations focus on factual arguments. In the factual argument, you will demonstrate to what degree the standards of performance apply to your subject. As in all factual arguments, the facts and examples you provide must be well documented. Personal experience—your test drive of a new car, for example—can be useful and convincing, but in most cases, that experience needs support from authoritative, unbiased sources (for example, an article on the car in a reputable magazine like *Road and Track* or *Consumer Reports*).

Any of the other supporting methods discussed earlier in this chapter (identification of effect, appeal to authority, comparison) can also be used in a performance evaluation. Of these, the most valuable is identification of effect. The crucial question in evaluating performance is almost always whether the person or object achieves its intended effect: Did the governor's administration achieve most of its goals? Did the camera produce good pictures? The argument will be largely factual if the effect has already occurred, and your primary job will be to document and evaluate the effect. In arguing that "Betsy Turner is a good violin teacher," you would cite the number of fine players she has produced (the effect of her performance as teacher) and briefly support your positive judgment of those players. In other cases, where the effect has not yet occurred, your argument is necessarily more speculative: "Based on the evidence we have, this car is likely to give you years of reliable service."

ACTIVITIES (8.8)

List in ranked order at least three standards by which you would judge the performance of the following. Then for one of the categories, write a two- to three-page essay demonstrating how well one person or object in that category meets your standards of performance.

1. An automobile for a family with three small children
2. A president of a college or university
3. A personal computer
4. A United States senator
5. A college reference librarian

Interpretations

The subject of an interpretive argument is the visible surface we wish to understand or explore further; it is the behavior, or event, or data that openly exist for all to observe. The interpretive term is the summarized explanation of the reality beneath the visible surface. In the interpretation "The iconoclastic world view of the brilliant physicist Edward Fredkin derives from his lifelong antiauthoritarian bias," the subject is Fredkin's "iconoclastic world view," and the interpretive term is "lifelong antiauthoritarian bias."

To write a solid interpretation, you must satisfy the following requirements: (1) the interpretive term must be clearly defined; (2) the interpretive term and the subject must be linked—not merely parallel or congruent, but attached according to some recognized principle; and (3) evidence must be supplied to support the interpretation.

Defining the Interpretive Term. Like evaluative arguments, interpretations work from assumptions about definition—about what elements constitute a certain condition or reality. In interpretations, we are stating that X (the subject) is Y (the interpretation). To prove or support this assertion, we must define Y in such a way that it restates X, or restate X in such a way that it coincides with Y. In the interpretive claim "Television news broadcasting is no longer news, it is entertainment," we must demonstrate the coincidence of our definition of entertainment on the one hand with what we see of television news on the other.

In the following passage, we see a similar assertion of coincidence, where Sigmund Freud equates literature (the subject) with the play of children:

Now the writer does the same as the child at play; he creates a world of phantasy which he takes very seriously; that is, he invests it with a great deal of affect, while separating it sharply from reality. Language has preserved this relationship between children's play and poetic creation. It designates certain kinds of imaginative creation, concerned with tangible objects and capable of representation, as "plays"; the people who present them are called "players."

The first step in assembling an interpretive argument is to consider whether to define and argue the interpretive term. As with evaluative arguments, you should define the term if you are using it in an unusual or controversial way, and you should justify that definition if you think your audience is likely to object to it. In the first example, the term *entertainment* probably should be defined, as it is a very broad and even subjective term. You might define the term as "any brief, self-contained, sensually pleasing performance that amuses but does not challenge." If your audience is likely to disagree with this definition, you will have to support it with the methods discussed in the preceding section, "Arguing the Definition," in this chapter.

Of course, you can work from an unstated definition, provided your argument clearly reveals the elements of that definition. The following example illustrates this tactic:

> Much of television news broadcasting is no longer news; it is entertainment. Most local and national news broadcasts, news shows like *60 Minutes, 20/20,* even public television news are putting out slick, superficial performances that are usually neither challenging nor controversial, but capture huge audience shares.

Here the definition of entertainment is contained in the characterization of television news.

Extensive interpretations of a series of events or continuing behavior work somewhat differently, though the basic principles are the same. In these cases—for example, an interpretation of a character's actions in a novel or of quarterly stock market activity—the subjects are usually explained in terms of a coherent and preestablished theory, system of thought, or belief. Instead of demonstrating the coincidence or equivalence of the subject and a single concept (like children's play or entertainment), these more ambitious interpretations reveal the existence of a series of related concepts—an entire system—behind the visible activity of the subject. The system identified could be Christianity, Marxism, Jungian psychology, feminism, Freudian drive theory, capitalism, semiotics—virtually any set of facts or principles logically connected to form a coherent view of the world.

Examples of this kind of systematic interpretation are especially prevalent in artistic and literary interpretations, though they are not limited to these contexts. A feminist interpretation of a literary figure like Emily Dickinson would work from a thorough understanding of feminist theory. The interpretation might explain

Dickinson's poems in terms of the tension between her vocation as a poet and the very different expectations that nineteenth-century society had for women.

However compelling such an interpretation, readers are not likely to be swayed if they strongly object to the interpretive system—to the Freudian, or Marxist, or feminist model of human behavior. Even if the construct used to explain the subject is not formally named, the principles contained in that construct must seem at least plausible to your readers. If you interpret modern American history on the basis of tensions and conflicts between different social and economic classes, your readers may not give your interpretation fair consideration if they are opposed to this set of principles. On the other hand, a good interpretation can often help readers gain sympathy for a philosophy or point of view they were previously hostile to or ignorant of. When you write interpretations, you should be sensitive to your audience's beliefs and be prepared at least to acknowledge their probable objections as you proceed. If you do so, you may convince some hostile readers, bringing them to accept not only your interpretation but also at least some aspects of your underlying point of view.

Establishing Coincidence.   All interpretations must demonstrate coincidence between the subject and the interpretive term. Coincidence in this context can mean equivalence (as in "Television news is the same as entertainment"), substitution ("Although marriage looks like a romantic partnership, it is often a formalization of female dependence"), or revelation ("Behind his warmth and friendliness is a cold and impenetrable shield of defenses"). The challenge of interpretations is in demonstrating these coincidences.

When the interpretive term is concrete, this task is comparatively easy. We can recognize such concepts as entertainment or economic dependence; they are verifiable. Once we agree on the meaning of the term, a simple factual argument will demonstrate the applicability of the term to the subject. If we know what economic dependence is, we can detect it in a relationship with little difficulty or little guesswork, provided we have the necessary facts.

But what about detecting "a cold and impenetrable shield of defenses," or "an unresolved Oedipal conflict"? These descriptions are legitimate and typical interpretive terms, yet no one ever saw a defense mechanism or an Oedipal conflict. How do we argue the operation of an essentially unverifiable concept? The answer is that we proceed in much the same way as with causal arguments. Just as a cause and its effect must be linked by some acceptable motivational principle that accords with human experience and observation, so must the interpretation (the less visible reality) relate to the subject (the visible reality) according to an acknowledged principle of experience.

If we argue that an apparently ambitious student's hesitancy to apply for a glamorous, high-pressure job reflects her ambivalence about success, we are assuming that our readers would accept the principle of ambivalence and recognize its symptoms—in this case, behavior guaranteed to threaten one's stated goals. This interpretation will be meaningless to a reader who knows nothing about these ideas. Because few interpretive arguments can afford the space necessary to educate a reader about its assumptions, you must carefully consider what principles of experience your audience is likely to acknowledge.

Documenting the Interpretation. Interpretations need documentation or evidence. As well as explaining your subject through an acceptable principle of experience, you will need to document your interpretation through examples taken from your subject. Even when your subject and interpretation are very narrow, you must offer such evidence. In the earlier example of the student's hesitancy to apply for a job, you could support your theory of ambivalence by describing the student's professed ambitions, the nature of the job, and her chances of getting it if she applies, as well as her refusal to apply. Different arguments will provide different kinds of evidence, so it is difficult to generalize about the best kind of evidence. But your interpretation must point to a number of concrete examples drawn from the condition or behavior of your subject.

The Possibility of Multiple Interpretations. Most subjects lend themselves to a number of different interpretations, and these interpretations are not necessarily mutually exclusive. This becomes obvious when we think of the many theories that could be offered to explain why you skipped breakfast this morning: maybe you simply had no time to eat; maybe you weren't hungry; maybe you were punishing yourself by depriving yourself of food; maybe you resent paying outrageous prices to food service. We would need more evidence to know which, if any, of these theories applies to your situation, but it is perfectly conceivable that a number of them could apply.

Because of the likelihood of multiple interpretations, you should try to resist a strongly dogmatic and inflexible tone in interpretive arguments. You do not need to acknowledge constantly the possibility of other explanations, nor should you sound tentative about yours, but don't present your argument as if it were immutable, inarguable dogma.

ACTIVITIES (8.9)

1. Write a brief interpretation (approximately 250 words) of a recent event or activity. Your interpretation should include the interpretive term, the kind of coincidence, and the supporting evidence. Then write a different interpretation of this same event or activity, again including all the necessary elements of an interpretation. When you have completed these two essays, write an essay of approximately 250 words explaining which interpretation you find more plausible and why. Some possible events or activities: a recent election, a political scandal, a friend's recent success or failure in some endeavor, or an athletic contest.

2. Find in newspapers or magazines two different interpretations of a film that you have seen recently. Write a two- to three-page essay describing the different views, stating which interpretation you find more plausible and your reasons for that view. You may have reservations even about the interpreta-

tion you favor. Be sure to state those as well. (Give your instructor a copy of the two reviews.)

S U M M A R Y

Arguing Evaluations

- All evaluations include a subject to be judged and an evaluative term applied to the subject.

- Before you argue the evaluation, you must ensure that your readers recognize and accept your definition of the evaluative term. When automatic acceptance seems doubtful, you must argue your definition. Definitions can be argued by appeals to assumed reader values, appeals to authority, identification of effect, and comparison. In evaluations of multiple subjects, you may have to rank the qualities defining your evaluative term and justify that ranking.

- Evaluating your subject consists of demonstrating, through a largely factual argument, the applicability of the evaluative term to your subject. Evaluations can also be supported through appeals to authority, identification of effect, and comparison.

- Evaluations are made in ethical, aesthetic, functional, and interpretive terms. In *ethical evaluations,* the focus is on applying the ethical standard (evaluative term) to the subject, not on defining that standard. *Aesthetic evaluations* typically work from standards currently accepted within the field, demonstrating the applicability of these standards to your subject. *Functional evaluations* typically work from a number of ranked standards in terms of which the subject is measured. *Interpretations* establish a coincidence between the subject and the interpretive term by linking them through an acknowledged principle of experience.

- Applying the syllogistic model to your evaluative claim can help you test its reasonableness.

SAMPLE ETHICAL EVALUATION

The following essay on euthanasia, based on an essay written by college student Robert Conway, is an example of an argument of ethical evaluation. The argument contains a stipulative definition of the subject (euthanasia) and an evaluative term (*moral rightness*). It appeals to authority in its references to traditional religions and ethical systems, and it employs identification of effect in discussing what could happen if euthanasia were not allowed. It also refutes one counterargument. This evaluation is somewhat unusual in that its claim ("I wish to argue the moral rightness of euthanasia") comes in the middle of the essay. As we noted in Chapter 3, claims can be found in the beginning, middle, or end of arguments, or they can be merely implied. The placement of the claim in the middle of the essay is effective here because the definition of one of the terms of the claim (euthanasia) is one key support for the argument; the claim is immediately more acceptable to potentially hostile readers if they accept the stipulative definition that has preceded it.

THE MORAL JUSTIFICATION FOR EUTHANASIA

Euthanasia is usually defined as the act of allowing death to occur in someone who is terminally ill but whose life may be prolonged through continued medical treatment. Despite the frequent equation of the terms, euthanasia should not be confused with mercy killing. Mercy killing involves an action which <u>causes</u> death. It is the direct and intentional taking of a human life, and that is murder. Tacking the word "mercy" onto "killing" is really an inexcusable attempt to justify murder by stressing the motive rather than the act itself.

We should restrict the use of the term "euthanasia" to simply <u>allowing</u> death to occur through the withholding of life support systems. Free of life maintained by drugs and machines, the body simply dies in a natural, inevitable way. For those unfortunate people who suffer from terminal diseases or horrific accidents, and the loved ones of those people, this natural death comes as a great relief and a welcome end.

Often writers on this subject divide euthanasia into two categories: positive or active and negative or passive, with active meaning mercy killing and passive meaning euthanasia as I have defined it (Ladd 164). But the meaning of the term should not be stretched so far, because the positive and negative versions are so different that it is necessary to have a clear and

unmistakable line drawn between them. Using the same term
for both acts makes it far too easy to confuse them.

That said, I wish to argue the moral rightness of
euthanasia. To my knowledge, none of the world's great
religions or ethical systems would dispute the appropriateness of euthanasia for terminally ill patients.
According to my limited study, these creeds and systems
accept the inevitability of death, with caution to
humanity about the folly of trying to prolong life beyond
its natural limits. The Book of Ecclesiastes in the Bible
tells us:

> To every thing there is a season, and a time to
> every purpose under heaven:
> A time to be born, and a time to die; a time to
> plant, and a time to pluck up that which is
> planted (3.1,2).

And classical Greek mythology warns us of the folly
of desiring immortality without also securing perpetual
youth in the story of Tithonus, who aged into a mere shell
of a human being, in one version of the myth finally being
turned into a grasshopper (Hamilton, 289-290). Those who
make immortality possible are also punished in Greek
mythology, as we see in the story of Aesculapius, the
healer whom Zeus punishes by death for bringing a dead man
to life (Hamilton, 280-281).

Closer to our own time, in a work of the eighteenth
century, the Struldbruggs in Swift's Gulliver's Travels
are still another caution against the folly of trying to
surpass human limits. The Struldbruggs are immortal but
continue to grow older and older, leading miserable lives,
a burden to themselves and to their society (Swift,
167-173; pt.3, ch.10).

We must also consider the incredible psychological
and financial stress on families of patients whose lives
are prolonged even though there is no hope of restoration
to a reasonable life. Often these families must devote

much or even all of their financial resources to this effort, while also undergoing the stress of watching the prolonged suffering of a loved one--with no real hope that this suffering might lead to a cure of the illness. Perhaps even worse than the strain on the families is the strain on the patients themselves, who, if aware of what is going on around them, are often experiencing great pain and are terribly frustrated by their own incapacity. For these patients, the natural outcome of their illness is far more humane than an artificial extension of a life that can no longer be satisfying.

Some opponents of euthanasia will counter that no illness is truly hopeless, since some day science may find a cure for all terminal illnesses, for death itself. Wouldn't it make sense to keep patients alive until that day? Perhaps it would, if society could bear the tremendous cost, and if we had the slightest shred of evidence that such a day were even possible. So far we do not: what science shows us is that individual organisms are mortal and that immortality, if it exists at all, belongs to the species. Those who look to scientific research as an argument against euthanasia seem to have a quarrel not so much with euthanasia as with death itself.

Of course, anyone who studies this issue soon discovers numerous questions with no simple answers, including, as the theologian Roger Shinn notes, questions about infants born with serious disabilities and about the definition of a meaningful life (23-30). Even the distinction between killing and allowing life to end must be examined in the context of specific decisions, as the philosopher John Ladd points out (164-186). Nevertheless, though we must be cautious, we can reach some conclusions. Euthanasia, as I have defined it and as I hope others will define it in the future, is consonant with traditional morality and with the acceptance of human mortality that traditional morality requires. Furthermore, it is the most

humane and realistic approach to the suffering of
terminally ill patients.

WORKS CITED

Hamilton, Edith. Mythology. New York: New American
     Library, 1969.

The Holy Bible. Authorized King James Version. New York:
     Harper and Brothers n.d.

Ladd, John. "Positive and Negative Euthanasia." Ethical
     Issues Relating to Life and Death. Ed. John Ladd. New
     York: Oxford University Press, 1979, pp. 164-186.

Shinn, Roger L. "Ethical Issues." New Options, New
     Dilemmas: An Interprofessional Approach to Life or
     Death Decisions. Ed. Anne S. Allen. Lexington, Mass.:
     Lexington-Heath, 1986, pp. 23-30.

Swift, Jonathan. Guilliver's Travels. Ed. Louis A. Landa.
     Cambridge, Mass.: The Riverside Press-Houghton
     Mifflin, 1960.

SAMPLE INTERPRETATION

In her essay "*Fifth Business:* Childhood Fathers the Man," student Deborah
O'Reilly interprets the behavior of three characters in the novel *Fifth Business,* by
Canadian writer Robertson Davies. The subject of her interpretation is the adult
lives of these three men, and the interpretive term—the summary of the operating
reality beneath the visible surface—is the influence of childhood experience on
these lives. Deborah argues that although each character is renamed as a young
adult, a significant coincidence exists between these reborn, adult identities and
the childhood identities. The principle linking the subject with the interpretive
term is a familiar tenet of psychological development: the powerful influence of
childhood experience on adult behavior. In the section of the essay excerpted here,
ample evidence supports the interpretation of the book's narrator and protagonist,
Dunstan Ramsay; Deborah cites Dunstan's loathing of his mother, his choice of career, his fascination with magic. As in all good literary interpretations, textual passages are used to document the writer's reading of the work.

FIFTH BUSINESS: CHILDHOOD FATHERS THE MAN

WHAT'S IN A NAME? In the novel Fifth Business, by
Robertson Davies, the three central characters seem to

believe that taking on a new name will dissociate them
from their origins and mark the beginning of new lives.
Dunstable Ramsay sheds the family name of the mother he
loathes and becomes "Dunstan." Percy Boyd Staunton opts
for the fashionable name "Boy" as a more appropriate
reflection of his new image. And finally, the frail,
victimized little boy Paul Dempster becomes the grand
"Magnus Eisengrim." While adopting a new name may provide
a sense of rebirth, of new identity, neither Dunny, Boy,
nor Magnus can escape the powerful influence of their
early lives.

   Let us look first at Dunstable "Dunstan" Ramsay.
Dunny's new name did not originate with him; it was a
parting gift from Diane on the night they agreed not to
marry. "'Let me do one thing more for you,' she said. 'Let
me rename you. . . . St. Dunstan was a marvelous person and
very much like you--mad about learning, terribly stiff and
stern and scowly, and an absolute wizard at withstanding
temptation"' (92-93). Dunstan "liked the idea of a new
name; it suggested new freedom and a new personality"
(93). Since Dunstable was his mother's maiden name, it is
easy to understand how Dunny could so readily give it up.
His loathing for his mother is most evident when he
recalls his reaction to the news of his parents' death:
"But as I lay in that hospital I was glad that I did not
have to be my mother's own dear laddie any longer. . . . I
knew she had eaten my father, and I was glad I did not have
to fight any longer to keep her from eating me" (81).

   But Dunstan's beginnings in Deptford had an impact on
his life that a mere name change could not erase. The most
obvious link to the past is his continuing obsession with
Mary Dempster. Since the day she was hit by a snow-covered
rock intended for the young Dunstable, he has been unable
to relinquish responsibility for her. Indeed, at the time
of her death, decades later, he is in effect her guardian
--the only person accepting responsibility for her.

In addition, Dunstan's choice of a teaching career had its beginnings in the Deptford library, where he used four-year-old Paul Dempster as audience for his inept magic tricks. According to Dunstan, "my abilities as a teacher had their first airing in that little library, and as I was fond of lecturing I taught Paul more than I suspected" (p. 37). Dunstan also remains fascinated with magic long after his performances for Paul, although he never mastered the techniques. In fact, it is that fascination that leads him into his important friendships with Magnus and Liesl.

Much as Dunstan wishes to turn his back on the troubles and perversities of his childhood in the little town of Deptford, he realizes late in life that total dissociation from that childhood is impossible: "I boarded the train . . . and left Deptford in the flesh. It was not for a long time that I recognized that I never wholly left it in the spirit" (p. 107). The man that Dunstable Ramsay became was irrevocably indebted to the boy that Dunstan Ramsay once was.

WORKS CITED

Davies, Robertson. Fifth Business. New York. Penguin Books, 1970.

SUGGESTIONS FOR WRITING (8.10)

1. Write a two- to three-page evaluation of a course you have taken or are taking in college. Your evaluation will be primarily a functional evaluation, with one of the crucial questions being whether the course actually achieves its intended goals. The evaluation can also include an ethical component: was the course good for your soul whether or not it achieved its intended effects?

2. Write a three- to four-page argument for or against euthanasia based on your reading of the sample student paper at the end of the section on evaluation. Do you agree with the definition of euthanasia given there? What about the other supporting arguments? Are there other arguments for euthanasia, or do you have what you believe are more powerful arguments against it?

3. Write a combination interpretation and evaluation (three to four pages) of a recent artistic or entertainment event you enjoyed: a film, play, novel, concert, or something similar. Your evaluation will be primarily aesthetic, but it may be ethical as well.

4. Write an essay of approximately five to six pages on the issue of whether capital punishment is morally justified. You may consider issues other than ethical ones, but your emphasis should be on the ethical aspects of this question. Be sure to cite and refute viewpoints opposed to your own.

9

Arguing Recommendations

Making *recommendations* (sometimes called *proposals*) is a common assignment for writers in business, education, and government, where major innovations are almost always initiated by a formal written proposal. Many organizations even devise a particular format to which formal recommendations must conform. While these formats can vary considerably in visual details of presentation, the material included is usually consistent. This chapter is concerned not with the varieties of physical format but with the substance of practical recommendations—the material that must be included and the arguments that must be made.

Recommendations are a hybrid form of argument; they draw on methods and principles frequently used in the other three categories of argument. For the most part, skill in arguing recommendations consists of understanding the particular application of certain familiar methods of support.

In any recommendation, you must establish a current situation and a probable future situation—you must argue facts and effects. How central either type of argument is to your recommendation depends on the emphasis demanded by the particular situation. If your recommendation emphasizes the present—that is, a *current* problem—much of your argument will be factual. If it emphasizes the future—the probable results of the changes you recommend—your argument will be causal, establishing the probable effects of the implemented recommendation. Regardless of their emphases, all recommendations make evaluative arguments; they include a judgment of the current situation (it is inefficient, unfair, incomplete, and so on) and/or a judgment of the proposed recommendation (it will be more efficient, more equitable, more thorough).

AUDIENCE NEEDS AND VALUES

Successful recommendations always work from an understanding of the needs and/or values of their audiences. Such an understanding should inform all kinds of arguments, but it is particularly important in recommendations, because you are asking your audience to *do* something, and people are more likely to take action if there is a possibility that their needs or desires will be satisfied as a consequence. Thus, when preparing recommendations, you should pay particular attention to the early stage of audience identification: Who is your audience? What are their needs and values likely to be regarding your claim? Can you responsibly appeal to these in your argument?

For example, if you were a personnel director of a large corporation recommending the institution of paternity leave, you would need to consider *what* sorts of appeals would move upper management, who will make the decision to accept the recommendation. Citing the psychological benefits for the children of employees would not be likely to influence vice-presidents—not because they are indifferent to how children are raised but because as corporation vice-presidents they have other primary responsibilities. But such a recommendation might be successful with this audience if it appealed to the well-being of the corporation, citing such benefits as employee morale, increased efficiency, and corporate reputation.

Although your recommendation must appeal to the needs and/or values of its audience, it will usually not identify them explicitly. In the paternity leave example, while you would identify the positive effects of the proposed plan, you would probably not have to devote time to convincing your audience that these effects are desirable. Provided your assumption about their values is correct, you can trust them to recognize the desirability of the effects on their own.

When Your Values Differ from Assumed Reader Values

Recommendations actually work with two sets of values—the reader's *and* the writer's. To succeed, a recommendation must appeal to the right reader values, but it actually originates in values held by the writer. In the examples discussed previously, we have implied that the assumed values of the audience are identical with the values of the writer. Often, this is the case.

Sometimes, however, the two sets of values are different, particularly when the recommender and reader are members of very different groups—consumer and corporation, for example, or student and faculty. Often, the value that moves you to recommend a particular change is not the value that will move your reader to implement your recommendation. In these cases, you must be aware of what the different values are; as long as they are related and not in conflict, their difference will not weaken your recommendation.

We can observe this principle in the following example of an unhappy customer writing a letter to the local transit authority recommending improvements in bus service. The writer's judgment of the current situation is based on what he perceives to be his rights as a paying customer—primarily the right of good service, which he is being denied. His judgment also originates in more specific needs—physical comfort, the importance of getting to work on time.

However, the value to which he is appealing in his reader is different, although clearly related. If his reader—the manager of customer services at the transit authority—chooses to take action on the strength of the recommendation, he will do so because of the importance to the transit service of the value of *customer satisfaction*. No business, even one that holds a virtual monopoly, as most transit authorities do, can afford to ignore the importance of customer satisfaction; the risks are ultimately too great.

In this example, the values of customer rights and customer satisfaction are not synonymous, but they are *causally* connected: if this customer's rights are being served, he will be satisfied. Not only is there no conflict between the two, but one follows from the other; thus they can happily coexist in this recommendation.

Here is the letter to the transit service:

Mr. John O'Brien
Manager, Customer Service
Metro Transit
Our Town, USA

Dear Mr. O'Brien:

I am writing to complain about the quality of the morning bus service for Bus #15, which runs from the Maplewood Shopping Center to Main Street downtown along Winton Avenue. By the time the bus scheduled to stop at 8:16 gets to my stop at Eleventh Street, it is usually late (in March, by an average of fifteen minutes) and always overcrowded, with standing room only even for elderly passengers. During the month of March, the bus was so overcrowded that ten people at my stop were denied a place: four on March 5, three on March 13, and two on March 20. Many of us have tried to take the earlier 7:44 bus, but the situation is essentially the same for that bus as well. Most of us cannot take a later bus because of our work schedules.

As you might expect, your customers are very unhappy. We feel we are being cheated of the service we deserve for the high fares, and we would like some action taken to improve the situation. To prove to you that I have a lot of company in my unhappiness, I am enclosing with this letter a petition signed by all the regular users of the 8:16 bus. Some of these riders have simply given up and use their cars to get downtown. More will certainly do so in the future if the situation does not improve.

I am sure that now you are aware of this problem, you will take steps to correct it. I look forward to hearing from you about what those steps might be.

Very truly yours,
Patrick Booth

In writing any kind of recommendation, you *must* identify to yourself the values from which you write and those to which you appeal in your readers. Often, these values are the same. But if they are not, they can only coexist in your recommendation if they are directly related and nonconflicting, as they should be in the case of the transit service and its unhappy customers. When you do recognize a conflict, you must find other values on which to base your appeal. You cannot convince an audience of cigarette smokers that the sale of cigarettes should be restricted because smoking is, as you believe, a stinking, filthy habit. But you might make some headway with an argument citing the risks of secondary smoke to loved ones—a risk that might concern even the most dedicated of smokers.

ACTIVITIES (9.1)

1. In each case below, the value cited to win the audience's agreement for the recommendation is not appropriate. For two of the following, write a paragraph on each describing another value that would be more appropriate.
   Sample recommendation: a longer school year for elementary and secondary students.
   Audience: elementary and secondary teachers.
   Inappropriate value: more work from teachers.
   Alternative value: a greater opportunity to ensure student's mastery of skills.
   a. **Recommendation:** earlier closing of a college cafeteria.
      Audience: college students.
      Inappropriate value: shorter hours and fewer headaches for cafeteria staff.
   b. **Recommendation:** a new federal tax on gasoline.
      Audience: truck drivers.
      Inappropriate value: reduced reliance on trucks for transporting goods.
   c. **Recommendation:** a curfew for everybody under the age of 16.
      Audience: those under 16.
      Inappropriate value: those under 16 can't be trusted.
   d. **Recommendation:** a law requiring motorcyclists to wear helmets.
      Audience: motorcyclists.
      Inappropriate value: reduced claims against insurance companies and therefore increased profits for insurance companies.
   e. **Recommendation:** a shorter work week.
      Audience: employers.
      Inappropriate value: more leisure time for employees.

2. For two of the following, write a paragraph describing a value shared by the two opposing groups.
   Example: Republicans and Democrats.
   Common value: concern for the national interest—the country as a whole.
   a. Planners of a new highway; homeowners whose property is in the path of the new highway.
   b. Managers of a company; workers on strike against that company.
   c. Parents planning to take away a child's allowance as punishment for bad behavior; the child in question.
   d. Planners of a large rock concert; neighborhood groups opposed to the concert because of noise.
   e. Proponents of legislation restricting the use of handguns; opponents of this legislation.

RECOMMENDATIONS EMPHASIZING THE PRESENT

Many recommendations concentrate on the problems or shortcomings of a current situation, leaving a proposal for change to another argument. The goal of such arguments is more to demonstrate *that* something needs to be done than *what* exactly that something is.

To accept this kind of recommendation, readers must first be given an accurate and, in most cases, detailed picture of the current situation. If they don't grasp the situation as it is, they won't be in a position to agree or disagree with your judgment. Thus the first part of recommendations emphasizing the present is a factual argument.

Establishing the Current Situation

Let's return to the example of the letter to the transit authority. The letter clearly states the reasons for dissatisfaction, and gives details about how this situation affects many people, not just the writer of the letter. In this case, the most effective information is numbers—how late the bus typically is and how many times people have been left behind at the bus stop. To get these figures, the writer had to conduct a little survey over a period of time. The reporting of the circumstances and results of the survey constitute a major part of the letter.

In such a recommendation, inclusion of accurate details is critical. For one thing, readers are going to take exact figures—such as are found in the letter—much more seriously than irate vagueness. Exaggerations like "Huge numbers of people are regularly prevented from riding the 8:16 bus" are far less meaningful than exact figures.

Second, misrepresenting the facts, whether purposefully to strengthen your case, or negligently through sloppy research, will almost always be detected. You can be sure that the recipient of any recommendation is going to investigate the situation before taking action; if the results of that investigation differ substantially from your figures, your recommendation certainly will not be acted on.

Evaluating the Current Situation

As noted earlier, all recommendations contain some evaluation. In recommendations emphasizing the present, the subject of the evaluation is the current situation. If you have a good understanding of your audience and their priorities, you will probably not need to write a fully developed evaluation complete with defined evaluative term. The transit authority letter, for example, does not require an explicit judgment of the situation presented. Any reader, whether an official of the transit authority or an occasional passenger, will recognize that the conditions described are undesirable. You could point to this fact for rhetorical emphasis, but the judgment will be implicit within the factual presentation.

Sometimes your recommendation will be addressed to readers who won't immediately recognize the problems associated with a particular situation. In such cases, you will need at least to identify *what* is wrong with the situation. In other words, you will need to supply a clear and limited evaluative term or terms. For example, a professor's schedule of assignments on a syllabus is counterproductive or unfair to students or is hopelessly unrealistic. Having established the standard according to which you are judging the situation, you can proceed with the evaluation according to the suggestions in Chapter 8, remembering the importance of considering your audience's needs and values.

Applying the Toulmin Model

As we mentioned in Chapter 5, the Toulmin logical model works particularly well with recommendations, helping you to detect possible weaknesses of reasoning or wording in the structure of your argument. An argument recommending improvements in a company's employee benefit package that concentrates on the shortcomings of the current package (i.e., emphasizing the present) would fit into the Toulmin model in the following way:

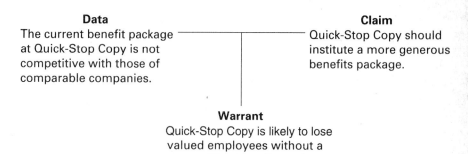

Data
The current benefit package at Quick-Stop Copy is not competitive with those of comparable companies.

Claim
Quick-Stop Copy should institute a more generous benefits package.

Warrant
Quick-Stop Copy is likely to lose valued employees without a competitive benefits package.

The data in the formula above are the current situation, and the warrant is the link between that situation and the recommendation itself (claim). In this case, the warrant is a causal claim with an implied evaluation: poor benefits will cost Quick-Stop Copy valued employees, which is not a desirable effect. Whenever your warrant is not immediately acceptable, you will have to provide support (backing) for it. Here, the backing would be the support that is necessary to justify the causal and evaluative claims embedded in the warrant. In arguments of recommendation, the warrant is usually the place where needs and values are assumed. The example above assumes that readers of the argument would be moved by the risk of losing employees. But if readers turn out to be executives who are planning to downsize the company, this particular warrant would probably not be effective.

ACTIVITIES (9.2)

1. For two of the situations below, what kind of evidence would indicate a need for major change? Make a list of this evidence and then write a description of this evidence in a summary paragraph.

    a. Traffic at an intersection
    b. Someone's physical appearance
    c. A friend's choice of a career
    d. A company's health care benefits
    e. The local court system

2. Using the material you developed for number 1 above, create two claims of recommendation. Then apply the Toulmin model, indicating what additional support or backing would be necessary.

Demonstrating the Probable Results of No Change

One way to convince an audience of the need for change is by demonstrating what is likely to happen if the current situation remains as it is. If you can show that maintaining an existing policy or practice will produce undesirable effects not currently obvious, by all means do so; it is an effective strategy. Of course, not all current situations lend themselves to such a strategy; often, maintaining a problematic practice will not create more problems, though it may ensure that current problems will not disappear.

An argument proposing an expansion of the local airport could be supported by a prediction (or argument of effect) of probable effects of the current policy. If you think the airport is too small for the number of flights it handles, you could point out (1) the possibility of an accident resulting from the current heavy traffic, and (2) the legal risk the local government is running if there were such an accident at this seriously overcrowded airport. If you can argue a plausible causal connection between the current policy and these very undesirable results, you will strengthen your recommendation considerably.

RECOMMENDATIONS EMPHASIZING THE FUTURE

Recommendations emphasizing the probable future effects of the proposed changes require more from a writer than those concentrating on a current situation. The biggest practical difference between the two recommendations is that in the second you must do more than identify current problems: you must come up with a new plan. These recommendations move beyond the general claim that something must be done; they also identify, reasonably and convincingly, what that something is. A recommendation emphasizing the future will be effective if it can demonstrate (1) that your proposal is likely to produce desirable effects, and (2) that the proposal is practicable.

Presenting the Recommendation

The presentation of your proposed plan or recommendation must be clear and immediately intelligible to your audience; readers cannot agree with a plan if they don't understand it. Different situations will demand different degrees of detail in this presentation. Sometimes, a rather general recommendation will be appropriate, as when you are not directly responsible for making the recommendation or overseeing the change. In other cases, particularly when you have some responsibility for the operations of the group in question, a detailed recommendation will be necessary. The following is an example of a general recommendation and a specific recommendation for the same issue:

1. *General* (Written by a group of angry homeowners requesting that the town supervisor take steps to reduce or eliminate the problem of speeding in their neighborhood.)

> Because of the well-known and recurring problem of speeders in the Village Lane neighborhood—a problem we discussed with you two months ago and which you admitted was serious—we recommend that you take more decisive steps than you have taken so far to deal with this problem. We need something more than a patrol car stationed here for two or three nights, which deters speeders only until they realize the patrol car will not be here regularly. We need a more routine presence of the police, more signs posting the speed limit, perhaps even speed bumps in some of the more dangerous places. Since the Village Lane neighborhood consists of narrow streets and shallow front lawns, building sidewalks is simply not possible. For the safety of all in the neighborhood, particularly the children, the town must do more to help us.

2. *Detailed* (Same recommendation as the previous, written by a chastened town supervisor to the heads of the town police and highway departments after discussions with them on actions to help solve the Village Lane speeding problem. If the town supervisor wants to be reelected, he will send a copy of this memo or at least a summary of it to residents in the neighborhood.)

> At our meeting on May 10 we discussed the problem of speeding in the Village Lane neighborhood and agreed that the following steps should be taken:
> - A radar car will be stationed in the neighborhood at least six hours a week for the next six months, particulariy in the evening when the speeding problem seems to be most serious. At the end of six months we will review this policy. A meeting with Village Lane Neighborhood Association officers will be part of this review.
> - The highway department will place five new speed limit signs in the neighborhood at locations mutually agreed upon by the highway supervisor and the neighborhood association. In addition, the speed limit for the entire neighborhood will be dropped from the general town speed limit of 30 mph to 25 mph.
> - The highway department will place speed bumps at the sharp curves on McDonnel and McMurtrie streets, along with very clear warnings to motorists about the presence of the bumps.

These two examples illustrate only two possibilities; recommendations can be more or less detailed than the second example. Generally, the more concrete your recommendation, the more effective it will be, provided your plan reflects a sound understanding of the operations of the group that would accept and implement the plan. You need to remember, however, that there are occasions when a great deal of detail is inappropriate. Most editorials make recommendations without much detail; most politicians give few details in their speeches to general audiences. In deciding how much detail to give, you need to consider the audience's capacity for and interest in the details, as well as their role in carrying out the recommendation. In the case of editorials and political speeches, most audiences are not interested in a lot of detail and are not responsible for implementing the recommendation.

ACTIVITIES (9.3)

For one of the general recommendations below, list at least three specific recommendations that would give substance to the general recommendation.
Example: We need a city with cleaner air.
Specific recommendations: (1) encouragement of "Park and Ride" lots for commuters to decrease automobile traffic, (2) tighter inspection standards for automobiles' exhaust emission systems, and (3) restrictions on the burning of leaves and trash. After you have made this list of recommendations, write a short essay (250–500 words) briefly explaining each of the recommendations and how they relate to the general recommendation.

1. Our college needs more school spirit.
2. Americans need to be more tolerant of racial and ethnic diversity.
3. Adolescents must be made more aware of the dangers of alcohol.
4. American industry needs to put more emphasis on the quality of its products.
5. Students and professors must learn to see each other as human beings.

Arguing the Effects of Your Recommendation

At the heart of a recommendation with future emphasis is your identification and evaluation of the probable effects of the new plan. After presenting the recommendation itself, you must demonstrate, through an *argument of effect,* what the results of the implemented recommendation are likely to be.

As with all arguments of effect, this part of your recommendation will be successful if you can show that the changes you propose (the causes) are related to the results you predict (the effects) through established causal principles (as presented in Chapter 6).

If you were proposing that the fees paid to doctors for routine nonemergency visits be increased, you would have to identify the probable results of that change. Suppose you predict the following short causal chain as resulting from this increase: the higher cost will mean that patients will visit doctors less frequently for minor ailments or vague complaints, thus allowing doctors to concentrate on people who really need care. Most readers will accept the argument that people will be hesitant to spend more money for minor problems. There is an acceptable motivational link between raising costs and fewer visits: the link is the common desire to save money.

The second link in the chain also seems plausible: doctors will use at least some of their gained time working with patients who have serious ailments. But if you argued that the patients who visit doctors after the fee increase are the ones really needing attention, you would be on shaky causal ground. While there would probably be fewer frivolous visits to doctors, people with sufficient money might continue visits for minor or imaginary ailments, and some people on tight budgets might be deterred from making even necessary visits. This practical recommendation based on results might break down if the result expected is that only those having genuine need of medical attention will now visit doctors.

ACTIVITIES (9.4)

For one of the recommendations and projected results that follow, write a short essay of approximately two pages in length analyzing how likely you believe the projected results are. You may find some results more probable than others.

1. **Recommendation:** increase the price of tickets to films at the college theater from $2 to $2.50.
   Projected results: no significant decline in attendance; more revenue from tickets to allow the theater to rent better films, which will eventually lead to higher attendance.

2. **Recommendation:** allow students to take one course pass-fail.
   Projected results: students will feel under less pressure about grades and be more willing to take tough courses; the students will work just as hard in the courses they take pass-fail as they would have if they had taken the course for a regular grade.

3. **Recommendation:** increase school taxes to subsidize new athletic facilities at the high school.
   Projected results: greater community involvement in and identification with high school athletic teams; improvement in high school image; increased student enrollment.

Judging Effects in Terms of Assumed Needs and Values

For your readers to accept your recommendation, they must see as desirable the probable effect you identify. An effect will be desirable if it satisfies or agrees with needs or values important to the readers. In developing a recommendation, you will probably identify several probable effects. You must ask yourself which values each effect would satisfy and whether those values would be important to your readers. If you were to recommend a pass-fail option to faculty by telling them that students would now have more free time, you would probably not appeal to faculty values, since most faculty would not place much value on a decline in student attention to course work. You should not deny this probable effect simply because your audience may not like it, but your emphasis should be on effects that do appeal to their values.

As with recommendations emphasizing current conditions, you may not have to evaluate the proposed effects explicitly, nor cite the needs and values that those effects will satisfy. But you must be aware of the values to which your recommendation appeals.

When Some Effects Are Undesirable.   Few recommendations can promise exclusively positive results. But as long as the desirable effects outweigh the undesirable ones, your recommendation is worth making. When you know that along with the positive effects there may be some less desirable repercussions, you should acknowledge them in your argument. Provided you can demonstrate that the negative effects are less significant than the positive ones, you will not weaken your argument by mentioning them. In fact, an argument that acknowledges and measures its own weaknesses is usually more effective than one that fails to admit what any intelligent reader will recognize.

If you were on a committee recommending the building of a new expressway, you should admit that the building of the new expressway, whatever its ultimate advantages, will cause inconveniences. This is a more effective and responsible approach than ignoring altogether the obvious negative consequences of your recommendation. You will enhance your credibility by admitting what many people will know or suspect anyway.

Implementation.   To be successful, your recommendation must pass one further test: not only must it appeal to your audience's values, it must also be feasible. Even the most brilliant recommendation will be rejected if its implementation is fraught with difficulties. While a detailed implementation plan is not required of all recommendations, some indication of the feasibility of your plan will strengthen your argument. At the least, you must provide a general indication that the recommendation is feasible. There is no point in advancing a recommendation your audience will see as totally impractical, regardless of how desirable the results might be. Sometimes, your audience will expect a very detailed implementation plan, including a list of activities and the name of the person responsible for each activity, the dates for beginning and completing each activity, and the likely costs for each activity.

A crucial element of a general or detailed implementation plan is an analysis of costs. Many great ideas born in the heat of inspiration have failed to become reality because of a lack of cold cash; programs that many judge worthwhile (such as manned exploration of Mars) have been delayed because of their expense. Whenever you present a proposal and outline its benefits, you also need to project its costs as accurately as you can. Remember that these costs often include not only the cost of constructing a new building or starting a new program but also the continuing costs once the proposal is a reality. Your community may need a new and larger airport, or a new bus service for the elderly, or new day care facilities, but once these are established, there may be additional costs for just keeping the services going from day to day. The new and larger airport, for example, may need more employees to maintain it and may cost more to heat and cool than the old one did. These continuing costs are easy to overlook or to minimize; the great temptation in making a recommendation that you believe in strongly is to overstate the benefits and understate the costs. You need to fight this temptation, remembering that some of your readers will be expecting just such a miscalculation.

People tend to accept recommendations that can be implemented within existing systems more readily than those requiring radical changes. Most of us are reluctant to make major changes on the strength of what *might* happen, however convincingly the probabilities are argued. Other things being equal, people usually prefer the least disruptive course of action.

On the other hand, sometimes existing structures need to be shaken up and disruptive measures taken. Much of the world we live in, including the very existence of this country, is a result of radical changes. You should at least consider whether a drastic change will not be ultimately more effective and easier to implement than a piecemeal one. Sometimes piecemeal recommendations are like putting money into an old car that is going to break down anyway, or like eighteenth-century Americans hoping King George III and the British government would see the error of their ways. One test here, though a difficult one, is whether the piecemeal changes will improve the situation enough to justify the time and cost of the changes: the old car may not be worth keeping; on balance it was easier to leave King George than reform him.

Applying the Toulmin Model

The Toulmin model will help you evaluate the reasonableness and completeness of recommendations emphasizing the future. Using the third recommendation in the example about the Village Lane speeding problem, we can apply the Toulmin model as follows:

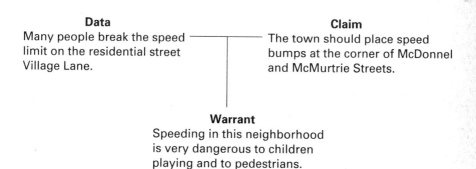

Data
Many people break the speed limit on the residential street Village Lane.

Claim
The town should place speed bumps at the corner of McDonnel and McMurtrie Streets.

Warrant
Speeding in this neighborhood is very dangerous to children playing and to pedestrians.

In this example, the warrant, which once again makes explicit the link between data and claim, is primarily an evaluative claim that would need further support, or backing, appropriate to evaluations. The warrant implies or assumes certain values on the part of the argument's readers: that it is not desirable to jeopardize the safety of children and pedestrians.

ACTIVITIES (9.5)

1. Each of the following are recommendations that many people believe are good ideas. Can you think of any drawbacks to these proposals that you would need to admit if you were recommending them? For one of the following, make a list of possible drawbacks and then write a brief paper (approximately 250 words) summarizing these drawbacks.
   a. Sending astronauts to explore Mars
   b. Passing elementary and secondary students from one grade to another only after they have passed strict competency tests
   c. Prohibiting smoking in all public facilities
   d. Increasing the school year by an average of one month for all elementary and secondary school children
   e. Requiring all states to implement a uniform speed limit of 65 mph on interstate highways

2. Prepare an implementation plan for some change you would like to make in your own life, such as studying harder, learning a new sport or hobby, or exploring a possible career. Your implementation plan should include the sequence of activities you will undertake, the dates you plan to begin and end each activity, and the costs, if any, of the project. See the recommendation report at the end of this chapter for a sample implementation plan.

3. Set up two of the following recommendations within the Toulmin model, indicating which elements (data or warrant) might need further support or backing.
   a. In order to reclaim their customers, U.S. airlines must initiate a series of monetary incentives, including reductions of first-class fares, increase of frequent flyer miles, and family fares.
   b. This company must practice a get-tough policy with those employees who refuse to comply with the no-smoking order; included in this policy should be deductions from paychecks, temporary suspension without pay, and the threat of discontinuance.
   c. My chemistry lab would be a lot more useful if there were fewer students, a professor with a Ph.D. in chemistry, and student tutors.
   d. If you want an A in this course, you will have to contribute to class discussion, hand in all your homework on time, and attend class faithfully.
   e. Our staggering divorce rate suggests that a course in marriage and relationships should be mandatory for all high school students.

RECOMMENDATIONS THAT CONSIDER
PRESENT AND FUTURE

The two types of recommendations we have discussed rarely occur in pure form; many recommendations contain some discussion of both the current situation and the future possibilities. Obviously, such recommendations will combine the strategies discussed in this chapter: they will present and evaluate the current situation, present the recommendation, and finally identify and evaluate the probable results of the recommendation. Because these arguments consider what currently exists and what could exist, they provide the groundwork for a useful comparative evaluation. After you have examined both the present and future elements of your argument, you may wish to compare the two explicitly—to demonstrate that the probable effects will be preferable to the current situation. If you have an accurate grasp of your audience's needs and values, you should be able to make this demonstration.

S U M M A R Y

Arguing Recommendations

- Recommendations emphasizing present conditions will include the following:
  - A presentation of the current situation/policy/practice (a factual argument).
  - An evaluation of this situation in terms of values/needs important to your audience. The judgment expressed and the value appealed to may be stated or implied.
  - When applicable, a presentation of the existing effects (causal argument) and a judgment of these effects.
  - When applicable, a presentation of the probable future effects (argument of effect) and a judgment of these effects.
- Applying the Toulmin model will help you judge the reasonableness of your recommendation.
- Recommendations emphasizing the future will include the following:
  - Presentation of the recommendation. The degree of detail in this presentation is usually dictated by your degree of responsibility for enacting the recommendation.
  - Identification of probable effects of your recommendation if it is implemented.
  - Evaluation of these effects (both desirable and undesirable) in terms of audience needs and values.
  - In some cases, a suggested implementation plan and an analysis of costs.

  Whether or not you include such a plan, those recommendations requiring minor changes to existing structures are generally more acceptable, though not necessarily more valuable, than those requiring radical restructuring.

- Recommendations considering present and future will include the following:
  - Presentation and evaluation of the current situation.
  - Presentation of the recommendation.
  - Identification and evaluation of the probable results of the recommendation.
  - In many cases, a demonstration that the probable effects of the implemented recommendation will be preferable to the current situation.

TWO SAMPLE RECOMMENDATIONS

The following sample recommendation report considers both the current situation and probable results of its implementation. The report is an example of what a student might include in a recommendation for a computer room in the dormitory. The format of the report, outlined here, is one of several possible formats for a recommendation report.

    I. Statement of Problem
   II. Statement of Recommendation
 III. Advantages of Recommendation
 IV. Disadvantages of Recommendation
   V. Costs and Implementation Plan

Many organizations and many professors have a preferred format for such reports; you would be wise to check whether there are such preferred formats before you begin to write this kind of report either at work or for a class.

This recommendation report is briefer and more general than many. If a report with the same proposal were being done by administrators in the Office of Computing, the report would undoubtedly include more detail on scheduling of the project, on the nature of the renovations, and on the kind of equipment that would be purchased. On the other hand, most recommendations by students to administrators would probably not include even a very general implementation plan, though including such a plan can help convince readers that the plan is carefully thought out and feasible. As we noted earlier, many recommendation reports have formats that differ from this sample. To be effective, they must at a minimum include a statement of the problem, a recommendation, a statement about the advantages of the recommendation that appeals to values of the audience, and some indication that the recommendation is feasible.

A Proposal for a Computer Facility in Marshall Dormitory
Prepared for
Dr. Hector Martinez,
Assistant Vice-President for Student Life
by Elaine Weston
Chair, Marshall Dormitory Student Committee
February 13, 1995

Statement of Problem

Currently many students living in Marshall Dormitory have difficulty getting access to a computer. The college's main computer facility is located over a mile away on the other end of campus and that facility is often overcrowded; many students find that they can use a computer only after eleven at night or before ten in the morning. Some students bring their own computers with them to college, but not all students here can afford their own computers. I surveyed all students living on the third floor of Marshall and found that only 25 percent had their own computers, while another 50 percent said they use computers at least occasionally for course work. Of this 50 percent, 45 percent said that they have sometimes found it hard to get access to one of the college's computers, and 35 percent frequently had this problem. Clearly, this lack of access to needed computers is a serious problem for Marshall students. When I spoke with Helen Borshoff, the Vice-President for Computing, she confirmed the severity of the problem and said that her organization is trying to deal with the problem within the constraints of its limited resources.

RECOMMENDATION

We recommend that the Office of Student Life work with the Office of Computing to convert the student lounge at the west end of the second floor of Marshall into a computer facility equipped with seven microcomputers, two terminals connected to the main academic computer on the other side

of campus, and three printers. Our discussions with the
Office of Computing indicate that the number of computers,
terminals, and printers is the maximum that would fit into
the amount of space available and that this range of
equipment would be most appropriate for student needs.
Since the need for more computers and more access to
computers is so pressing, we recommend that the necessary
renovations take place this summer so that the facility
will be ready by the beginning of the next academic year
on September 6, 1995.

ADVANTAGES OF RECOMMENDATION

If our recommendation is implemented, students who live in
Marshall will be able to use college-owned computers
without having to go all the way to the college facility.
There will also be more computers available than there are
now, and students without the means to buy their own
computers will be at less of a disadvantage than they
currently are. For students, then, there are significant
educational advantages if this proposal is implemented.

For the administration, there are several other
advantages as well. Construction of this facility will
alleviate at least some of the overwhelming pressure on
the main computer facility. Since the space for this new
facility already exists, renovating this space will be
less costly than adding new space somewhere on campus.
This new facility will also show the administration's
concern for increasing student access to computers, and it
will therefore help to reduce the growing tension between
students and administrators over this issue.

DISADVANTAGES OF RECOMMENDATION

Our recommendation does have some disadvantages. Probably
the most significant is the security risk of having a
small facility so far removed from the central computer
facility, which means that it would not make financial
sense to have someone on duty to guard the equipment.
Another disadvantage is that some space devoted to student

relaxation would be taken and used for another purpose. The placing of a computer facility in a dormitory also raises some new policy questions for the college, including whether only students in the dormitory could use the facility, or whether the facility would be open to all students of the college.

These disadvantages are real, but they can be dealt with. The Vice-President for Computing assures us that new electronic security devices reduce the need for security personnel. In a poll taken two weeks ago, the Marshall students indicated that they preferred to see the current lounge converted into a computer facility, with 68 percent expressing this preference, 18 percent opposing it, and 14 percent expressing no opinion. Finally, while this proposal does raise some new questions of policy, these questions must be addressed at some point in the near future anyway, as computers and computer facilities become more pervasive in the college.

COSTS AND IMPLEMENTATION PLAN

The following is a tentative and very general outline of the costs of the project as well as an implementation plan. These will have to be refined by the Offices of Student Life and Computing as they begin to work on the project. The Vice-President for Computing has assured us, however, that the costs and implementation plan we have outlined here seem reasonable. At her advice, we have not included personnel costs for the time of administrators, since these costs are difficult to calculate and are not usually included in the budgets for small projects of this kind.

Activity	Dates	Costs
Initial planning with students, Student Life and Computing Administrators	March	--

Work requests for construction; orders for equipment	April	--
Renovation of lounge	June-July	$15,000
Installation of security devices	Early August	$ 3,000
Purchase and installation of computer equipment	Late August	$30,000
Total initial costs		$48,000
Ongoing costs; maintenance on equipment		$ 3,000 per year

The following recommendation is a more general argument than the preceding formal proposal, but like the preceding argument, its central claim calls for a new course of action: "But we need to look at some of the actions taken in the name of fighting discrimination and promoting diversity to see if they are solving these problems—or just creating different ones" (paragraph 5). The writer, Pamela J. Hsu, demonstrates the need for this recommendation by citing and implicitly evaluating a number of consequences of the current emphasis on minority rights. Ms. Hsu's presentation of the current situation is based largely on her personal experience and observation. Her modest recommendation—a call for review of existing policies—is strengthened by appeals to authority (Daniel J. Boorstin, Pulitzer Prize–winner, and William Raspberry, syndicated columnist).

THE SIDE EFFECTS OF AFFIRMATIVE ACTION

PAMELA J. HSU

In the 1960s, the civil rights movement said people could not be denied things like employment based on race. In the 1970s, affirmative action injected women and minorities into the workplace. In the 1980s, diversity programs stressed appreciating differences among all people. But are we starting to see some negative side effects in the 1990s?

During the past several decades, many programs have promoted the education and employment of women and minorities. Minority scholarships are readily available in just about every field. And most corporations track hiring, retention and promotion of women and minorities, and aim to improve performance in these areas.

As a 24-year-old Chinese woman, I benefit from these programs. I received a generous minority internship/scholarship package from a major corporation one summer during college. When I applied to graduate school, one university offered me a fellowship specifically for minorities entering that particular field of study.

I know that these opportunities have provided a boost in my career. I appreciate them. But there are times when I wish I could have competed against everyone else. I believe my ability would have made me at least a strong contender against all applicants.

I know we have not reached that ideal scenario. I realize that problems still exist and that economic and social conditions prevent some children from getting any chance at all. But we need to look at some of the actions taken in the name of fighting discrimination and promoting diversity to see if they are solving these problems—or just creating different ones.

I'm noticing a growing number of white males who say they are now being discriminated against. I'm talking about the professor who warns his white male students that a particular graduate program may be difficult to get into because they are favoring women and minority candidates. I'm talking about a former employer who ran a department one person short for months, even though many applied for the job, because the position had to be filled by a minority. There's a difference between fairness and force fitting.

Daniel J. Boorstin, the Pulitzer Prize-winning historian and best-selling author, said it best: "We must give everybody a fresh start and not try to compensate for past injustices by creating present injustices."

A growing number of groups are voluntarily segregating themselves from others to preserve ethnic identity. Just take a look at the average college campus, and you'll find Greek houses for minorities and organized student groups for just about every ethnic population. But some may be developing blanket beliefs about their own ethnic group. I've heard that you aren't being true to yourself if you "act" white or you aren't really happy if you've assimilated. The fact that I'm Chinese in blood and American in behavior rubs some people the wrong way. They dub me a Twinkie—yellow on the outside but white on the inside.

I was raised to assimilate, and I don't regret that. Just because I live an American lifestyle doesn't make me any less Chinese. It's ironic that groups which intend to promote an appreciation of their culture among others sometimes fail to reciprocate the respect among their own.

Competition between minority groups may be breeding another problem. One minority group complains that a university gave such-and-such group this much money, and how come they didn't get the same? Columnist William Raspberry pointed out that more students these days search for "discrimination nuggets" because if they find enough of them, they can trade in at the administration building for an ethnic sensitivity course or a minority student center.

It's time to step back and refocus on our ultimate goal. The idea that minority status equals money needs to change. Financial assistance should be available for those who need a chance. Ethnic groups should preserve traditions but not alienate those who do things differently. Sharing traditions with other people and encouraging those who are interested to get more involved—even if they do not belong to that ethnic group—would truly promote diversity.

Detroit News, Sunday, May 22, 1994

SUGGESTIONS FOR WRITING (9.6)

1. Following the form of the first sample recommendation, write a recommendation report to improve some aspect of your college or university. Possible areas for improvement could include dormitories or apartments, the library, the curriculum in your major, or the food service. Make your recommendation as

realistic as possible by interviewing people with some responsibility for that area. From these people you should try to learn why the situation exists in its current form and how feasible your recommendation might be, as well as some sense of the costs of the project. The length of this report will vary with the complexity of the problem and your recommendation, though it might be wise to limit yourself to a maximum of approximately ten pages.

2. Almost every community has its share of white elephants: elaborate projects or expensive buildings that ultimately had to be abandoned or converted to some alternative use because their cost greatly exceeded their benefit to the community. Look for a white elephant in your community and analyze why the project never met its original intentions. Your professor can help you get started. You will almost certainly have to consult the local newspapers and then perhaps the local archives. Since your time is limited and there may be a great deal of documentation, you might have to restrict your research to newspaper accounts of what happened and why. As with option 1, the maximum length should be approximately ten pages.

3. Working from the principle of dissonance discussed in Chapter 2, write a general recommendation (along the lines of sample 2) in which you call for a reconsideration of a policy or system at work or school that you find problematic.

10

Writing and Image

In our contemporary society of sound bites and spin doctors, the concept of *image* has developed something of a negative flavor, suggesting superficiality and falseness. Public personalities pay a great deal of money to have distinctive images packaged and popularized—images that may bring them enormous success but that bear little relationship to the real people behind them.

This book uses the term *image* differently and more positively, to suggest the ways in which writing honestly reflects to the reader the kind of person the writer is. In successful arguments, writers project an image of intelligence, probity, and trustworthiness. There is nothing false or superficial about this kind of image: these qualities cannot be created out of thin air; they must be true *reflections* of the writer and thus are developed over time and through experience. But whenever you write, you should strive to project such an image, while also being aware that this image will need to be slightly adjusted to fit the context of a given argument.

Image consists of many elements. Most obviously, the quality of the argument itself—its intelligence, honesty, and accuracy—will impress your readers. But image is projected on a smaller scale as well—by the mechanics of your writing (grammar, spelling, punctuation, physical appearance). Stylistic elements also contribute to a positive impression: word choice, sentence construction, and figures of speech such as metaphor and analogy. Even the sound of your writing will convey a certain impression to your readers. Your style as a writer results from all the choices you make about language in your argument. Finally, a writer's image is partially a function of the *voice* he or she chooses for the occasion—the overall tone or mood of the writing.

This chapter will focus on some of the conscious choices writers of argument make about image—choices about voice, diction, metaphor and analogy, connotative language and slanting, and even about the sound of their prose. As you compose your own arguments, we encourage you to consider these elements and to make choices about them that accord with your subject, your purpose, and your audience.

THE ROLE OF VOICE

A writer's *voice* is the role that he or she takes for a particular occasion, almost like an actor taking on a part in a new play. To many inexperienced writers, voice suggests insincerity or fakery, but all of us continually "play" different roles. We behave one way in a classroom, another way playing basketball. We talk to our parents in one way and to our friends in another. Voice is simply the manifestation of this adaptability in writing.

The following simple example demonstrates the variability of voice:

Dear Mr. Jones:

At the suggestion of Ms. Hawkins, I am writing to inquire about an opening as an electrical engineer in your firm.

Dear Mom and Dad:

Hi and help! You won't believe this but I'm broke again. Boy, were my textbooks expensive this quarter!

The same student wrote both of these openings and was completely sincere in both cases, though the voices differ markedly. In the first case, the student was formal, polite, restrained. In the second, she was informal and very direct. In cases like these, the choice of a particular voice seems natural; the student did not spend much time or effort choosing these voices. But you can improve your writing by being conscious of the available choices and using them effectively. One crucial choice is between the formal and informal voices—the voices of the first and second letters, respectively. Using an informal voice in a formal situation can have disastrous effects. What would happen to our student if she wrote to Mr. Jones (whom she presumably does not know) in the following manner?

Dear Mr. Jones:

Hi and help! I ran into somebody Hawkins—I forget her first name—and she says you've got jobs. Boy, do I need one!

The Importance of Ethos

As the Greek philosopher Aristotle noted, one major element of any successful argument is the establishment of a positive *ethos* (or character)—that is, the portrayal of the writer as a sincere, upright person. Audiences are interested in the source of an argument and trust arguments from people who appear to have the traits they admire, including honesty and a concern for other people. They distrust arguments from people who are known to be dishonest, or selfish, or whose voice suggests those traits. As a writer, you must be aware of the importance of a positive ethos and demonstrate it in your own writing. In argument, a carefully considered voice can convince an audience that you are a principled person concerned not just with your own self-interest but with the general welfare. When your readers believe that you are this kind of person, they are much more likely to accept your argument.

The following letter from an angry student to her campus newspaper does not establish a convincing ethos:

> The grading policies of this college are rotten, just like everything else here at State. How can the administration put a student on probation for failing a course outside of her major? That's just outrageous. When I got an "F" in physics, they put me on probation even though I received at least a "C" in the courses in my major. I didn't want to take physics anyway, and the instructor really stunk. Now I'm not eligible to play on the women's basketball team! When are we students going to force the administration to get rid of this stupid policy?

The reasoning in this letter has many weaknesses, but the writer's failure to establish a convincing ethos also destroys the letter's effectiveness. The writer presents herself as lacking balance (is *everything* at State rotten?) and as concerned only about herself (what about the effect of the grading policy on someone other than herself?). Almost all readers of this letter would dismiss it as a howl of outrage over a personal problem, not an argument for them to consider seriously.

When Aristotle urged creators of argument to establish an effective ethos for their argument, he was not urging hypocrisy. Neither are we. In creating an ethos, you may present your best side, but this side is still part of you. The outraged student who wrote the preceding letter is presumably capable of balance and of concern for others. Before writing that letter, she should have moved from outrage to a broader perspective, using her own anger as inspiration but recognizing that expressing hurt feelings does not make an argument.

Good writers also create credible voices by being confident about their views but not more confident than their support warrants. A credible voice is neither dogmatic nor apologetic. Readers suspect writers, such as our angry student, who make sweeping claims—such as the one that everything at State is rotten—or forceful statements ("the governor is the dumbest woman in this state") for which they cannot possibly produce adequate support. On the other hand, they also suspect arguments that seem too wishy-washy: "I suspect it is probably true that this policy may lead us in the wrong direction." Student writers, especially when writing about fields new to them, are prone to be excessively cautious, which very quickly undermines readers' faith in the writers and their arguments.

As an example of an argument with a credible voice, let us return to the angry student, who has calmed down and decided to try another version of the letter.

> After a painful experience with the policies on probation and suspension here at State, I have concluded that these policies should be revised. The policy states that any student whose grades fall below a "C" average will

be placed on suspension, making that student ineligible to participate in athletic teams or many other extracurricular activities. The policy appears reasonable, but its effect is to place too much emphasis on courses outside of a student's major. Many students, including three of my acquaintances, have found themselves ineligible to participate in these activities even though they were doing acceptable work in their majors. I now find myself in a similar situation, ineligible to be on the women's basketball team yet earning grades of "C" or higher in my major.

The voice in this letter is that of someone who is honest about her own situation but also concerned for others, someone who allows for an apparently reasonable opposing view while remaining firm in her own.

ACTIVITIES (10.1)

1. Write a one-page letter to your parents or a friend asking for a loan of some money to help with your college expenses. Then write a letter to your college's financial office asking for the same loan. Make a list of the differences in the two letters.

2. Write one or two paragraphs stating why you should be given an award for your many outstanding contributions to your community. Your paragraphs must portray you as deserving this award, but they should not be boastful.

THE VIRTUES AND LIMITATIONS OF PLAIN WRITING

Most writing instructors and most writing textbooks today urge students to make their writing clear and straightforward, without obvious embellishments. The British novelist and essayist George Orwell gave the most famous formulation of the rules for this plain style in his "Politics and the English Language":

(i)   Never use a metaphor, simile or other figure of speech which you are used to seeing in print.

(ii) Never use a long word where a short one will do.

(iii) If it is possible to cut a word out, always cut it out.

(iv) Never use the passive where you can use the active.

(v)   Never use a foreign phrase, a scientific word or a jargon word if you can think of any everyday English equivalent.

(vi) Break any of these rules sooner than say anything outright barbarous.

The plain style Orwell urges arose as a reaction against the bloated and often dishonest prose of modern bureaucratic society, where military first strikes are called "anticipatory retaliations," visual materials in school curricula become "integrated systems learning designs," and simple sentences and direct expression disappear behind clouds of vague pomposity: "Please contact my secretary about an appointment regarding the project slippages in implementing the new on-line system." The writer could have said "Please see me about the delays in starting the new on-line system," but for too many writers today the first version seems more official, more important. A plain style of writing is an antidote to this swollen contemporary prose.

But plain writing carries its own risks, as Orwell notes with his sixth rule. Writers who use plain style exclusively risk writing prose that is clear but undistinguished, serviceable but dull. To combat this risk, we suggest the following additions to Orwell's rules:

(i) Don't be afraid to use metaphors, similes, or other figures of speech, provided they are not overworked.

(ii) When a long word is the best one, use it.

(iii) Use long sentences for variety and when they best suit your needs.

(iv) Dare to try something different.

(v) Break any of these rules rather than confuse your reader.

These rules do not contradict Orwell's; they are offered as friendly amendments—another point of view to keep in mind, a balance of the delicate scales of an effective style.

The following passage from the second paragraph of Henry David Thoreau's *Walden* is a good example of writing that succeeds by going beyond the plain style. We have annotated parts of this passage that demonstrate some of our rules for enriched prose.

Clever phrasing—
dare to try
something different

I should not talk so much about myself if there were anybody else whom I knew as well. Unfortunately, I am confined to this theme by the narrowness of my experience. Moreover, I, on my side, require of every writer, first or last, a simple and sincere account of his own life, and not merely what he has heard of other men's lives; some such account as he would send to his kindred from a distant land; for if he has lived sincerely, it must have been in a distant land to me. Perhaps these pages are more particularly addressed to poor students. As for the rest of my readers, they will accept such portions as apply to them. I trust that none will stretch the seams in putting on the coat, for it may do good service to him whom it fits.

Use long sentences
for variety

Use metaphors,
similes

METAPHOR AND ANALOGY

A *metaphor* is an implicit comparison of two dissimilar subjects so that some aspects of one (usually concrete and familiar) can be used to illuminate aspects of the other (usually more abstract or unfamiliar). "The twilight of her career" is a metaphor comparing something concrete and familiar, the end of a day, to something more abstract, in this case the end of someone's career. The "global village" is another metaphor, where the abstract concept of the globe or world (the entire population of the earth) is compared to the more familiar and concrete idea of a village. A *simile* is a comparison where the act of comparing is made explicit, usually through the use of *like* or *as:* "Falling in love is like getting caught in a warm spring rain." For our purposes, simile can be seen as a type of metaphor. *Analogy* is like metaphor since dissimilar areas are compared, but in analogy the comparison is extended through several points. The "global village" becomes an analogy when the world is compared to a village in several respects, including the need for certain agreed-upon laws and the importance of communication and cooperation among those in the community.

The following passage from the historian Barbara Tuchman demonstrates the value of metaphor in argument. In the first paragraph of "History as Mirror," Tuchman begins her argument by describing history as a mirror where we can see an image of ourselves.

> At a time when everyone's mind is on the explosions of the moment, it might seem obtuse of me to discuss the fourteenth century. But I think a backward look at that disordered, violent, bewildered, disintegrating, and calamity-prone age can be consoling and possibly instructive in a time of similar disarray. Reflected in a six-hundred-year-old mirror, a more revealing image of ourselves and our species might be seen than is visible in the clutter of circumstances under our noses.

According to Tuchman, studying the history of fourteenth-century western Europe is like looking into a mirror. In this mirror we can see a clearer image of ourselves than is available from just examining the present; in the present we are too absorbed in current details to get the "big picture." The "big picture" is what makes our lives tick: our motivations, desires, problems, crises, and triumphs. By using this metaphor of the mirror, Tuchman shows us briefly and clearly the value of history to our lives.

In the following passage, the psychiatrist Carl Jung offers us an example of an effective use of analogy in supporting an argument. Jung describes the mind of twentieth-century humanity through the analogy of a building.

> We have to describe and to explain a building the upper story of which was erected in the nineteenth century; the ground-floor dates from the sixteenth century, and a careful examination of the masonry discloses the fact that it was reconstructed from a dwelling-tower of the eleventh century. In the cellar we discover Roman foundation walls, and under the cellar a filled-in cave, in the floor of which stone tools are found and remnants of glacial fauna in the layers below. That would be a sort of picture of our mental structure.

Jung's analogy is effective because it clearly reveals his view of our minds, with the most recent cultural developments being in the most visible upper layers and the more ancient (and instinctive) behaviors being buried below, less visible from the outside but just as important as the upper layers. Of course, Jung could have described these characteristics of our minds in a more abstract language, similar to what we are using here to explain his analogy, but his description would have been less memorable than this picture of a house with a buried cave underneath. This example demonstrates how analogies can crystallize abstract ideas into a sharp picture that both clarifies the ideas and makes them memorable.

Metaphors can also be valuable means of discovery—doors that lead us to important ideas and arguments. All of us are naturally disposed to noticing correspondences, to seeing the threads of similarity that unify experience. We have all had the experience of being spontaneously struck by similarities between two seemingly different subjects. Usually, our minds hit upon such a comparison because it is apt, because it contains a truth that we may not consciously recognize. Upon close examination, these correspondences or metaphors that come to us can reveal important truths about both subjects and can generate and even structure a theory or argument. When the noted computer scientist Edward Fredkin was struck by the correspondences between the operation of computers and the operation of the universe, he followed up that metaphor, creating a controversial but intriguing theory of digital physics from the implications of a seemingly simple metaphor. Like Fredkin and others, you should be alive to the generating power of your natural metaphor-making tendency, letting it work for you in the ideas you develop and the arguments you write.

Some Cautions About Metaphor and Analogy

Metaphors and analogies can illuminate and generate ideas, but they can never *prove* a point. A writer cannot prove that a certain policy should be adopted by using a metaphor or analogy. Calling the world a village does not prove the need for world government. Furthermore, analogies, if pursued too far, inevitably break down because the two areas being compared are not identical; the world may be a village, but it is a village with more than five billion inhabitants, speaking thousands of different languages and following an incredible range of customs and beliefs. Some village!

Analogies can be risky if people take them too literally, as they did with the "domino theory" analogy in the 1960s and 1970s. The domino analogy compared countries in Southeast Asia to a row of dominoes. When dominoes are placed on their ends in a row, they will fall down one by one if the first in the series is pushed. According to the domino theory, these countries would fall to communism in the same manner. The domino theory was a major reason for American involvement in Vietnam; American strategists believed that the fall of South Vietnam to the communists would lead to communist control of all of Southeast Asia and perhaps all of Asia. South Vietnam and some other parts of Southeast Asia are now communist, but other countries in Southeast Asia are not and do not seem to be in any danger of falling under such control. The domino theory may not always be this faulty, yet the theory cannot become an excuse for failing to analyze the particular complexities of a specific situation. Real countries are always more complicated than dominoes.

ACTIVITIES (10.2)

1. For one of the following analogies, write a one-page essay analyzing ways in which the analogy illuminates aspects of the situation and ways in which it does not. Our discussion of the "domino theory" above is one example of this kind of analysis.
   a. Sexual politics
   b. The family of humanity
   c. The game of life
   d. The war of ideas
   e. The corporate ladder
2. Write a paragraph that develops an analogy. You may use one of the analogies in Exercise 1, provided it is not the one you used in that exercise. The paragraph by Carl Jung previously cited is one model for this development.

CONNOTATIVE LANGUAGE AND SLANTING

Good writers must be aware not only of the *denotations* of words but of their *connotations* as well. The denotation of a word is its explicit meaning, its dictionary definition; the connotation of a word is the meaning or meanings suggested by the word, the word's emotional associations. The denotation of the words *apple pie* is a baked food made with apples. In our society the connotations of "apple pie" are family life, patriotism, and innocence. Writers of arguments need to be sensitive to the connotations of words and use these connotations appropriately. A writer urging development of a suburban tract of land for offices and factories is more likely to succeed by describing it as a "High Tech Park" than as an "Industrial Development Area"; the term *High Tech* has a certain vogue, while "Industrial Development" smells of factory smokestacks. In Rochester, N.Y., developers of a new suburban office building appealed to the taste for the rural and natural by calling the building "Corporate Woods," though there are few trees anywhere in sight.

The example of "Corporate Woods" points out the risk in a heavy reliance on mere connotation. Beyond a certain point, words used for their connotative value cease to have any meaning at all; there are very few woods in "Corporate Woods" and nothing fresh in "lemony fresh" soap or in "fresh frozen" juice. And what is so natural about many of the products that advertise themselves as "naturally delicious"? Connotation is an inescapable element of argument, but it should not be used without regard to denotation. Some advertising does this and gets away with it, but most readers demand higher standards for other kinds of written arguments.

Writers are often tempted to use not only connotation but also blatantly emotional terms as illegitimate supports for their arguments. Suppose you were arguing for a new recreation center on your campus. You might refer to the necessity of having a place "where students could use their free time constructively, letting off the frustrations and pressures caused by rigorous scholastic demands." Here you are portraying students and their needs in a positive way—we tend to respect anyone subjected to "rigorous scholastic demands." But if you were arguing against the recreation center you could completely alter this impression by using words with negative connotations: "Do our spoiled and spoon-fed students really need another service catering to their already well-satisfied needs?" The respectable students of the first argument have become the undeserving parasites of the second. Words like *spoiled, spoon-fed,* and *catering* are negative words, and their application to the students in question affects a reader's impression of the issue. The words used *slant* the argument, even in the absence of sound evidence. As a writer of responsible arguments, *you* must not fall into the trap of letting such language suggest conclusions your argument does not support.

The temptation to slant is probably strongest in arguments of ethical evaluation; of all the arguments you write, these are the most personal, the most self-revealing, and thus the most important to you. For these reasons, they can tempt you to resort to irrational means to convince your audience. You are not likely to invest high emotional stakes in arguing that four-wheel-drive cars are superior to other kinds of cars, but you can be passionately committed to an argument for or against capital punishment or abortion. Slanting, while almost unavoidable in such cases, must not become a substitute for sound support for your argument.

ACTIVITIES (10.3)

Write two paragraphs describing the same object or activity, but favorably in one paragraph and unfavorably in another. Some possible topics: New York City (or some other city); a particular television show; a book you recently read. Be sure to describe the same qualities in both paragraphs.

THE MUSIC OF LANGUAGE

Any writer who ignores the importance of *sound* in argument is overlooking an enormously valuable tool of argument. We all know the power of advertising's jingles and catch phrases, which linger in our minds even when we wish they wouldn't. Less obvious but powerfully convincing is prose that holds our attention because of a fresh and pleasing combination of sounds. Such prose contains euphony and rhythm.

Euphony, which comes from Greek roots meaning "good sounds," is a pleasing combination of sounds. We usually think of euphony as a characteristic of poetry or some kinds of prose fiction, but it can and should be present in written arguments as well. Euphony, of course, depends on the ear of the reader or listener, but ears can be trained to become sensitive to this quality of prose, just as we learn to be sensitive to different qualities of music.

Rhythm is a recognizable pattern or shape of the flow of sounds through time. In prose, rhythmical units are often divided by grammatical pauses such as commas or periods, though a rhythmical break can also occur at some other place where we would pause to catch our breath if we were reading aloud. "I came, I saw,

I conquered" is a simple example of prose rhythm, with three short rhythmical units divided by commas. All of us have a rhythm to our prose just as we have a rhythm to our breathing or walking, and this rhythm can vary with the situation, just as our walking rhythm can. Good prose writers learn to know their prose rhythms, to develop them as they gain experience in writing, and to recognize and use the appropriate rhythm for a specific purpose.

The following passage from Toni Morrison's Nobel Prize lecture demonstrates a sensitivity to euphony and rhythm:

> The systematic looting of language can be recognized by the tendency of its users to forgo its nuanced, complex, mid-wifery properties, replacing them with menace and subjugation. Oppressive language does more than represent violence; it is violence; does more than represent the limits of knowledge; it limits knowledge. Whether it is obscuring state language or the faux language of mindless media; whether it is the proud but calcified language of the academy or the commodity-driven language of science, whether it is the malign language of law-without-ethics, or language designed for the estrangement of minorities, hiding its racist plunder in its literary cheek—it must be rejected, altered and exposed.

The passage demonstrates two key elements of effective prose style: parallelism and emphasis. *Parallelism* is the principle that equivalent thoughts demand equivalent expression, a principle that Morrison carefully follows with her repetition of the construction "whether it is . . . or." This series of repeated constructions also establishes a noticeable rhythm to the passage. The series is also arranged in order of *emphasis,* the worst offense of language reserved for the last ("language designed for the estrangement of minorities").

The passage contains other devices that enhance its appeal to the ear and emphasize its meaning. The repetition of the key word *language* gives aural coherence to the passage while also stressing its central concept. In the long final sentence, the contrast between the complexity with which the offenses of language are represented and the simplicity of the offered solution—"it must be rejected, altered and exposed"—brings the passage to an emphatic and compelling close.

Developing a sensitivity to language isn't easy, but it can be done, just as most people can develop a sensitivity to tone and rhythm in music. One way to do this is to listen to the sound of your prose as you read it aloud. If this seems awkward, make an audiotape of your reading, or read to a friend, or have a friend read your prose to you. When you are doing this, listen for spots that seem especially clumsy or difficult and note them for later review. These spots probably need revision. If you practice reading aloud for a while, you should begin to develop a "silent ear" that will give you a sense of how the words sound even without your speaking them aloud.

The sound of your prose *will* affect how readers react to your argument, even if they are not conscious of the role sound plays in written prose and even if they have not developed the skill to create sound-pleasing prose themselves. As the rhetorician Kenneth Burke has noted, audiences tend to identify with skilled speakers and writers and are likely to be carried along simply by the very structure of the prose. Even academics who practice extreme examples of Morrison's "proud but calcified language of the academy" are likely to be carried along by the rising force of Morrison's prose.

ACTIVITIES (10.4)

Of the following passages, choose the one you find most striking or memorable as prose. Write a one- to two-page essay analyzing why you find the prose effective. If you find this assignment hard to do without more information, describe why this is so and what information you need.

1. You know how it is, you want to look and you don't want to look. I can remember the strange feelings I had when I was a kid looking at war photographs in *Life,* the ones that showed dead people or a lot of dead people lying close together in a field or a street, often touching, seeming to hold each other. Even when the picture was sharp and cleanly defined, something wasn't clear at all, something repressed that monitored the images and withheld their essential information. It may have legitimized my fascination, letting me look for as long as I wanted; I didn't have a language for it then, but I remember now the shame I felt, like looking at first porn, all the porn in the world. (Michael Herr, *Dispatches.* London: Picador, 1978, p. 23.)

2. Commercial exploitation and growing population demands will speed destruction of rain forests as well as oceans, grasslands, lakes, and wetlands. *Pleading ignorance of these vital and fragile ecosystems can only spell global disaster. What can you do?*
   You can accept this invitation to support World Wildlife Fund. *We have a plan for survival. We need your help to make it succeed.* (Letter from the World Wildlife Fund. World Wildlife Fund, 1987, p. 1.)

3. The stars awaken a certain reverence, because though always present, they are inaccessible; but all natural objects make a kindred impression, when the mind is open to their influence. Nature never wears a mean appearance. Neither does the wisest man extort her secret, and lose his curiosity by finding out all her perfection. Nature never became a toy to a wise spirit. The flowers, the animals, the mountains, reflected the wisdom of his best hour, as much as they had delighted the simplicity of his childhood. (Ralph Waldo Emerson, "Nature," in *Essays and Lectures.* Ed. Joel Porte. New York: The Library of America, 1983, p. 9.)

4. Many adults carry high school around with them always. It is a unique, eccentric, and insulated social system, a pressure cooker where teenagers rush from one class to another, shoved into close quarters with twenty-five or thirty others their age they may love, hate, care little about, or hardly know at all. It has its own norms, rituals, vocabulary, and even its own way to tell time—not by the minute and hour but, as sociologist Edgar Friedenberg has pointed out, by periods. As the setting for the adolescent search for identity, high school is, Kurt Vonnegut wrote, "closer to the core of the American experience than anything else I can think of." There is life after high school, but what we do as adults is powerfully shaped by those years. (Myra and David Sadker. *Failing at Fairness: How America's Schools Cheat Girls.* New York: Charles Scribner's Sons, 1994, p. 99.)

5. Yes, Virginia, there is a Santa Claus. He exists as certainly as love and gen-
erosity and devotion exist, and you know that they abound and give your life
its highest beauty and joy. Alas! how dreary would be the world if there
were no Santa Claus. It would be as dreary as if there were no Virginias.
There would be no child-like faith then, no poetry, no romance to make toler-
able this existence. We should have no enjoyment, except in sense and
sight. The eternal life with which childhood fills the world would be extin-
guished. (*New York Sun*, 1897.)

SUMMARY

Writing and Image

- The image you project through your writing is the result of a number
  of conscious choices you make about your style, your voice, and your
  use of language.

- You should write clearly, but you should also use various strategies to
  enrich your prose, including metaphors, similes, or other figures of
  speech, long words and sentences when appropriate. In general, dare to
  try something different.

- Metaphor and analogy can be valuable for illuminating and generating
  an argument, but they can never prove a point.

- You must be sensitive to the connotations of words, but you must defend your position with adequate support, not merely with connotation
  or open slanting.

- You should be sensitive to, and use, euphony and rhythm in your prose.
  Two common devices for creating these qualities are parallelism and
  emphasis.

SUGGESTIONS FOR WRITING (10.5)

1. Write a one-page essay describing a friend to another friend. Then rewrite this
   essay as a speech describing your friend at a ceremony where he or she will
   be receiving an award. Write a one-paragraph description of the differences
   between the two versions.

2. Pick a famous brief essay or speech such as Kennedy's "Inaugural Address,"
   Lincoln's "Gettysburg Address," or Martin Luther King, Jr.'s, "I Have a Dream."
   Using this essay or speech as a model, try to capture some of the spirit of the
   original while using your own words and ideas on some topic of your choice
   in a two- to three-page essay. Pay particular attention to frequently recurring
   patterns of sentences and try to use some similar patterns in your own essay.

II

Openings and
Closings

An argument's opening and closing—the first and last impression you make on the reader—require careful attention. Closings—whether a general conclusion or a specialized summary—are, of course, almost always written late in the process, when you know exactly where your argument has gone. Some writers compose introductions before the body of the argument, but many delay them until the end of the first draft, when they know more clearly what is to be introduced. In the following pages we discuss the importance of effective openings and closings and make some suggestions for beginning and ending your arguments.

INTRODUCTIONS

Because it is the readers' initial experience with your argument, your opening—whether a formal introduction or the first paragraphs of your document—must be particularly appealing to your readers. Unless circumstances compel your readers to read your argument, they are not likely to finish it if its beginning is murky or trite or generally uninviting.

The context of your argument—the occasion and audience for which it is written—as well as its length, tone, and level of complexity, will influence the style and content of your introduction. Regardless of how you choose to introduce your argument, the basic purpose of any introduction is the same: to engage the reader. In most cases, introductions will successfully engage readers if they are clear and inviting. Of these two features, clarity—the precise and accurate transmission of carefully considered ideas—is probably the easiest to achieve, though for many writers it comes only with careful thought and considerable revision. To be inviting, an introduction must contain material that by itself stimulates the readers' interest, as well as arousing curiosity about the rest of the document. Because being inviting does not come naturally to everyone, we offer some opening tactics that can make your arguments appealing to readers.

Tactics for General Introductions

Introduction by Narrative.   Writers of "general interest" arguments (nontechnical arguments, such as newspaper editorials, intended for a broad audience) often gain their readers' attention by opening their essay with a specific anecdote or short narrative. This kind of opening contains two appeals to which most readers are susceptible: first, in its narrative approach, it satisfies our delight in being told a story; and second, it gains our interest by its *particularity*. Particularity—details about people, places, and events—gives readers a firm context as they begin exploring an unknown text. A *Time* magazine essay, "The Demagogue in the Crowd," begins with the following paragraph:

> The audience leaped to embrace the speaker while sitting still. They ate him up. His words were devoured the ways seals snap at fish. You could see the words settle in the crowd's bellies: 25,000 satisfied customers packing New York City's Madison Square Garden last Monday night to hear Minister Louis Farrakhan, head of the Nation of Islam, bring his dual message of self-help and hate. The message of hate predominated. How the crowd hungered for that meal. At the words of defiance they stood and roared. At the in-jokes they laughed joyfully. At the derisive words they smiled and sneered. The converted attended the preacher.

The writer of this essay, Roger Rosenblatt, begins his largely reflective, philosophical essay with an active narrative paragraph, securely set in time, place, and principal characters. While his essay refers to Minister Louis Farrakhan repeatedly, Rosenblatt's real subject is the danger of hate, a claim he gives the reader at the beginning of his fifth paragraph. References to Farrakhan serve a unifying and specifying function in the essay, but the essay's scope is wider than the first paragraph suggests. The particularity and the narrative quality of the opening capture a reader's attention more completely than would an abstract and generalized statement about the dangerous combination of hate and demagoguery.

Introduction by Generalization.   Good introductions can also begin with a strong, unambiguous generalization related to the readers' experiences, as in the following opening paragraph of an article by David Brown published in a medical society journal:

> Few honorable professions have as much inherent hostility toward one another as medicine and journalism. Ask a doctor to describe journalists and you are likely to hear adjectives such as "negative," "sensationalistic," and "superficial." Ask a journalist about doctors, and you will probably hear about "arrogance," "paternalism," and "jargon."

Broad statements such as this should be limited and developed in succeeding sentences or a succeeding paragraph. In the second paragraph of this essay, the writer both justifies and develops the generalization made in the first paragraph.

The descriptions are the common stereotypes and not wholly inaccurate, for the two professions occupy distant worlds. Physicians are schooled in confidence and collegiality; journalists seek to make knowledge public. Physicians speak the language of science; journalists are largely ignorant of science. Physicians inhabit a world of contingencies and caveats; journalists inhabit a world where time and audience require simplification. Physicians are used to getting their way; journalists are used to getting their story.

This paragraph's development of the idea contained in the initial paragraph is echoed by the writer's syntax (the arrangement of his words): the last four sentences, neatly divided by semicolons into opposing clauses, emphasize the focus on this professional opposition.

Introduction by Quotation. Some introductions begin with quotations that are eventually connected to the topic of the essay. While perhaps overused and over-taught, this technique *can* work if practiced thoughtfully. The writer using an opening quotation must be sure that it can be made to apply to the subject in an interesting way, and that the quotation is interesting, provocative, or well written (preferably all three). The following paragraph in an essay by Marilyn Yalom is a successful example of this technique:

When Robert Browning wrote his famous lines "Grow old along with me!/The best is yet to be,/The last of life, for which the first was made," he was undoubtedly not thinking about women. The poet's Victorian optimism is difficult enough to reconcile with the realities of old age for men, and virtually impossible when we consider the condition of older women in the nineteenth century.

As in the article about the antagonism between the medical and journalistic professions, the initial statement is immediately explained and developed in the succeeding sentence. Here, in fact, the explanatory sentence is also the claim of this essay on the older woman in Victorian England and America.

Other Types of Introductions. Many other tactics can be used to make an essay inviting to a reader: the use of startling statistics, a brief historical survey of the topic (which can have the same charm as the narrative introduction), a particularly startling or shocking statement (provided it has something to do with the essay's content), or even a direct announcement of the essay's subject (as in "This article is about bad writing"). Any of these tactics can work as long as they are finally relevant to the rest of the essay.

Introductions in Professional Writing

Introductions written in a professional context according to an established format do not need to be as inviting as our previous examples. Because audiences of professional reports are usually more captive than the casual reader of the essay on the back page of *Time* magazine, writers of these reports have to worry less about being original in their introductions. Rather than trying to attract potential readers to their argument through an effective introduction, these writers are more concerned with serving the needs of a known audience that can use the report for their jobs. Introductions in such cases will usually be successful if they are precisely representative of the content of the report. Company policy often dictates the form of a preliminary summary: some companies require an initial outline, others an abstract, still others an executive summary reflecting both structure and content. When the form is not dictated, the most useful is the summary of structure and content.

We'll use as an example an analysis of problems in customer relations assigned to a customer service representative of a local grocery chain. In her report, the representative first identifies, describes, and documents the different conditions she has found to be damaging to good customer relations: inadequate customer check cashing privileges, a time consuming refund policy, impolite carry-out personnel, and inaccurate advertising of sale prices. She then estimates the loss of business resulting from each problem. Finally, she recommends possible solutions to the problems she has identified. Her report is clearly written and organized, but it is also lengthy and complex; unquestionably, it needs an introduction that will prepare her readers not only for the content of the report but also for the arrangement of the report's material. Her preliminary summary will prepare her readers for the sequence of the argument's main points, and it will serve as a useful reference should the readers become confused while reading the body of the report.

A structure and content introduction to the report about difficulties in customer relations might read as follows:

> This report examines the recent quarterly decline in business at the seven Goodbelly stores. It attributes this loss of revenue to at least four remediable problems in the area of customer relations: (1) inadequate check cashing privileges, (2) a time consuming refund policy, (3) lack of concern for customers by carry-out personnel, and (4) inaccurate advertising of sale prices. It is estimated that these difficulties may have cost Goodbelly's as much as $300,000 in revenue in the past three months. This report concludes by recommending specific personnel and policy measures to be taken to ease these difficulties and to regain the lost business.

Without being painstakingly mechanical, this brief paragraph identifies the central claim of the report (that the decline in revenue is due to poor customer relations) and prepares the reader for the structure and content of the argument. While an introduction such as this one may not engage a reader who has neither an interest in nor obligation to the company, its concise and accurate representation of the report's content will be extremely useful to the obligated reader.

General Suggestions About Introductions

We conclude our discussion of introductions with a list of suggestions.

1. Try writing your introduction *after* you have written a first draft of the argument. Often, there's no point in agonizing over a preliminary summary for business or technical reports or a more catchy introduction for a general interest argument before you know exactly how the argument is going to unfold. Even if you are working from a fairly detailed outline, structure and content will change as you compose. On some occasions, a catchy introductory sentence or group of sentences may come to you early, which gives you a hold on the overall structure, tone, and style of your essay. Don't let these sentences get away!

2. Don't make your introduction too long. Even the most interesting, captivating introduction is going to seem a little silly if it's twice as long as the argument itself. The turbot, a variety of anglerfish, has a head that takes up half of its total body length and is one of the most ridiculous-looking fish to swim the seas. Don't follow its example.

3. Make sure your introduction is truly representative of the entire argument. If you are writing a preliminary summary, be sure all the main points of the argument are referred to in the introduction. In a less formal argument, don't let your desire to be engaging lure you into writing an introduction that is stylistically or tonally inconsistent with the rest of the argument. In short, the opening paragraph should never look as if it has been tacked on merely to attract reader interest, with no thought about its relationship to what follows. Rather, it should resemble an operatic overture, beautiful in its own right, but always preparing its audience for what is to follow.

ACTIVITIES (11.1)

1. For one of the following writing tasks, write two different introductory paragraphs using two of the tactics discussed in the preceding section: narrative, generalization, quotation, startling statistics, a brief historical survey, a startling statement, or an outright announcement of claim. Then write a two- to three-sentence description of the different effects of the two introductions.
   a. An essay on a relative whom you admire
   b. An essay on a law or policy of the federal government that you strongly support or oppose
   c. An essay on your favorite food
   d. An editorial in your local newspaper advocating lower local taxes
   e. A report to your supervisor (or a parent or a friend) explaining why you have failed to accomplish all the goals you set for yourself six months ago

2. For one of the following claims, write an introductory paragraph, as in the following example:

   Claim: Biking is both enjoyable and good for our health.
   Introductory sentences and claim: Too often in life we learn that what we enjoy is bad for our health. When we are children we learn that too much candy is bad for us. We also learn that certain foods or activities we don't especially like, such as eating spinach or going to the dentist, are good for

us. Sometimes we may feel that enjoyment and good health are incompatible, but that despair arises only for those who have not discovered the joys of biking. Biking is one activity that is both enjoyable and good for our health. (Note: These introductory sentences are general, but you could introduce your claim with a specific anecdote or illustration.)

   a. Reading fiction is not an escape from life; it helps us to understand life's complexities.

   b. Jogging may be healthy for many people, but it can be dangerous for those with certain cardiovascular diseases.

   c. Today's generation of young people is realistic about the world of work and the economic difficulties our society faces, but it is also idealistic in its hopes for the future.

   d. Despite the tremendous changes in our society in the last thirty years, baseball is still an enormously popular sport.

   e. If costs keep rising as they have been, a college education may become an impossible dream for most young Americans.

3. The following sentences are first sentences of opening paragraphs of essays. These paragraphs could end with a claim, though they do not have to. For one of these sentences, write the rest of the paragraph.

Example of an opening sentence: Aside from death and taxes, Americans share one other inevitable experience: being caught in a traffic jam.

Sample opening paragraph: Aside from death and taxes, Americans share one other inevitable experience: being caught in a traffic jam. Despite energy crises, pollution alerts, the trend toward smaller cars, and the development of expressways, traffic jams are still a common experience in all large metropolitan areas and even in smaller towns and cities. Americans may see themselves as problem solvers, but they have not yet solved this problem of traffic jams. America still needs a coherent and workable policy on the automobile's role in mass transit.

   a. Unsolicited mail, popularly known as junk mail, arrives in my mailbox daily.

   b. Despite our enormous technological advances, many age-old problems remain unsolved.

   c. When you are driving in the Northeast or the industrial parts of the American Midwest, you don't have to search too long to find an abandoned factory or mill.

   d. I remember almost fondly the worst class I ever had.

   e. Individuals vary enormously in what they look for in friendships.

CONCLUSIONS

Once you have selected and presented the best possible support for your argument, you may feel that you have exhausted all the material relevant to your position, that you have nothing more to say on the subject. But you cannot consider your argument finished until you have provided a final closing, a conclusion that rounds out your argument, giving your readers a satisfying sense of closure. Most readers feel uncomfortable with open-ended writing, with writing that is not somehow rounded off at the end. Readers expect this closure in all kinds of writing—in letters, in imaginative literature of all kinds, and in written arguments.

Closings are not always easy to write, particularly because by the time we get around to thinking about writing an ending, we are often tired of the whole argument. But you don't need to be a master rhetorician to write an effective ending. A conclusion that is direct, precise, and appropriate to the occasion will serve its purpose well. Depending on the context, the length can be as short as a paragraph or as long as a chapter in a book.

Types of Conclusions

General arguments can have three basic types of conclusions: the findings or results of an investigation, a recommendation or a set of recommendations, or a more general closing that looks back to the essay or points to other considerations related to the central claim.

Findings. The first of these types, the findings or results of an investigation, usually ends an argument of fact, such as the reporting of a scientific experiment or a case study. Some casual arguments, such as certain historical studies, also end with results or findings. In reality, these findings or results are the argument's claim, which may be given in general form early in the argument and then with more detail at the end, or they may be given only at the end. An example of a findings or results conclusion is the second-to-last paragraph of an essay titled "Particle Accelerators Test Cosmological Theory".

> Preliminary results from the machines indicate that there are at most five families of elementary particles. David B. Cline of the University of California at Los Angeles and the University of Wisconsin at Madison . . . has shown that the lifetime of the $Z°$ boson [a subatomic particle] is approximately what one would expect with just three families. Experimental uncertainties, however, allow for two additional kinds of neutrinos [another subatomic particle] and hence two additional families. . . . For the first time accelerators are counting neutrino types and getting a small number, one that was predicted by cosmological theory."

Recommendation. A second common type of conclusion is a recommendation or a set of recommendations, typically found in a recommendation report. This type of conclusion tells the readers exactly what the argument expects of them. If the first type of conclusion tells the readers what they should *know,* the second tells them what they should *do.* An example of this type of conclusion is found at the end of "A Proposal for a Computer Facility in Marshall Dormitory" in Chapter 9 of this book. The proposal ends with a "Costs and Implementation Plan" section that spells out in some detail the actions that need to be taken. In the case of this proposal, the more general recommendations came earlier, so ending with more specific steps is a suitable way to conclude. In many other cases, the most appropriate conclusion will be a general recommendation, as in this last paragraph from an essay titled "U.S. Economic Growth."

> Only if we increase investment in both capital and technology in all sectors of the U.S. economy (particularly manufacturing) and improve the quality of labor at all levels can the American standard of living rise at an acceptable rate. In the present highly competitive world market the U.S. has some historically demonstrated advantages, but it must take the longer view and pursue those seemingly trivial increases of a few tenths of a percentage point in growth rate each year.

General Closing.   The general closing is what we usually think of when we think of conclusions. This type of conclusion can work in several ways: it can move from the specific argument to a statement of the argument's broader significance, it can suggest future directions for research, or it can raise related issues. The general closing suggests a movement *onward* (where we go from here) or a movement *outward* (how this specific argument relates to other arguments), though the emphasis in any case will vary between these two elements.

The following paragraph (the closing of Janet Sternburg's opening essay in her collection titled *The Writer on Her Work: Contemporary Women Writers Reflect on Their Art and Situation*) exemplifies a conclusion that moves to a statement of an argument's broader significance:

> This collection offers, I believe, an expanded version of what is central to women writers. Against crippling and mutually exclusive definitions, these essays suggest that multiple choices are possible. Against the fragmentation caused by conflicting demands, they suggest that the various parts of the self can nourish one another. This book stands in relation to a well-documented history of women whose artistic gifts have been damaged by prevailing circumstances. Against the need to justify the worth of our experience . . . women writers are claiming the truths of that experience. Against the silence of the past and of immediate forebears, we are speaking for those who did not speak. Against the fear of stopping, we are trusting in our continuity as artists. Nor is our situation truly solitary; it can be richly populated, as it is here in this book which is, most simply, women writers in each other's company.

A conclusion pointing to new directions and future possibilities is the last paragraph of the essay cited previously, "Particle Accelerators Test Cosmological Theory."

> The next step promises to be even more exciting. As new accelerators are completed and begin producing more data with fewer uncertainties the

cosmological limit of three or at most four families will be checked with extreme accuracy. . . . The machines will probe the early universe with an effectiveness that no telescope will ever match.

A conclusion that raises related issues is the last two paragraphs of a famous essay by Jose Ortega y Gasset titled "The Dehumanization of Art," an essay on the tendency of modern art to move away from portraying the human figure and move toward a "pure" art of form and color.

Should that enthusiasm for pure art be but a mask which conceals surfeit with art and hatred of it? But, how can such a thing come about? Hatred of art is unlikely to develop as an isolated phenomenon; it goes hand in hand with hatred of science, hatred of state, hatred, in sum, of civilization as a whole. Is it conceivable that modern Western man bears a rankling grudge against his own historical essence? Does he feel something akin to the *odium professionis* of medieval monks—that aversion, after long years of monastic discipline, against the very rules that had shaped their lives?

This is the moment prudently to lay down one's pen and let a flock of questions take off on their winged course.

In raising related issues, as Ortega does, you need to be careful that the issues are not too far afield from the main thrust of your argument. Ortega is asking questions about the meaning of the modern quest for a pure, abstract art; thus he is staying close to the main point of his essay, which is to describe some characteristics of this type of art.

These three subcategories of a general closing—significance, future directions, and related issues—can of course overlap. Ortega's related issues are issues of significance, presented as questions to ponder. In addition, a conclusion can contain more than one of our three basic types. The second to last paragraph of "Particle Accelerators Test Cosmological Theory" presents the results of the research, while the very last paragraph presents a statement on future directions of this research. Generally speaking, any results or recommendation conclusion could also have added to it a more general conclusion that opens the argument outward. However, with arguments aimed at restricted audiences, such a strategy may not be necessary.

A word of caution about all conclusions: the conclusion must not lie outside the boundaries of what you can legitimately claim in your argument. You should not, for example, turn an argument about the weakness of a certain school's curriculum into a conclusion uniformly condemning all schools, though your conclusion could suggest that the case you have examined may not be an isolated one. You should not, in other words, overgeneralize from the evidence you were able to use to support your argument. Nor should you use your conclusion as the place to launch a whole new argument or make claims that do not have some basis in what has preceded. In his conclusion to "The Dehumanization of Art," Ortega makes some suggestions about the significance of "pure art," but these suggestions will not come as a surprise to a careful reader of his essay, and they are presented as no more than possibilities, not as bold new claims.

SUMMARIES

A conclusion differs from a *summary,* which is a restatement of the main points of your argument. In writing most short or medium-size essays (500 to 5,000 words), you will not need a summary at the end of your argument; final summaries are typically found in very long essays, essays with difficult subject matter, or in books. We have, for example, used sentence summaries at the end of each chapter of this book because we want to stress certain key points to an audience new to much of this material.

Writers of written arguments or their editors sometimes provide a summary of the basic points preceding the essay. These summaries are usually either separate from or at the very beginning of the arguments and usually take one of two forms: the *abstract,* often used in academic or technical research, and the *executive summary,* often used in business reports and proposals.

An abstract is a summary, typically in paragraph form, that states the essential points of the essay so that readers can grasp these points without having to read the essay; in other words, the good abstract can stand alone, meaningful by itself. If the readers can read only the abstract, they will of course miss much of the argument, especially its support, but they will at least know what the argument's main claims are. With the flood of information confronting us all, abstracts have the obvious value of helping us decide what research needs further investigation and what can be left alone.

The following summary by King-Kok Cheung of her essay on Alice Walker's *The Color Purple* and Maxine Hong Kingston's *The Woman Warrior* is a good example of an abstract:

The Color Purple and *The Woman Warrior* exhibit parallel narrative strategies. The respectively black and Chinese American protagonists work their way from speechlessness to eloquence by breaking through the constraints of sex, race, and language. The heroines turn to masculine figures for guidance, to female models for inspiration, and to native idioms for stylistic innovation. Initially unable to speak, they develop distinctive voices by registering their own unspoken grief on paper and, more important, by recording and emulating the voices of women from their respective ethnic communities. Through these testimonies, each written in a bicultural language, Walker and Kingston reveal the obstacles and resources peculiar to minority women. Subverting patriarchal literary traditions by reclaiming a mother tongue that carries a rich oral tradition (of which women are guardians) the authors artfully coordinate the tasks of breaking silence, acknowledging female influence, and redefining while preserving ethnic characteristics.

Executive summaries are often longer than abstracts, though they should not usually be longer than a page. Like abstracts, they give the main points of an argument, but they may also contain some background on why the report was written and on the scope of the original study. If the executive summary is of a recommendation report, the major recommendation should be included in it. Like abstracts, executive summaries should be written to stand alone; the readers should be able to get the major points of the report without referring to the report itself.

The following is a sample executive summary with a format that might be used by a group auditing the overall effectiveness of a university computer center:

> Audit completed a review of the Johnston Computer Center in February 1994. The Johnston Computer Center is one of three academic computing centers at the University and contains terminals and microcomputers for up to 200 onsite users, with access also available for up to 50 offsite users, making it the second largest of such centers at the University.
>
> The objectives of our review were to determine whether present and planned Center operations are fulfilling user needs and in compliance with University policies and procedures for computer security.
>
> In our opinion, the Center's operation is satisfactory in meeting the needs of its users and in using its internal resources to meet these needs, but unsatisfactory in meeting security policies and procedures.
>
> Our survey of Computer Center users indicated that user satisfaction is high and that Center personnel are responsive to user needs. While system response time has deteriorated in the last six months because of an unexpected increase in user demand, Center management has addressed this problem by encouraging users to use the system during nonpeak hours and by recommending a hardware upgrade to the Vice President for Systems and Computing.
>
> Our review of security showed that unauthorized users could gain access to and change another user's files. Since the Center's computers are not directly connected to the University's administrative computers, which do contain other security safeguards, the University does not face a risk to its financial and personnel records because of these deficiencies. The student and faculty academic files contained in the Center's computers are at risk, however. The Center has reported three such instances of tampering in the last six months. Center management is eager to address this problem but will need additional resources to purchase software and to obtain the necessary technical assistance.

Executive summaries have become increasingly common as business executives and other managers find themselves confronted with an overwhelming number of reports to read. The executive summary allows readers to decide if they want to read further, or if the summary alone provides enough information. Unlike abstracts, which are often intended for a specialist audience, executive summaries usually have a nonspecialist audience of higher managers who may be very far removed from the technical details of the report. The executive summary should allow for the audience's lack of familiarity with these details by avoiding specialized vocabulary whenever possible and by defining any specialized terms that are used. Executive summaries can be very difficult to write because they demand great attention to the readers' needs and great precision in wording. They are also typically written after the report or essay is finished, when the writer wants to relax or move on to a new project, not concentrate on writing a summary of something already finished. The writer of the executive summary needs to remember, however, that for some important readers this summary may be the only part of the report they will ever see.

SUMMARY

Openings and Closings

- The context of your argument will influence the style, content, and length of your introduction, but all introductions should be clear, engaging, and appropriate to the occasion.

- Some useful tactics for general introductions are:

  Introduction by narrative

  Introduction by generalization

  Introduction by quotation

- Introductions of arguments in formal, professional writing should be precisely representative of the content of the report.

- Conclusions are usually one of three basic types: findings or results, a recommendation or set of recommendations, or a general closing. Which type of conclusion you use depends on the type of argument. Findings or results typically conclude reports of scientific experiments or case studies. Recommendations conclude recommendation reports. General closings are used for other types of arguments, especially interpretations and evaluations. The general closing has three subtypes: a statement of significance, suggested directions for research, and a raising of related issues.

- Do not confuse a conclusion with a summary. A summary is a restatement of the main points of your argument. There are three types of summaries: the ending summary, the abstract, and the executive summary. *Ending summaries* are typically found in books and in very complex or very long essays or reports. *Abstracts* and *executive summaries* are typically found at the beginning of or separate from the arguments on which they are based. Readers should be able to understand an abstract or an executive summary without referring to the report or essay on which it is based.

SUGGESTIONS FOR WRITING (11.2)

1. Write a one- to two-page essay that describes the kind of introductions you used in your last two or three essays. Were the introductions engaging? Would the essays have been substantially different if you had used a different type of opening? Would they have been better? Why? Be sure to give your instructor a copy of each of the essays you discuss.

2. Locate a section of a newspaper or magazine that presents several editorial or opinion essays (the *Sunday New York Times* Op Ed page is an excellent source; your local Sunday paper may have its own version). Examine the types of conclusions used for the three pieces and write an essay of two to three pages describing the type of each conclusion, its effect on readers, and its overall effectiveness. Which of the three do you find the most effective? Why? Be sure to give your instructor a copy of the Op Ed page you use for this assignment.

3. Write a one-paragraph abstract of one of your last papers, making sure that readers will be able to understand the abstract without reading the paper. When you hand in this assignment, give your instructor both the abstract and the paper on which it is based.

12

Revising

Revising your argument means stepping back from the argument and seeing it whole. *Revising,* as its Latin roots ("re"—again; and "visere"—to look at) indicate, is to see again, to have a new vision of the entire work. Sometimes this new vision can lead to dramatic changes in the introduction, the claim, the support, or the style of your argument, though close attention to these issues while you are writing the first draft can greatly reduce the need for such changes. Even the most careful work on the first draft, however, cannot prevent your having to make some changes. Good writers know that they must allow time and attention for revision.

WRITING A FIRST DRAFT, REVISING, AND EDITING

Some college students, knowing that revising could mean serious changes in their draft, avoid the process altogether or reduce it to a perfunctory check for poor spelling or grammar. These students confuse revising with editing. Editing is a careful check of language usage, spelling, grammar, punctuation, and consistency of a manuscript. Revising, as we have noted, is a more profound look at the manuscript's entire content, shape, and style. Revising involves a great deal of judgment on your part, because questions about claim, support, and style rarely have simple black or white, right or wrong, answers. Most questions about editing do have right or wrong answers. There are only so many ways to spell a word or punctuate a sentence correctly.

Writing your first draft, revising, and editing require different attitudes and employ somewhat different skills. Writing the first draft requires energy and egoism to keep you going through the bumpy parts; revising calls for detachment and reflection; and editing demands close attention to detail. Attempting a "perfect" first draft is actually one of the most dangerous and laborious ways to write. It is dangerous because you will lack the necessary distance to judge the quality of your argument, and laborious because you are trying to combine these three separate tasks. To some extent, of course, revising and editing occur during the writing of any draft; we all make minor changes in wording, organization, and mechanics even in the early stage of writing, and sometimes we decide on major changes as we write. Inserting these changes then makes sense, but you still need to set aside time for revising and editing, making each your major preoccupation in separate reviews of the manuscript.

Many college students feel that they don't have time for anything but a first draft, but in fact they usually do. Students of roughly equal ability and with roughly the same amount of time available work in amazingly different ways, some finishing their work with plenty of time to spare, others doing everything at the last minute. Most students who claim that they were forced to write their papers just before the due date mean that writing the paper was not their highest priority and they could get motivated to write it only by the pressure of a deadline. Especially with word processing, writers who write a first draft, leave it for awhile, and then revise it do not spend any more time writing than those who try to write just one polished draft.

SOME SUGGESTIONS FOR SUCCESSFUL REVISING

We offer here some suggestions that should help you to revise your arguments more effectively. These are not ironclad rules, but our own experience and the experience of many other writers indicate that following these rules can make revising easier and more effective.

Suggestion 1: Give Yourself Some Breathing Space

Whenever possible, allow some time between finishing the draft and beginning to revise, usually a minimum of twenty-four hours. This "breathing space" will provide the necessary distance between you and your work, allowing you to view the manuscript more objectively and thus be ready to make major changes if they are needed. Setting aside time also allows the more recessed parts of your mind to churn the material over, giving you new perspective and allowing you to become more comfortable with what you feel is worth keeping and less comfortable with those parts of the manuscript you will change or discard. Even when you are not consciously thinking of the manuscript (and the smart thing to do is to try not to think about it too much), your subconscious will be active, working for you even when you have stopped consciously working. This "churning" process can be enormously valuable. If you do not take advantage of it, you are denying yourself an opportunity to improve your work simply by waiting.

Suggestion 2: Avoid the Red Pen

As you are reviewing the draft, you need to avoid the lure of the red pen—the temptation to make small mechanical changes even before you have read and assimilated the entire manuscript. When you begin revising, you need to figuratively tie your hands behind your back and *just read.* Read the entire draft through, asking yourself how the draft works as a whole: Does the introduction catch the reader's attention and give the reader a sense of what will follow? If there is a claim, is it clear? Does the rest of the argument support the claim? Is the organization the most effective for this argument?

Suggestion 3: Review Your Original Purpose and Audience

In writing a first draft, writers risk losing touch with their original purpose and their intended audience, becoming so fascinated by the composition itself that they lose track of why they started the composition in the first place. When you revise, you need to make sure that you have successfully fulfilled your original purpose for your intended audience (your purpose and audience could change, of course, but that should be your conscious choice).

Part of distancing yourself from your manuscript is putting yourself into the mind of your readers, trying to see your argument through their eyes. Have I met my original purpose? If I intended, for example, to recommend a course of action, have I done so? Are my vocabulary and use of specialized terms appropriate for my readers? Have I understood and appealed to what is likely to motivate them? Will they know what I want them to do after they have finished reading the argument?

Suggestion 4: Review Your Overall Organization

In making sure your argument works, you need to review not only your purpose and audience but also your overall structure, making sure that the parts fit together well, that nothing crucial is omitted, and that the structure is lean, with a minimum of repetition. If you find it hard to keep the structure in mind, you might try reproducing it in an outline form like the one that follows. This outline should reflect what you actually wrote, not what you intended to write.

    I. INTRODUCTION (if appropriate)
   II. CLAIM (if appropriate)
 III. SUPPORTING ARGUMENTS:
      A.
      B.
      C.
      D.
 IV. CONCLUSION OR SUMMARY (if appropriate)

If you actually wrote the argument from an outline, you should not look at it until you have completed this new one. If you have trouble constructing this outline, your manuscript almost certainly has structural problems that need correction.

At this stage you need to review the issues raised earlier on in the discussions of claims and introductions: If I have a claim, is it clearly stated? If I have an introduction, does it adequately program the readers for what will follow? Is my introduction interesting if it needs to catch the readers' attention? You also need to deal with the issues raised earlier about organization: Should I include a refutation of one or more opposing arguments? Is my ordering of the support most effective for the essay?

Suggestion 5: Review Your Argument's Coherence

Even the most carefully organized argument can puzzle readers if the relationship between its parts is not indicated in some way. In certain professions and businesses, standard formats include headings like "Introduction," "The Problem," "History," and so on. But such headings are inappropriate in many settings. You can make the elements of your argument *coherent*—establish their relationship to one another and to the whole—by using simple transitional words and expressions that indicate the nature of the relationship.

Words like *therefore, thus, so,* and *consequently* identify a conclusion and its evidence. Words like *but, however,* and *on the other hand* indicate exceptions to a stated point. You can alert your reader to the introduction of each new piece of support by using indicators such as *first . . . , second . . . , and, furthermore,* and *finally.* Transitional words and expressions such as these are enormously useful to readers of arguments, particularly when the argument is long or elaborate. They help readers understand how one statement or section that might otherwise seem a digression or irrelevancy relates to what has gone before or what might come later.

As well as using such brief signposts, you can also be quite direct about the role of different parts of your argument. Public speakers are often very explicit about the function of crucial parts of their speeches: "Let me give you two reasons why this land should be developed," or "To conclude, I'd like to remind you of a few lines by Walt Whitman." Such obvious signs are crucial when there is no written text for an audience to follow and ponder. But indicators such as these can be used in written argument as well, especially when the parts are many and complex.

Suggestion 6: Review Your Style

During revising you also need to examine the style of your argument, and when necessary, modify it. As we discussed in Chapter 9, style is an important component of the argument's total image, and image plays a major role in an audience's acceptance or rejection of the argument. The writer who complains that readers failed to appreciate his strong argument because of poor style doesn't really understand that style is a part of good argument. Poor style can be just as damaging to an argument as a vague or unsupported claim, and compelling style is just as helpful in convincing an audience as abundant evidence.

The appropriateness of voice in your argument is a question of style. In Chapter 10 we discussed the crucial role of a credible voice in winning over a reader. You need to review the voice of your argument to ensure that it presents a positive ethos and a reassuring confidence in your position.

In reviewing the style of your manuscript, you should ask yourself if you have followed Orwell's rules for clarity in writing, along with the friendly amendments offered in Chapter 10. You should also check to see if you have (1) used connotation effectively, (2) avoided slanting, (3) used metaphor and analogy effectively, and (4) paid attention to the sounds of words. Some of these questions will naturally occur during your consideration of a claim (if you have one) and the organization of its support, as well as during your review of audience and purpose.

Suggestion 7: Review Your Argument for Fallacies in Reasoning

In Chapter 5, we introduced some basic concepts of logic that can help you set up a reasonable argument. As we noted, informal fallacies, to which even the best arguments are susceptible, are most easily detected during the revision stage. As a final step in reviewing your argument, read it through to detect any fallacies you might have unwittingly committed. Pay special attention to those fallacies that are particularly common in the kind of argument you have written.

Suggestion 8: Use a Word Processor

As you begin to revise, you may be disheartened to know that revising can lead to drastic overhaul of your argument, but if you want to create the most effective argument possible, you will not forsake the opportunity to make improvements. As a growing number of writers know, using a word processor can make revising much easier than it used to be. With word processing, you can switch entire sections of a draft around with relative ease, change words swiftly and even "globally" so that one word replaces another throughout an entire essay, and make corrections with no trace of crossed-out words and letters, no telltale blotch of white ink. Because revision can mean not just a second draft of an argument but a third or even a fourth draft, word processing can save you a great deal of time as you move from one draft to the next. If you own a computer with word processing software, or if you have access to one, you should use this valuable tool. The computer will not make you a better writer, but it will give you the chance to make yourself a better writer.

ACTIVITIES (12.1)

1. Write an outline of a paper or a draft of a paper that you have written for this class, using the format given in Suggestion 4. Then exchange this paper or draft with one of your classmates, while keeping your outline. Now prepare an outline of your classmate's paper, again using the same format, and then exchange outlines with your classmate. Compare your classmate's outline with your own. Do the two outlines agree on what the claim is and what the supporting arguments are? If there are disagreements, discuss these with your classmate. Find out why he or she saw your argument working in a dif-

ferent way than you did. Remember that if there is disagreement, you cannot simply assume that your classmate is wrong and you are correct: the purpose of your argument is to convince the reader, not yourself. After this discussion, make a list of the changes or possible changes you would make in your paper in a next draft.

2. Write a one- to two-page essay describing the voice you created in one of your earlier essays. What means did you use to create this voice? How credible is this voice?

SUMMARY

Revising

- You should plan on spending separate portions of time writing a draft, revising, and editing.

- Allow breathing space between writing a draft and revising it. In your first review of the draft, concentrate on how the draft works as a whole.

- In revising, you need to review your original purpose and audience, organization, adequacy and logic of support, and style.

- Knowing the principles of logic can be a significant help in reviewing your draft.

- Using a word processor makes revising significantly easier.

AN EXAMPLE OF REVISION

Having read your manuscript all the way through at least once, and preferably twice, you are now ready to make major changes if they are needed. By avoiding the red pen until you have reviewed the entire manuscript, you are more likely to recognize the need for such major changes, and less likely to get lost in grieving over minor errors.

The following sample student essay (based on an essay written by a student) is a good example of how revising can correct major problems in an argument. What follows is the first draft of the essay, along with the student's notes for revision, which he wrote in the margins during a second and third reading of the draft.

```
When we think about computers, we usually
think about how helpful they are to us: they
enable us to process huge amounts of data,
```

prepare large written documents with an ease
undreamt of even twenty years ago, and by
acting as the "brains" of robots, help us
perform dangerous or monotonous tasks. But we
often fail to think of the negative side of
computers, including the threat they pose to
our privacy. Also, in many cases computers are
replacing human labor in factories and
offices.

Drop- this idea not followed up

One thing computers are used for is to
store information about people. These computers contain databases, which are collections of discrete data that are divided into
fields, such as age, sex, income, and place of
residence. A user of a database can pull
information out of the database on everyone
who fits a category made up of some or all of
these fields, such as every male between
thirty and forty who earns between thirty and
fifty thousand dollars a year and lives in
Florida. An example of a database is the
Internal Revenue Service's database, which
contains basic information on tax returns
along with demographic information on those
who pay taxes. Other databases contain credit
histories within them. If you have someone's
Social Security number, you can find out just
about anything you want about them. Not just
anybody can do this, but there are already too
many people who can.

overstated →

A separate point, not related to ¶. Also, I have no proof.

wordy, vague ←

If it isn't bad enough to have someone go
through all the information about you in one
database, databases can even be linked to
other databases because of the increased
networking power of computers today. Having
this ability leads to the potential problem of

Too many
separate ideas
in this ¶:
Networking,
human error,
lack of paper
copies. These
need separate
treatment.

wrong information being kept on a person
(especially if no written records are kept).
Computers do fail, but the most important
reason why a database would contain wrong
information about someone would be because
someone typed in incorrect information. If the
police used computer databases to keep track
of criminal records without having another
record of them on paper somewhere, anyone
could input harmful data on innocent people
that could cause them a great deal of misery.

If the major problem with the accuracy of
information in databases is human error, then
perhaps new forms of electronic entry of data
will eliminate some of these errors. Our phone
bills are one example of a completely electronic
system. But these phone bills can tell someone
who wants to know everybody we called and when
we called them. Our phone companies could be
recording everything we say as well.

No evidence.
statement
undermines my
credibility.

In our society privacy is regarded as a
right—a right that is being threatened by the
increasing use of databases to maintain large
amounts of information on all of us. A number
of privacy bills have been passed but are
almost useless because they are so hard to
enforce. Violating someone's privacy is hard
to detect, and successfully prosecuting
someone for this offense is harder still.

Ideas need
development.
Is situation
hopeless?

Not relevant
to what
I've written.

Is this
conclusion
justified by
what I've
written?

Computers are enormously valuable tools,
but they can be misused to violate privacy
and to manipulate people. We have a population
explosion today and yet we replace people
with computers. We must carefully examine the
role of computers in our society and learn to
control them before they control us.

This essay reflects poor planning by the writer: it contains some errors that a careful consideration of the claim and its support before the actual writing would have probably prevented. Fortunately for the student, he noticed many of these problems during a careful review of the draft and made a list of them.

1. Claim—I have a combination claim focusing on the privacy issue and the issue of computers replacing human labor, but I do nothing with the second issue. I should drop the second issue and concentrate on the first.
2. Organization—My ideas aren't clearly presented and organized, especially in the third paragraph, which talks about the three separate ideas of networking, human data entry errors, and lack of paper or "hard copy" backups. All of my paragraphs must be clearly tied to the privacy threat.
3. Support—I don't really support my argument because I talk a lot about the threat of invasion of privacy but give no actual cases. I need to distinguish clearly between the potential for abuse and actual cases. Is there a real possibility for abuse? Also, my conclusion about humans controlling computers before they control us isn't warranted by what I've written, since I've offered no suggestions for controlling computers.
4. Style—I undermine my credibility with sweeping statements like "If you have someone's Social Security number, you can find out just about anything you want about them." Some of my writing could be much tighter, including wordy expressions like "If it isn't bad enough to have someone go through all the information about you in one database. . . ."

When writing a second draft, the student tried to correct the problems he saw in the first. This draft still has some problems, but it is stronger then the first. In this draft the student has also added source references.

When we think about computers, we usually think about how helpful they are to us: they enable us to process huge amounts of data, prepare large written documents with an ease undreamt of even twenty years ago, and by acting as the "brains" of robots, help us perform dangerous or monotonous tasks. But we often fail to think of the negative side of computers, including the threat they pose to our own privacy. This threat may not seem immediate, but it is growing with the increasing power of computers, and so far society has done little to deal with it (Roszak, 181).

One thing computers are used for is to store information about people. Computers often use databases, which are collections of discrete data that are divided into fields, such as age, sex, income, and place of

residence. A user of a database can pull information out
of the database on everyone who fits a category made up of
some or all of these fields, such as every male between
thirty and forty who earns between thirty and fifty
thousand dollars a year and lives in Florida. An example
of a database is the Internal Revenue Service's database,
which contains basic information on tax returns along with
demographic information on those who pay taxes. Other
databases contain our credit histories, our history of
contributions to a specific organization, our personnel
records with our employers, or a variety of other
information. Businesses and other organizations already
use this information to bombard us with targeted
advertising through the mail; the information could be
used to monitor our opinions and activities (Roszak,
182-187).

Databases can be made even more powerful by being
linked to other databases through networking. The
increasing capabilities of network systems raise the
possibility of a wide variety of information on us being
shared by numerous databases. Such information on specific
individuals would be a boon to marketers trying to find
target audiences, but individuals could end up with their
records of contributions to an organization in the hands
of the IRS, or their IRS files in their employers'
personnel records without their even knowing it.

So far at least, cases of deliberate abuse or
manipulation of databases to violate an individual's
privacy have been relatively rare. Far greater problems
have arisen because of errors in the entry of data in
databases, with such undesirable results as individuals
receiving bad credit ratings because of erroneous reports
of unpaid bills or even some cases of innocent individuals
being denied government jobs because their names appeared
on computer lists of people belonging to subversive
organizations (Sherman, 344). The risk of these kinds of
errors may increase with the increasing use of "on-line"

entry of data into computers, where a paper copy (called a "hard copy" in computerese) of the transaction is not necessary, leaving no trace outside the computer system of the source of the error. These errors threaten our privacy, because this supposedly "private" information can mislead others, damage our reputation, and enormously complicate our lives. Common sense suggests that with the increasing amount of "private" data being kept on all of us, the likelihood of harmful errors also increases.

Most such errors are caused by human mistakes, but even computers can develop "glitches." Furthermore, even errorless electronically entered data can pose threats to our privacy. Our phone bills are one example of a completely electronic system which is almost always error-free. Yet these phone bills can tell someone who wants to know everybody we called and when we called them. The information may be accurate, but in the wrong hands it can be seriously misused.

In our society, privacy is regarded as a right--a right that is being threatened by the increasing use of databases to maintain large amounts of information on all of us. A number of computer privacy laws have been enacted in the last twenty years, including the Medical Computer Crimes Act of 1984, the Cable Communications Policy Act of 1984, the Financial Privacy Act of 1978, the Fair Credit Reporting Act of 1974, and the Family Educational Rights and Privacy Act of 1974 (Organization for Economic Co-operation and Development, 22). One aspect of all these laws is the protection of individuals from unwarranted use of data about them. But violating someone's privacy is hard to detect, and successfully prosecuting someone for this offense is harder still.

Nevertheless, protecting individual privacy against the threat posed by large databases is not a hopeless cause. The growing list of computer privacy laws indicates that the public is not blind to the threats posed by computers, though much needs to be done to make these laws

meaningful. Even consumers can help, by insisting that
their names not be sent to others when they subscribe to a
magazine or join an organization. Faced with such
insistence and the possibility of losing customers or
members, many groups will stop sharing these lists.

Computers are enormously valuable tools, but they can
be misused to violate our privacy. While the threat to our
privacy is real, the situation is not yet severe. We still
have the time to control this threat before the threat
begins to control us.

WORKS CITED

Organisation for Economic Co-operation and Development
(OECD). Computer-Related Crime: Analysis of Legal
Policy. Information on Computer Communications Policy
10. Paris: OECD, 1986.

Roszak, Theodore. The Cult of Information: The Folklore of
Computers and the True Art of Thinking. New York:
Pantheon, 1986.

Sherman, Barrie. The New Revolution: The Impact of
Computers on Society. Chichester, U.K.: Wiley, 1985.

This second draft attempts to deal with the problems the writer saw in the
first. Read it carefully in light of the issues he identified. How did he solve (or at
least try to solve) the problems he noted? What further changes do you believe
would be necessary in a third draft?

ACTIVITIES (12.2)

Read the following draft of a student's essay (actually a composite of several
essays) and make a list of what you feel the major revisions need to be. Compare
your list with those of your classmates, then revise the essay in accordance with
your list. Compare your revision with some of those done by your classmates.

Student Government: Why No One Cares

Being an engineering student here at High Tech, I have
very little free time. My time is entirely devoted to
academics. Occasionally I will have a few hours free on the
weekend, but then I work part-time at odd jobs. Tuition here
is very high.

I am one of many busy students here who simply doesn't have the time to take an interest in student government. This same fact is true for most of us. Most of us don't even know one person who is in student government and could not tell you what student government actually does.

We are very ignorant about student government and what role we can play in it. Speaking for myself, even if I saw posters announcing a meeting about student government, I would not attend. Most of my fellow students would not either. What can just one student do? None of us has much of a voice in how things are run. The administration really runs the show here at High Tech, not the students. I believe that if the student government started putting up more posters and getting out more publicity about its activities, students would be more interested in its activities even if they did not attend them.

It is a whole lot simpler to just ignore what's going on and to assume that the student government is looking out for our interests than to take the trouble to get involved. Besides, life isn't all that bad around here, so why should we spend a lot of time and effort trying to improve a situation most of us already find satisfactory? By the time we solved some problem, we would be ready to graduate anyway.

SUGGESTIONS FOR WRITING (12.3)

1. Revise a paper you wrote earlier in this course, following the advice outlined in this chapter. Make a list of the major differences between the original paper and your new version and indicate very briefly why you made these changes.

2. For this assignment the class should be divided into groups of three or four. Each group will collectively write a three- to four-page paper (750 to 1,000 words), starting with a group outline, each student then writing a particular section of the paper. When this first draft is written, the group will get together to discuss the draft and then revise it again in light of the group discussion, with each student revising his or her own section. The group will then discuss this second draft and choose one student to prepare and edit a final version consistent in style and tone. Some possible topics follow.
   a. The uses of word processing in revising papers
   b. Social life on your campus
   c. The changing nature of the job market

3. Write a paper on the steps you usually follow in writing arguments—not the steps you believe you should follow or the ones you would like to follow, but the ones you actually do follow. Start with where you get your ideas and move through writing the first draft and on to whatever steps you take before you arrive at a final edited version. Describe how efficient you find this process in terms of the time you spend, and how effective you find it in terms of creating a convincing argument. Do you believe there are ways this process can be improved so that you could write better arguments in a reasonable amount of time?

Credits

Index